Online Marketing

Ralf T. Kreutzer

Online Marketing

 Springer

Ralf T. Kreutzer
Berlin, Germany

This book is a translation of the original German edition „Online-Marketing" by Kreutzer, Ralf T., published by Springer Fachmedien Wiesbaden GmbH, part of Springer Nature in 2021. The translation was done with the help of artificial intelligence (machine translation by the service DeepL.com). A subsequent human revision was done primarily in terms of content, so that the book will read stylistically differently from a conventional translation. Springer Nature works continuously to further the development of tools for the production of books and on the related technologies to support the authors.

ISBN 978-3-658-35368-1   ISBN 978-3-658-35369-8   (eBook)
https://doi.org/10.1007/978-3-658-35369-8

This Springer imprint is published by the registered company Springer Fachmedien Wiesbaden GmbH part of Springer Nature.
The registered company address is: Abraham-Lincoln-Str. 46, 65189 Wiesbaden, Germany

Preface to the First Edition

Dear Readers,

The triumph of online marketing can no longer be stopped. Every business would do well to consider in what form they should make use of online marketing. Outsiders who do not engage online in one form or another will be marginalized in the long run and disappear from the market. Because those who are not found online no longer exist for ever-widening circles of users!

Therefore, today, it is more important than ever to know the most important levers and success factors of online marketing and to use them skillfully. This work is intended to provide an introduction to this. The classic fields of online marketing, such as the design of the corporate website, search engine marketing, online advertising and online PR, e-mail marketing, mobile marketing, and especially social media marketing, are presented transparently in their essential fields of action.

In implementing what you have read, I wish you a "good hand" and much success at all times!

Yours sincerely

Ralf T. Kreutzer
Berlin, Germany

Contents

About the Author

Ralf T. Kreutzer has been Professor of Marketing at the Berlin School of Economics and Law as well as marketing and management consultant since 2005. He spent 15 years in various management positions at Bertelsmann (last position head of the foreign division), Volkswagen (managing director of a subsidiary), and Deutsche Post (managing director of a subsidiary) before being appointed Professor of Marketing in 2005.

Through regular publications and lectures, Prof. Kreutzer has provided significant impetus on various topics relating to marketing, dialogue marketing, CRM/customer loyalty systems, database marketing, online marketing, digital Darwinism, dematerialization, digital transformation, change management, strategic as well as international marketing, and artificial intelligence. He has advised a large number of companies in Germany and abroad on these topics and trained and coached executives at middle and top management level. Prof. Kreutzer is a sought-after keynote speaker at national and international conferences and also moderates world café formats and other interactive forms of group work.

His most recent book releases are *Digitaler Darwinismus – der stille Angriff auf Ihr Geschäftsmodell und Ihre Marke* (Digital Darwinism – the silent attack on your business model and brand) (2nd ed., 2016, together with Karl-Heinz Land). *Digital Business Leadership – Digitale Transformation – Geschäftsmodell-Innovation – agile Organisation – Change-Management* (2017, together with Tim Neugebauer and Annette Pattloch), *Führung und Organisation im digitalen Zeitalter kompakt* (2018), *Digital Business Leadership, Digital Transformation, Business Model Innovation, Agile Organization, Change Management* (2018, together with Tim Neugebauer and Annette Pattloch), *Toolbox für Marketing und Management* (2018), *Toolbox for Marketing and Management* (2019), *Künstliche Intelligenz verstehen* (2019, together with Marie Sirrenberg), *Understanding Artificial Intelligence* (2020, together with Marie Sirrenberg), *B2B-Online-Marketing und Social Media* (2nd ed., 2020, together with Andrea Rumler and Benjamin Wille-Baumkauff), *Die digitale Verführung* (2020), *Voice-Marketing* (2020, together with Darius Vousoghi), *Praxisorientiertes Online-Marketing* (4th ed., 2021), *Toolbox für Digital Business* (2021), *Kundendialog online und offline – das große 1x1 der Kundenakquisition, Kundenbindung und Kundenrückgewinnung* (2021), *Social-Media-Marketing kompakt* (2nd ed., 2021), *E-Mail-Marketing kompakt* (2nd ed., 2021), *Praxisorientiertes Marketing* (6th ed., 2022), *Digitale Markenführung* (2022, together with Karsten Kilian), and *Toolbox Digital Business* (2022).

List of Abbreviations

AI	Artificial Intelligence
among others	among others/and others
App	Application (as a term for an application)
ASP	Application Service Providing
B2B	Business-to-Business
B2C	Business-to-Consumer
CDI	Cross-Device Identification
CLS	Cumulative Layout Shift
ConPO	Contacts per Order
CPA	Cost per Action
CPC	Cost per Click
CPCoup	Cost per Coupon
CPI	Cost per Interest
CPL	Cost per Lead
CPM	Cost per Mille (Cost per 1,000 Impressions; Price per 1,000 Impressions)
CPO	Cost per Order
CPR	Cost per Redemption
CRM	Customer Relationship Management
CRO	Conversion Rate Optimization
CTA	Call-to-Action
CTP	Customer Touchpoint(s)
CTR	Click-Through Rate
DAU	Dumbest Assumable User
DiSoLoMo	Digital, Social, Local, Mobile
DMP	Data Management Platform
DR	Direct Response
DSP	Demand Side Platform
e.g.	for example

E-Commerce	Electronic Commerce
esp.	in particular
FAQs	Frequently Asked Questions
FAZ	Frankfurter Allgemeine Zeitung
FCB	First Choice Buyer
FID	First Input Delay
FMCG	Fast Moving Consumer Goods
GTC	General Terms and Conditions
HB	Handelsblatt
HTML	Hypertext Markup Language
i. S.	in the sense
i.e.	that is
if applicable	if applicable
in principle	in principle
incl.	inclusive
KISS	Keep It Short and Simple
KPI	Key Performance Indicator
LCP	Largest Contentful Paint
M-Commerce	Mobile Commerce
NDN	Non-Delivery Notification
o. s.	or similar
O2O	Online to Offline
OTS	Opportunity to see
POP	Point of Purchase
POS	Point of Sale
PPS	Pay per Sale
PR	Public Relations
QR	Quick Response
ROI	Return on Investment
ROMI	Return on Marketing Investment
RSS	Really Simple Syndication
RTB	Realtime Bidding (Realtime Advertising)

SaaS	Software as a Service
SBF	Strategic Business Fields
SBU	Strategic Business Units
SEA	Search Engine Advertising
SEM	Search Engine Marketing
SEO	Search Engine Optimization
SERPs	Search Engine Result Pages
SLA	Service Level Agreement
SSL	Secure Sockets Layer
SSP	Supply Side Platform
SWOT	Strengths/Weaknesses/Opportunities/Threats
SWYN	Share With Your Network
TCP	Thousand-Contact-Price
URL	Uniform Resource Locator
USP	Unique Selling Proposition

Instruments, Success Factors and Goals of Online Marketing

Contents

© Springer Fachmedien Wiesbaden GmbH, part of Springer Nature 2022
R. T. Kreutzer, *Online Marketing*, https://doi.org/10.1007/978-3-658-35369-8_1

1

Learning Agenda

What is online marketing? What are the different forms of online marketing? In this chapter you will be familiarized with the most important terms and forms of online marketing. After reading …

- ▶ Section 1.1 you understand why online marketing has gained importance.
- ▶ Section 1.2 you can trace the development of online marketing.
- ▶ Section 1.3 you will master important success factors of online marketing.
- ▶ Section 1.4 you know the general expectations and motives of online users.

1.1 Instruments of Online Marketing

As users, we encounter **online marketing** in a wide variety of forms (cf. ◘ Fig. 1.1). The online presence of a company in the form of a **corporate website** is a particularly important form of online marketing: The homepage as the entry page represents the virtual entrance door to a company and thus becomes the supporting **pillar of online marketing**. The corporate website

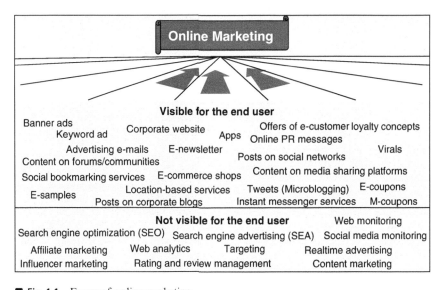

◘ **Fig. 1.1**   Forms of online marketing

itself comprises the entirety of a company's content presented under a URL, i.e. an Internet address (e.g. ► audi.com). The focus of a corporate website is either the company itself or its products, its services and/or the respective brands. Links to the company's activities in social media or to blogs, social bookmarks and online communities can be communicated on the corporate website.

Anyone who is on the Internet is also confronted with various forms of **online advertising**. One of these is **banner advertising**. Banners are advertising formats that are integrated into websites in a wide variety of ways. Anyone who uses search engines as an online user comes across **keyword ads**, i.e. paid advertisements on the search engine results pages. In addition, we are confronted daily – intentionally and unintentionally – with a multitude of **advertising e-mails** and **e-newsletters**, the receipt of which we have usually only partially requested.

Another form of online marketing is **e-commerce**, which involves the electronic initiation and processing of purchase processes and thus e-commerce. There are also – partly complementary to this – **customer loyalty concepts** that also or exclusively take place in online media (e.g. in the form of an app). If they are only implemented in the online area, these are called **e-customer loyalty programs**. If online and offline elements are combined, we speak of hybrid systems. Many of the loyalty cards in circulation today reward both online and offline purchases.

E-coupons are used to try to trigger certain behaviors. *Amazon,* for example, offers coupons worth € 10 to encourage participation in a customer survey. Such e-coupons can also be communicated as part of banner advertising to encourage online users to visit the website or subscribe to a newsletter. **E-sampling** also takes place in the sense of the electronic sending of a product sample, e.g. in the form of e-books, in order to motivate users to engage with the corresponding offer. In addition, there are forms of **online PR** or **online public relations** that companies use to present themselves and their offerings to the public.

In recent years, the importance of **social networks** (e.g. *Facebook, LinkedIn*) has increased significantly. In these, millions of people are networked with each other and form an interesting target group for the advertising industry due to the high density of information about the individuals. In addition, **forums and communities** can be found on the Internet, which – only partially initiated by companies – offer platforms for a comprehensive exchange of information. Furthermore, **social bookmarking services** create the opportunity to mark interesting websites and inform others about one's own website preferences.

1

Via **media sharing platforms** (such as *Instagram*, *TikTok*, *YouTube*) it is not only possible to present one's own creations online. Rather, these platforms also offer companies the opportunity to present themselves through their own videos, presentations and photos. This approach can be particularly successful if the "story behind the story" is presented, e.g. a "making of" an advertising spot. At the same time, these media sharing platforms are also the field of action for many digital opinion leaders who cover a wide variety of topics here (keyword "influencer marketing").

Blogging is no longer limited to private individuals. Companies are increasingly setting up **corporate blogs** to inform their own employees as well as external target groups about relevant processes in the company and to enter into a dialogue with them. These developments are flanked by **microblogging services** such as *Twitter*, which companies use for direct communication with their target groups and also to provide services. The term **microblogging** is derived from the fact that posts on these blogging services are limited to a certain number of characters. **Instant messenger services** are now becoming increasingly important (*WhatsApp* and *Facebook Messenger* come to mind here). These services can be used to send text messages, but also text, image, video and audio files. In addition, location information and contact data can be exchanged between individuals or in groups.

Finally, **mobile marketing**, which is becoming increasingly important, opens up a wide range of opportunities for companies to come into contact with mobile users. **Location-based services** make it possible to tailor messages and offers to the respective location of the user. In this context, **apps** and the corresponding app marketing are becoming increasingly important. "App" is an abbreviation for "application", i.e. a software program that is used by a mobile device and has a variety of possible uses. For example, **mobile coupons** can be sent. In addition, online media also offer an exciting scope for using **viral marketing**, so that advertising messages in particular spread epidemically on the net as virals.

Behind the visible forms of online marketing for the end user, there is a second level of fields of action for companies that "play on" these in order to operate their online activities successfully. This includes, for example, **keyword advertising** (also called **search engine advertising** or SEA). The results of this are visible to the user of search engines in the form of keyword ads. In the hit lists of the search engines, the activities of **search engine optimization** (SEO) become visible to the searchers. In search engine optimization, companies try to appear in the most prominent position possible in the hit lists of search engine providers in the so-called "organic hit list" by means of a specific design of their online presence.

The activities of **affiliate** marketing also belong to the "in the background" running activities of online **marketing**. Through these, one's own online advertising becomes visible on the websites of third-party companies or also on private websites in order to reach a larger target group. A central basis for successful online advertising – which is also not always visible to the user – is the various forms of **targeting**. For this purpose, e.g. the search and surfing behaviour on the Internet – partly in connection with other user data – is evaluated in order to derive needs profiles and product and service interests. These are used as a basis for the placement of online advertising. In this context, so-called **real-time advertising** or **real-time bidding** (RTB) is increasingly being used, in which online banners are booked automatically. In addition, a wide range of analysis options are opening up to companies in order to record not only the behaviour of online users, but also the effects of their own online activities. When behavioural data on websites is analysed, this is referred to as **web analytics**. Click-stream analyses and web tracking are used here, for example.

In contrast to **web analytics**, the acitivties of **web monitoring** attempts to gain insights into the perception of one's own services or one's own company and its competitors on a **meta-level**, i.e. on a level above the real communication (e.g. between customers and a company). In the case of this so-called "information about information", the aim is, for example, to distill particular clusters of praise and complaints, expressed expectations, concrete product suggestions or even trends from the multitude of opinions expressed on the Internet. In essence, the aim is to listen as closely as possible to online users. When monitoring focuses on social media platforms, it is referred to as **social media monitoring**.

In recent years, content marketing has become increasingly important. The term **content** is used to describe any form of content, which can include sound, text, still and moving images. **Content marketing** is about winning over (potential) customers by presenting exciting content. To do this, companies need to think more like publishers and ask themselves what content is relevant to readers. Thinking purely in terms of sales is not appropriate to this approach. In essence, content marketing is about creating and distributing relevant content in order to attract the attention of a defined target group and to build a positive reputation in order to attract buyers for one's own services (see also ► Sect. 1.3).

❯ In a nutshell: Brands and companies become publishers themselves in the course of content marketing.

1

Influencer marketing is also very important today. This means the integration of (digital) opinion leaders in order to have them report – ideally positively – about one's own offers. If customers are acquired for this purpose, we speak of a **rating and review management** – the professional acquisition and handling of customer reviews (cf. Kilian and Kreutzer 2022 for an in-depth discussion of these three areas).

Based on these diverse characteristics, **online marketing** can be defined as follows:

> **Notice!**
>
> **Online marketing** encompasses the planning, organization, implementation and control of all market-oriented activities that make use of mobile and/ or stationary end devices with Internet access to achieve marketing goals.

Online marketing uses online tools both for the marketing of digitized products and services and for the marketing of non-digitized products and services. For this purpose, information can be presented online in a wide variety of forms. Online marketing can support pure online sales channels, pure offline sales channels as well as any combination of these within the framework of multi- or omni-channel sales. In **multi-channel sales**, the individual sales channels are relatively unconnected to each other. In **omni-channel sales**, the aim is for all the sales channels used to complement each other optimally. In addition, instruments of classic offline communication (such as TV advertising, posters, advertising letters and print ads) can be used to "fire up" online activities (cf. in-depth Kreutzer 2021a; Böckenholt et al. 2018).

Online marketing has a special focus on two classic instruments of marketing: **communication policy** and **distribution policy**. Online marketing enriches and supplements "classic" marketing with a **variety of innovative concepts**. In some areas, there is a significant shift in communication budgets, e.g. from classic to online communication. In addition, more and more stationary providers are tapping into the possibilities of e-commerce and thus supplementing their distribution channels.

> **Notice!**
>
> **E-commerce** is understood as the electronic initiation and handling of purchasing processes and can refer to physical and non-physical products as well as services.

❯ To put it in a nutshell: In my opinion, it always makes sense to speak of **online marketing** when it clearly goes beyond communication in general or advertising and when several marketing instruments are integrated into a concept. Where this is not the case, we should speak more precisely of **online communication** or **online advertising**.

1.2 Development of Online Marketing

In addition to the stationary and mobile telephone network, the central basis for today's online marketing is the **Internet**, which has been accessible to more and more users since 1991. The Internet enables the use of Internet services that allow the international transfer of data in a wide variety of forms (including e-mails, IP telephony and, above all, via the World Wide Web). Data is transferred via standardized Internet protocols. The terms "Internet" and "World Wide Web" are often used interchangeably because the World Wide Web is the most widely used Internet service. In summary, these applications of the Internet are also referred to as **Web 1.0**.

New technologies enabled the emergence of the so-called **participatory web**. The term **Web 2.0** was coined for this in 2004. The core characteristics of Web 2.0 are the **active participation of users** and thus the **exploitation of the Internet potential** through the possibility of making changes to much of the content available on the Internet themselves or presenting their own creations by any user. In addition to broadband access, easy-to-use software and low-cost access to the Internet have led to a variety of new applications. This includes, for example, the development of **wikis**, whose content can not only be read by users, but can also be changed online directly in the web browser (e.g. *Wikipedia*).

Easy-to-use blog development software also opened up more opportunities for online users to present themselves. The term **blog** is an abbreviation of the artificial word weblog formed from web and log(book). Blog is classically translated as online diary. In addition, **media sharing platforms** allow broad user groups to upload their own photos and videos or presentations (e.g. on *Instagram*, *TikTok* and *YouTube*). **Social networks** also enable many millions of users to build up their own online presence without much effort and to post their own content here.

Increasingly powerful **end devices** (also called "devices") facilitate access to the Internet and the possibilities offered there. These devices allow access not only "around the clock", but increasingly also mobile. The dynamics that can be observed in the adoption of new devices and service offerings can be

1

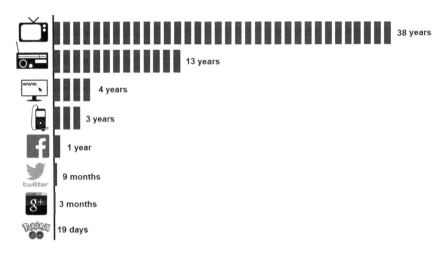

38 years

13 years

4 years

3 years

1 year

9 months

3 months

19 days

◘ **Fig. 1.2**   How long did it take to gain 50 million users?

seen in ◘ Fig. 1.2. While **radio** and **television** still needed 38 and 13 years respectively to gain 50 million users, the Internet managed to do so in 4 years and the *iPod in* 3 years. *Facebook* gathered a user community of 50 million after 1 year – and *Twitter* after just 9 months. *Google+'s* adoption was even faster, with 50 million users after just a quarter of a year. In 2016, *Pokémon Go*, a game built on augmented reality, managed to hit 50 million users in 19 days. The driver behind this increasing pace of technology adoption is a perceived relevance from the user's perspective.

As a result of these technological possibilities, more and more previously passive **consumers** of Web 1.0 are becoming **producers of Web 2.0**. This development is reflected in the term **prosumer** as a mixture of producer and consumer. The core of Web 2.0 is therefore **user-generated content**, i.e. the posting of content online that has been generated by non-professional online users themselves. In addition to the photos and videos already mentioned, this also includes comments, ratings, articles and audio files. **Web 2.0** thus describes the phenomenon that content and pages on the Internet can no longer be created and changed only by selected specialists or companies, but by the community of online users themselves. Web 2.0 is therefore not a stand-alone online marketing tool, but opens up many additional platforms and opportunities for companies to access and involve online users.

When **assessing the engagement of online users**, however, we must bear in mind the **10:20:70 rule** (cf. ◘ Fig. 1.3). Studies show that – across countries –

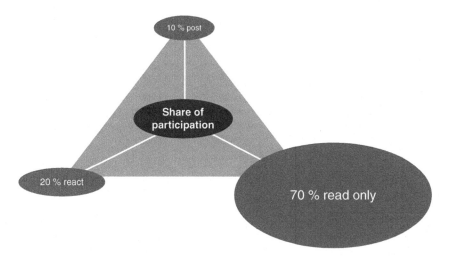

◘ Fig. 1.3 The 10:20:70 rule

around 10% of users are very active and, for example, post their own articles in blogs or online communities and write reviews. This does not refer to "private" social media activities. About 20% of the users react to such entries – while a "silent majority" of about 70% is only active in reading.

> To put it in a nutshell: It is important for companies to identify the 10% of opinion leaders on the Internet and ideally to win them over as multipliers for the company.

More than 4.5 billion people already access the Internet today – and the trend is still rising. Not only the Internet is a driver of online marketing. Also the development of telephony, specifically the dramatically increasing **spread of mobile telephony** as well as the high **penetration of mobile devices with Internet access** as an additional communication channel to customers enforces this trend. The increasing performance of mobile end devices with often falling prices as well as the expansion of the technical infrastructure in many countries of the world have led to the fact that more and more online applications can be used on the move. This is why the motto for online projects in Western industrial nations is often: **mobile first!** This is to ensure that applications work well, especially on mobile devices. In China the slogan is often already: **mobile only** with the dominating application of the **all-in-app** *WeChat*.

1

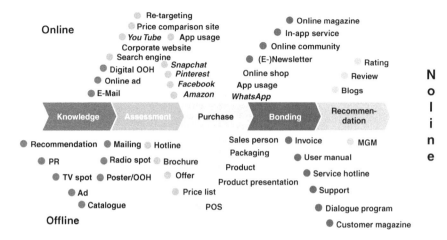

Fig. 1.4 Example of a customer journey – from online and offline to noline

Companies need to focus on the so-called **customer journey**. This "journey" comprises the various phases that a customer goes through before deciding to purchase a product or service. Today, this customer journey must be increasingly thought of across online, offline and device boundaries in order to ensure an integrated communication. A look at a typical customer journey in ◘ Fig. 1.4 shows which tasks are associated with this, and which **online and offline touchpoints** can be used. However, the touchpoints shown there represent only a small selection of the possibilities. At the same time, it becomes clear that the boundary between online and offline is becoming less important because prospective customers (also called prospects or leads) and customers can continuously switch back and forth between the different worlds – even when mobile. That is why it is better to speak of **noline** today instead of online and offline. Consequently, marketing concepts are to be developed and implemented "noline". Then the recipient does not have to put together the individual communication morsels and process steps – only to discover that they do not fit together at all!

> **Notice!**
>
> An exciting thought experiment:
> Let's look at each touchpoint as an independent sales employee. How satisfied are we with the respective performance of our sales staff – online and offline?

Digital

Social

Local

Mobile

◘ **Fig. 1.5** The DiSoLoMo trend

However, one central aspect of the **digital customer journey** has changed. Whereas in the past in stationary sales the product selection usually came after the supplier selection, in e-commerce the reverse order often dominates: **the product selection is followed by the supplier selection!**

The **dynamics of the available online options** will intensify even further. The so-called **DiSoLoMo trend**, which encompasses the dimensions **digital, social, local** and **mobile**, indicates the emerging development (cf. ◘ Fig. 1.5).

The **challenges of digitization** for companies lie first of all in the fact that more and more physical objects are being digitized and thus freed from the restrictions to which gravity had subjected them (key words: "**dematerialization**"). This applies to books, newspapers, magazines – and thus to information in general. The digitization of music and moving images fuels the success of streaming providers (e.g. *Amazon Music, Amazon Video, Netflix, Spotify*). Objects lose the limitations associated with a physical object through digitization. E-books, for example, can be sent to the other side of the world in seconds and can be produced with "zero marginal costs". A particular challenge for many business models is the **digitalization of buying and selling**. This involves online trading or e-commerce. Other services are increasingly being "dematerialised", for example in the case of insurance companies and banks (see Kreutzer 2022b for more details). These developments are

1

receiving an increasing boost from the emerging triumph of **artificial intelligence** (cf. Kreutzer and Sirrenberg 2020).

In addition, social media is creating unprecedented **countervailing power for companies**. We encounter the prefixed word "social" in more and more applications, from "social TV" to "social commerce" and "social plug-ins" to "social CRM" (customer relationship management). Companies would do well to take this **social component** into account when designing customer relationship management.

In addition, the **localization of users** and thus the regionalization of supply and demand will gain in importance. Many offers gain relevance if they are related to the user's location. City tips, coupons for stationary retail and weather forecasts come to mind here. This localization can not only refer to cities and shopping centers, but also include in-store navigation. This can provide additional buying impulses in the store. In addition to this **location-based communication**, location-based communities are also gaining in importance, which come together (spontaneously) through **check-in services**. Furthermore, **mobile access** to online services is increasing dramatically through the use of smartphones, tablet PCs and smartwatches.

❯ In a nutshell: the development of online marketing is closely intertwined with the goals, strategies and instruments of direct or dialogue marketing. Many of the success factors and solution concepts that have promoted the triumphant advance of dialogue marketing over the past few years now provide the ideal basis for its continuation in online media. The synthesis between the central building blocks of dialogue marketing and the new possibilities of online marketing will enable companies to make interesting advances in efficiency and effectiveness.

1.3 Success Factors and Design Options for Online Marketing

Good news first: the increased use of online marketing does not mean that our knowledge of marketing and customer behavior suddenly becomes obsolete – quite the opposite. The central requirements for successful marketing, as they were developed and discussed in the context of the behavioral science foundations of marketing also retain their validity in the online age. Consequently, the overarching **success factors of marketing** must be consistently taken into account when designing online marketing. These success factors are summarized in ◼ Fig. 1.6 as the **octagon of marketing** and are

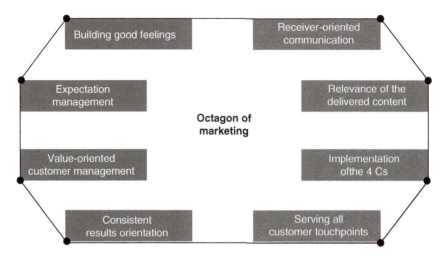

◙ Fig. 1.6 Octagon of marketing

discussed below. You can check for yourself how consistently your communication – as a private person, but above all as a company – is oriented towards these factors!

- **Every customer is first of all looking for good feelings!**

Marketing in all its forms should lead to the creation of "good feelings", especially among the prospective customers and customers of a company. For this reason, all marketing activities must be systematically and regularly assessed to determine whether they contribute to the positive mood of (prospective) customers. Consequently, it is the task – not only of marketing management – to contribute to the **creation of positive feelings** among the relevant target persons across all communication and distribution channels as well as through the company's own offers. This also applies to other stakeholders, such as investors, political decision-makers, cooperation partners – and last but not least, the company's own employees. If the focus is on prospects and customers, this is referred to as a positive **user experience (UX).**

- **Conception and implementation of receiver-oriented communication**

Many forms of corporate communication in general and of addressing prospective customers and customers in particular – whether online or offline – are still designed with a **sender-oriented approach.** Here, the company wants to communicate something and implements this without regard to the recipient of the message. **Indicators of a lack of receiver orientation** can be found

1

in a wide variety of places in companies: rates of unread deleted e-mails and e-newsletters of over 95%, bounce rates when visiting one's website of over 80%, response rates for mailings of well under 1%, coupon redemption rates in the low single digits or far below. In the online age, ad blockers and spam filters are an answer to irrelevant targeting. We need to listen to customers much more – and respond to the expectations of the target group. Because as a **result of the lack of reciever orientation** in the development of market-oriented communication offers, it is often only the company's own product managers (and possibly those of the competitors) and in-house lawyers, in addition to the marketing managers themselves, who completely read a company's advertising messages!

A **self-analysis** can provide exciting insights here: when was the last time you read a mailing (incl. various inserts), an e-newsletter, a larger text on a website or a product brochure completely? However, most companies still assume – wrongly – that their messages are read more or less completely.

❯ To the point: **we're texting for non-readers today!**

In order to make the recipient orientation "comprehensible", the **persona concept** can be used. **Personas** are fictitious archetypes that represent the target group and give them "a face" and "a name". They are described like a real person and have a life story, hobbies, philosophy of life, etc. up to a name and a picture. When designing marketing, these personas can be referred to again and again, for example to answer very specific questions about online marketing. Here, we speak of **consumer personas** or **buying personas** (for more information on the persona concept, see Kreutzer 2019, pp. 59–61).

❯ In a nutshell: communicative messages must not be **sender-oriented** if they are to achieve their goal. Instead, these messages must be consistently designed with the **recipient in mind**, i.e. geared towards the target person. What is needed here is a return to the core of marketing: **thinking in the customer's head – and feeling in the customer's heart**. This includes not trying to sell products and services, but their **benefits** – and from the receiver's perspective!

■ **Relevance of the delivered content**

Directly connected to the recipient orientation of the communication or the entire marketing is the focus on the **relevance of the delivered content** – however perceived through the eyes of the target persons! Has the company really understood what the customer is about? Does the offer actually provide a contribution that is desired by the customer – and which can therefore contribute to the creation of the good feelings? When were the customers last asked about their expectations? Are these expectations also known in the company – at the responsible places?

A first important step to ensure receiver orientation and thus relevance with the target persons is **listening**. Therefore, a procedural concept is advocated here, which has proven itself as a general guiding idea in the company – but also in the private sector. It comprises the four steps:

▬ **Listen – Learn – Act – Control.**

A good conversation always begins with an appreciative listening (**Listen**) in order to record needs, interests and moods. The second step is the **Learn** phase which is about identifying the relevant contexts, interpreting behavioural patterns and developing approaches to solutions. After the **Act** of implementation, the **Control** phase follows. This process is the only way to build a learning organization.

> To the point: Nothing is as unstable as user preferences. Moreover, online marketing opens up new possibilities every day, the effects of which need to be tested. That's why it's always good to listen, to keep testing new ways to gain and keep the interest of users!

In the context of delivered content, there is another form of marketing, which is referred to as **content marketing**. This is understood to be an orientation of marketing in which relevant and thus valuable content is created and provided for specific target groups. These processes are initiated with the aim of acquiring or retaining certain target groups or motivating them to engage in a certain way. This is also intended to achieve higher-level marketing goals – mostly sales, but also, for example, donations to a fundraising company (such as *Greenpeace* or *UNICEF*). A particularly common use is in newsletters. Here, articles, charts or white papers from service providers (e.g. from consultancies such as *Boston Consulting Group*, *Gartner* or *McKinsey*) are often offered with the aim of proving one's own competence in certain fields and, in the course of the download process, to obtain an opt-in for further support by e-mail or for contact by telephone. White papers are discussion papers which, in the form of an article, a report and/or a study, help the reader to advance knowledge or provide concrete decision-making support.

It is important that content marketing is not to be understood as a one-off action, but as a process in the course of which the defined target groups are provided with "exciting content". Consequently, content marketing does

1

not aim directly at a sale, but rather indirectly via the building of competence, sympathy and trust. This is why we also speak of **communication across the board**, because the target – as in a game of billiards – is not approached directly, but rather across the board.

■ Implementation of the "4 Cs" in marketing

The 4 Cs stand for continuity, consistency, consequence and competence. In order to achieve the necessary orientation function for the stakeholders, but especially for the leads and customers, a long-term validity of central guiding ideas of marketing is to be strived for. A high degree of **continuity** contributes to this, for example with regard to the corporate vision, the underlying values as well as the strategy and positioning of companies and/or brands. Anything else is more likely to lead to confusion and thus uncertainty among the target audience. This jeopardizes the emergence of a trustworthy image on the corporate and/or supply side. Therefore, not every new trend should be immediately translated into measures. Instead, it should be checked for example whether a commitment to *Clubhouse*, *Snapchat* or *TikTok* is actually target-oriented in the long term.

The additional **consistency** helps to achieve a coherent overall appearance of the company across all marketing instruments (keyword "omni-channel communication"). All inwardly and outwardly directed measures – be they online or offline – must be oriented towards the core objectives of the company in order to create a coherent corporate and/or product identity. In order to achieve this consistency in cross-media campaigns across all online and offline media, it is recommended that the results of the agencies involved are not only brought together after completion. In contrast, a procedure in which all agencies responsible for communication receive a briefing in one place and at one time, on the basis of which they then work together, can be much more effective. In this case, consistency is already ensured during the campaign development process. The results are then presented in just one document. In some cases, the clients also combine the agencies into separate units in order to ensure a high degree of consistency in their work.

In addition, the measures introduced and recognized as correct should be implemented with **consistency**. All too often, first-class strategies lose their power of persuasion during implementation – or come to nothing because the first resistance leads to giving up. This is especially true for the concepts of corporate blogs and corporate communities discussed later. But it also applies to corporate engagements on *Facebook*, *Instagram*, *Pinterest*, *Snapchat*, *TikTok*, *Twitter* & Co. These activities should be based on a solid strategy in order not to be discontinued after only a few months because content, personnel and/or budget for a continuation are lacking. An abrupt end of such a social media engagement would otherwise be a blow to the very people who feel most connected to the company and are therefore the first to take up an engagement.

The basis of everything is **competence**, which must not only be given in the area of the company's core services, but also, for example, in social media marketing. Due to the many opportunities for prospective customers and customers to exchange information about companies and their services in blogs, forums, communities, on rating platforms, etc., it is becoming increasingly difficult for companies to survive on the market with "poor performance". For this reason, a process of re-qualification must be set up throughout the entire company – across all hierarchical levels and not just with a focus on online marketing (cf. in-depth Kreutzer 2022b).

The dangers of a lack of continuity, consistency, consequence and competence must be systematically prevented. The consideration of these requirements gains additional importance for companies through the integration of further (online) instruments. After all, a coherent overall picture should still be created in the target persons' minds when companies use different channels in communication and distribution and interact with prospects and customers here. The requirement to deliver a convincing overall picture remains; however, it is much more difficult to implement.

- **Serving all relevant customer touchpoints**

Customer touchpoints are the points of contact between (prospective) customers and the company. This includes contacts with the salesperson in the retail trade as well as those with the field sales force or employees in the customer service center. The company's online presence with its own website, invoices (ideally designed as a "love letter to the customer"), e-mails, e-newsletters, advertising banners and corporate blogs as well as online forums and communities operated by the company also represent such touchpoints. These touchpoints can be addressed in the pre-sales, sales and/or after-sales phases. Many approaches to the management of customer touchpoints focus on the contact points of the company's own sphere, which the company itself "manages".

However, this leaves many (new) touchpoints unused and uncontrolled, which a leads or customer accesses in the run-up to or parallel to a purchase or product use or the use of a service. This includes not only the exchange in the private environment, but also the engagement with companies and their offers on the Internet – beyond the company-controlled presences. However, blogs, communities and fan groups, rating platforms and social media that

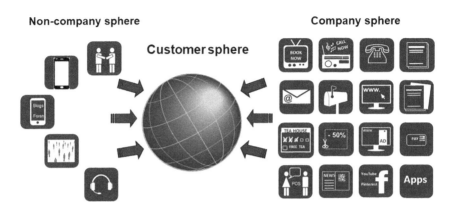

Fig. 1.7   Extended concept of customer touchpoints

are not managed by the companies themselves are also becoming increasingly important for the acquisition of information by prospective customers and customers (cf. **Fig. 1.7**). Therefore, these must also be integrated into the touchpoint management.

Many companies still neglect the contact points of the non-corporate sphere – as they are beyond direct control and influence. Nevertheless, these contact points have a central influence on the decision-making behavior of prospects and customers. Finally, statements in online forums are attributed a higher **credibility** than the content of corporate communication (cf. **Fig. 1.8**; based on Nielsen 2015). Consequently, touchpoint management must be further developed accordingly in order to also take these other touchpoints into account in corporate communication.

The study by Nielsen (2015) addressed the question of **trust in various sources of information worldwide**. For this purpose, 30.000 people were surveyed. **Figure 1.8** shows the top-2-box results, combining ("complete trust" and "high trust"). According to the study, **personal recommendations** have the highest trust potential with 78% of the mentions. This is followed by **online recommendations** with 60%. Only after these ratings come **brand websites** 54%, followed by **editorial content** with 52% and **TV advertising** with 45%.

The **play on all relevant touchpoints** must correspond to the aforementioned 4 Cs in order to convey a coherent impression across channels and media – oriented to the **customer journey** already discussed (cf. **Fig. 1.4**). This also raises the question of how this customer journey and customer

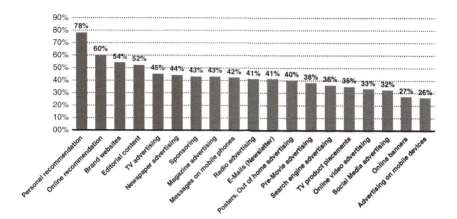

■ **Fig. 1.8** Which of the following forms of advertising do you trust?

expectations of it have changed. In addition, it must be examined which of the **customer touchpoints** – in the eyes of the customers – have gained in importance and which have lost. All customer communication – online and offline – must be aligned with this.

- **Consistent result orientation of marketing activities**

In many cases still little developed – but indispensable for a broad acceptance of marketing in the company – is a consistent orientation of all marketing activities towards the **achievement of profit contributions**. This means that the managers responsible for marketing must make greater efforts to make their performance contribution to the achievement of corporate goals visible and thus also assessable. The magic formula for this is called: **Return on Marketing Investment** (ROMI). For this reason, it is important to ensure that points for success control are planned and meaningful key performance indicators (KPIs) are defined as early as the conception stage of marketing activities.

> To put it in a nutshell: companies should not carry out marketing measures whose success cannot be measured. Consequently, already in the conception phase of a marketing action, it is necessary to "think along" how its success can be measured. In addition, all activities should be systematically evaluated for their contribution to success. This is the only way to make marketing activities more successful from time to time.

1

■ **Value-oriented customer management**

Value-oriented customer management represents a specific form of the target orientation of marketing. In many companies, **customer value** – an example of a particularly important key performance indicator – is still not a central control variable. Why? Because in the vast majority of companies, customer value is still not determined. However, a determination of the customer value must not stop at the recording of the turnover – even more so determined ex post (i.e. retrospectively). It is a question of a current or, even better, future-oriented value of each individual customer, which ideally goes beyond pure sales and captures the **forecast customer contribution margin** (cf. on different concepts for determining customer values Kreutzer 2021a, pp. 28–43).

In the **B2B market** (business-to-business), it is often easier to determine this target figure because the number of customers served is often lower here and, at the same time, a higher information density per customer is achieved. In the **B2C market** (business-to-consumer) – for example in stationary retail – there is often a lack of data to determine customer value. But how can a targeted acquisition of new customers and a potential-oriented customer development take place if the value of the leads and customers acquired via different channels is not known?

> In a nutshell: Even if it is tedious: Every company should try to determine the – ideally future – value of its customers!

■ **Expectation management**

Consistent expectation management is another requirement. Through communication – in private as well as in business – expectations are consistently built up in the counterpart. Anyone who promises "delivery within 48 hours" and delivers the goods after 4 days is visibly producing disappointment. That's why I think it's an underestimated task in marketing and especially in communication to consistently steer the customer's expectations into an area that the company can actually live up to. Only those who deliver more than promised will trigger enthusiasm – a central prerequisite for satisfying customer relationships in the long term. If this succeeds, the desired "good feelings" also arise more easily in the target persons, which closes the circle of the relevant requirements.

> In a nutshell: The **points of the octagon** mentioned above provide an **orientation framework**. Not only the classic marketing instruments, but also the entire online marketing must be aligned with this framework. Consequently, the central guiding ideas, mechanisms of action and general laws on which marketing has been based up to now also apply when entering the online sector.

These overarching success factors are complemented by **specific design options for online marketing**. These have led to online marketing being integrated to an ever greater extent into the value chain of companies and also making a significant contribution to the customer experience. At the same time, the budget share of online marketing, especially in the communication budget of companies, has increased significantly in recent years. The central design options for online marketing are outlined below (cf. Kreutzer 2021b, pp. 40–75; **Rusnjak** and **Schallmo** 2017).

- **Stronger focus on target persons and target groups**

Some online marketing instruments (e.g. e-mails, e-coupons, online advertising, push messages, *WhatsApp* messages) allow a stronger focus of the respective messages on individual target groups or target persons than is usually possible with a classic TV spot or an advertisement in a popular magazine such as *Vogue* or *Time*. In this way, targeted e-mails can be sent to the company's own prospective customers and customers or to rented addresses. The prerequisite for this is that permission has been granted to address them by e-mail (cf. the relevant requirements of the General Data Protection Regulation in Europe).

In the **B2B market**, for example, companies celebrating a milestone anniversary in the coming year can be targeted. These can be offered the preparation of a commemorative publication or the organisation of the company anniversary. Or managing directors can be approached in order to offer specific seminars to these managers. In the **B2C market,** the members of the *Pampers Club* – based on an app – can receive tailored information. In this way, the (promotional) messages reach the desired recipients with pinpoint accuracy (cf. further Kreutzer 2021a, pp. 230–245).

- **Higher individualizability of the transmitted messages: target-oriented (behavior-oriented) addressing of the people**

In some cases, the online tools used offer the possibility of individualising the messages transmitted with regard to the target persons in conjunction with the focus. This is possible with **telephone calls, e-mails, e-newsletters, e-coupons** and **push notifications**. Here, tailored offers can be made on the basis of a known prospect or customer history (such as purchases in the online shop). A company can learn more and more about its prospects and customers here; a **learning relationship** is created (cf. Peppers and Rogers 2017, p. 1).

Individualization based on this can also be achieved by generating **individualized purchase recommendations in real time** (i.e. immediately) during a

1

telephone conversation with a customer – based on the customer's personal purchase history. These can be displayed on the screen of the customer advisor in the customer service center. Such personal recommendations are also presented by *Amazon*. To achieve this *Amazon* compares the information and purchasing behavior of a person with that of other *Amazon* customers on the basis of shopping cart analyses – and today increasingly through AI-based analyses. Here we can speak of a **recommendation engine**.

By **analyzing the surfing and search behavior of online users**, it is determined in which content environments (from photo portals to websites of newspaper publishers to erotic sites) a person is "on the go" online. This method is called **behavioral targeting** (cf. in-depth Kreutzer 2021b, pp. 221–223). Based on this information, online banners can be provided in a context-oriented manner. Further possibilities for individualisation arise from the **evaluation of profile data** that members deposit with social networks. For this, members must give their consent to the data evaluation in advance.

With **predictive behavioral targeting** or **lookalike targeting** the provision of online advertising is aligned with the **expected behaviour of the online user**. For this purpose, information on navigation and search behaviour is linked with further data from other online users in order to "extrapolate" to the expected behaviour or to expected areas of interest. For this purpose, information on age, gender, interests or overall lifestyle is used, which was provided in the course of (anonymous) online surveys. By extrapolating the behaviour of a subset to other online users, their expectations are to be better recognised and served. In this way, forecasts about their areas of interest can also be made for online users without clear characteristic profiles, and advertising delivery can be geared to these. The persons identified in this way are also referred to as **lookalike audiences** or **lookalike targeting**. A prerequisite for their identification, however, is that a sufficiently large number of visitors allows a statistically stable extrapolation.

The variety of targeting options contributes to the **reduction of scattering losses in the target group approach**. However, a higher degree of individualization in the recipient leads to an **increase in the relevance of the offer** and thus promotes the likelihood that the recipient will exhibit the behavior desired by the company.

■ **Offer immediate response options**
Many online marketing tools can achieve a **higher level of attention** in part due to an immediate call-to-action (CTA). A call-to-action is a short descriptive instruction that tells the reader or user exactly what to do. Less

activating CTAs are "click here" or "download here". Stronger CTAs state the achievable benefit and read, for example, "7 SEO tricks" or "Your path to resilience". Through a CTA, the person being addressed can react immediately and, for example, place a request for information or an order. "I'll look at that again later" is often omitted here. However, this also means that the call-to-action must be designed very attractively in order to trigger an action immediately! In addition, companies should be prepared for quick reactions.

- **Short response times on the supply and demand side**
The online tools make it possible to react promptly or even in real time to certain developments – such as the order volume or the demand for certain information. For example, an ongoing acquisition campaign via e-mail or e-newsletter or a keyword campaign can be stopped if delivery bottlenecks are foreseeable. At the same time, tailored information can be provided by the company – in the decision-making processes still underway at the prospective customer. Thus, in the case of shopping cart abandoners whose e-mail address has already been recorded, it is possible to ask "nicely" about the reason for the abandonment or – much better – what is still missing for a successful conclusion (on these problem-solving questions, see Kreutzer 2019, pp. 24–26). The results obtained here can in turn be recorded promptly and used to further optimize the actions. Moreover, even poorly performing online banner campaigns can be optimized or terminated after a few hours or days. Finally, the Cost per Click is available here and can be compared with the results achieved.

- **Possibility for personal interaction**
If the **telephone** or a **chatbot** is used in the course of online marketing, the focus is even on direct dialogue (cf. in-depth Hundertmark 2021). Such dialogues can also be continued through the use of **digital assistants** such as *Alexa* and *Google Home* (cf. Kreutzer and Vousoghi 2020). Here, not only does the possibility exist to gain a variety of information in direct conversation, but also to present individualized solutions. Such solutions make an important contribution to customer acquisition as well as customer retention. On many websites there are also **call-back buttons**, through which a call-back request is signalled to the company. In e-mails, a link can also be integrated to announce a call-back request. All these offers enable a personal dialogue.

- **Short lead time of online actions**

The lead time for online campaigns is very short for many instruments. For example, an appeal for donations can be sent by e-mail to registered donors (with e-mail permission) just a few minutes after a disaster becomes known. In contrast, a mailing appeal with a larger circulation has a lead time of several days, even if many steps have already been prepared. Online banners and keyword ads can also often be developed and "armed" within minutes.

- **Applicability even with small marketing budgets**

Many online marketing tools can be implemented even with **small budgets**. Renting 1000 e-mail addresses (with permission) to target plastic surgeons in Germany is just as possible as contacting 50 customers by phone that a dealership has identified based on an analysis of the probability of buying a new car. However, this is only possible if the dealership has obtained permission to call in advance. Those who want to work with *Google Ads* or with advertising on *Facebook* for the first time can start doing so with just a few Euros. Publishing content via posts on *Facebook*, *Instagram* or *LinkedIn* do not come with significant costs. However, there are costs for the creation of the content.

The possibility to become very focused and thus also cost-effective with the instruments of online marketing is particularly interesting for **niche providers** and **small companies**. Advertising banners can be placed in the online environments that are interesting for the relevant target groups only.

- **Global reach**

A decisive advantage of the Internet is its global reach. All online users worldwide can access the Internet presence of *Montblanc* or *Esprit,* unless government censors deny access. This comprehensive degree of dissemination offers almost unlimited possibilities in the procurement and provision of information – for suppliers and customers alike.

- **Comprehensive and timely evaluability of the results of online marketing tools**

Instruments of online marketing often aim at an immediate reaction of the addressed persons via different (online) reaction channels. Therefore **reaction data** are available very quickly. With the help of this data, the respective success of the initiated measures can be determined – even with ongoing campaigns. **Test concepts** can also be placed more easily in order to identify the "best working" variants in advance of a comprehensive deployment (keyword "pre-test"), e.g. through **A/B testing** (cf. Kreutzer 2021a, pp. 168–171).

If the **surfing behaviour** is tracked, success can be monitored on an hourly or daily basis. It quickly becomes visible which target achievement can be expected. Such an evaluation of success can be carried out not only on the online instruments used alone, but also in connection with the target groups and sub-target groups addressed. In this way, it can be determined which online instrument guarantees the highest target achievement for which group, in order to optimise the use of the instrument specifically for the customer and/or segment.

- **Performance-oriented payment of integrated partners and service providers**

Many forms of cooperation with partners or service providers in online marketing are remunerated on the basis of performance. Then companies no longer pay for the placement of online ads alone, but for the leads or customers they acquire. This is often the case with affiliate marketing and many forms of online advertising. This is referred to as **performance marketing** or **performance-oriented marketing**. However, performance marketing is also referred to when the results of marketing campaigns can be quickly recorded – for example, in comparison to measures aimed at brand building.

In order for the instruments of online marketing to exploit their potential for the entire marketing presence, their comprehensive **integration into the company's marketing concept** is necessary. In many companies, it is still the case that different organisational units are responsible for the tasks of classic and direct or online communication. In addition, different agencies are usually responsible for PR, advertising (often still separated into TV and print), dialogue marketing, POS marketing, event marketing and online marketing (possibly differentiated for online advertising, search engine optimization, keyword advertising, affiliate marketing, etc.).

There are often additional **cognitive firewalls** between the departments and/or the people in charge. These "firewalls in the heads" impede or prevent goal-oriented communication. Then the integration of the various measures cannot succeed. A convincing and consistent appearance towards prospects and customers is missed. The associated **silo mentality** in the sense of thinking in closed units (e.g. departments or specialist areas) must be consistently overcome.

1

❯ In a nutshell: The **customer as the target object of corporate marketing** should not be the only one to determine whether the measures are comprehensively coordinated. But he still is too often. Then there are references in classic advertisements to websites that are not active at the time of placement. Or they are not equipped with the promised information. Then important **synergetic potentials of integrated communication** remain unused. These potentials must be exploited through an **integrative planning and implementation process**. All customer-oriented activities are to be planned and implemented in an integrative approach – in a noline process as mentioned before (cf. ◘ Fig. 1.4).

1.4 General Expectations and Motives of Online Users

In order to understand the changes in expectations and the motives of online users, it is first necessary to analyse people's basic need structures (cf. ◘ Fig. 1.9). Starting from one's own "I", this **map of needs** strives for the needs of connectedness on the one hand and freedom/autonomy on the other. These needs are in tension with each other. The **striving for connectedness** includes the need for security as well as for relatedness to a partner, the family, a group, a team, a company. Here one tries to be part of something bigger. The negative form of this are dependence on others and self-sacrifice. In contrast to this is the **striving for freedom/autonomy.** Associated with this is the pursuit of power and control. If this need is served in an uncontrolled way, loneliness can be the result.

Another basic human need is the **striving for creativity and development.** This is about creating and achieving something. Excessive expression of this need can lead to excessive demands. Somewhat detached from these three basic needs is the **striving for being**. This is about being accepted because one "is" – not because one achieves something. In the ideal state of being, flow sets in. In these situations the physical challenge experienced and one's own performance are in absolute balance. A dominance in living out this need for "being" can be the feeling of boredom and uselessness, if the person himself does not find satisfying answers for himself for the arrangement of his own existence. The totality of these four needs, which each person feels in varying degrees of intensity, represents an important **driver of human behavior.**

Derived from these basic human needs, the **motives for specific behaviours on the Internet** can be determined (cf. ◘ Fig. 1.10). A motive represents the reason or the drive for people to do something. In the case of the

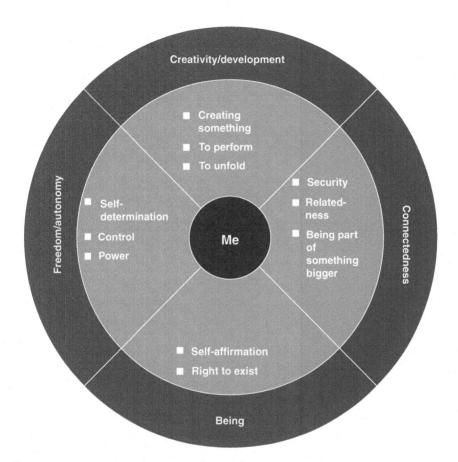

□ Fig. 1.9   Needs map – basic human need structures

target group of leads and customers as online users, which is particularly important for us, a distinction must be made between commercial and non-commercial motives for their actions. **Commercial motives** include the desire to purchase certain products or services at the lowest possible price. This motive leads to visiting price comparison sites. Commercial motives also lead to the online sale of one's own services or other products or services without already engaging in e-commerce as a professional provider. For these semi-professional sellers, platforms such as *Etsy,* but also more broadly positioned providers such as *eBay* or *Amazon,* offer interesting market access. This makes important contributions to satisfying the needs for autonomy

1

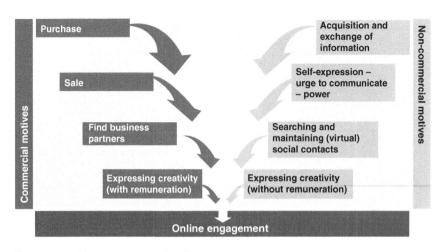

□ **Fig. 1.10**   Motive structures of online users

and especially for creativity. In addition, the search for business partners (certainly also a potential employer) can be promoted through networks such as *LinkedIn*. These activities pay off in the pursuit of connectedness.

Commercial motives are also available for **click workers** or **crowd workers**. These are online users who apply for jobs on a fee basis on online platforms (e.g. ▶ jovoto.com). These jobs involve tasks that can usually be worked on independently and flexibly in terms of time with online access.

In addition, there are a large number of **non-commercial motives** that are leading to more and more time being spent online (cf. □ Fig. 1.10). The dominant driver behind this is the quest for connectedness – or simply the desire to "pass the time". The basis for this is the acquisition and exchange of information, which is supported by online research via search engines and can pay off in terms of commercial goals. The evaluation of or participation in rating platforms, blogs, forums and communities also satisfies the need for connectedness. The latter concepts additionally offer the possibility of making one's own contributions, thus satisfying the motives of **self-expression** and the **urge to share** as specific manifestations of the need for creativity. The totality of these motives leads to the fact that many millions of *Facebook*, *Instagram* and *Pinterest* members elaborately design their profiles and pinboards, maintain them daily and provide them with texts, videos, photos and/or sound recordings.

With the freedom/autonomy-based urge to communicate can also be a **striving for power**. Until now, customers were predominantly part of an unorganized, invisible "mass". This could hardly exert a lasting influence on companies. Now, individuals can vote on social networks via the Internet and put the fear of God into companies by posting on blogs, forums and communities. All in all, based on the **power of the masses**, a previously unknown position of power is emerging, which companies must first learn to deal with. These shifts in power are also reflected in the fact that customers are increasingly demanding services via social media. The particularly critical aspect of these **social services** from the company's perspective is that the service provision takes place in front of the "interested public" – and everyone can see whether the company is "performing" or "failing".

This also changes the significance of previous opinion leaders in the public sphere. In the past, (public) opinion was primarily shaped by representations in the discussions led by **(professional) opinion leaders** in (mass) media. The voices of the (supposed) experts dominated. In the future, the greater dissemination and active use of social media will not only make it more difficult for previous experts to convey their monopolies of opinion, but will also result in a much greater diversity of opinion. This has to be absorbed organizationally in the companies. At the same time, the **influencer marketing** must be given greater importance (cf. Kilian and Kreutzer 2022; Kilian 2020; Kost and Seeger 2020).

The motive of **expressing one's own creativity** can refer to the further development of third-party services. This includes the participation in the development of *Lego bricks*. It can also refer to answering complex research questions that are presented by companies at ▶ innocentive.com. Commercial motives can also play a role here if creative achievements are rewarded by companies. The creativity motive can also refer to the design of third-party services that the customer wants to purchase himself. This is the case with the concepts of ▶ spreadshirt.com or ▶ mymuesli.com. The introduction of one's own creativity can at the same time refer to the motive of **self-profiling** (need to be) in the relevant reference group, which can support the search for and maintenance of (virtual) contacts as an expression of the striving for connectedness. This represents the main motive for many users to engage in social media.

A study by Sherman et al. (2016) provides exciting findings in this regard: **Likes have the same effect on the brain as chocolate**. Likes for posts, photos, videos or other creations set classic reward mechanisms in motion in the brains of young people, as is the case when they win money. Whether the likes come from "real" or "supposed" friends is irrelevant. This **digital reward effect** was determined by studying the processes involved in social media use in the brains of 32 teenagers. It became clear how important the **opinion of**

1

others on social media is: the more likes a photo had already received from others, the more likely the participants were to give it a positive rating – regardless of what was actually in the photo (e.g. cigarettes or alcohol). Here we can speak of **conformity constraint** or **peer pressure**, which also has an effect in "digital" form in the social networks. **Recognition** is an important motive for action here!

❯ To the point: An analysis of the **need structures** and **motivational landscape of online users** provides an important background for action when designing marketing and communication measures. Only the comprehensive consideration of the presented findings ensures what is indispensable for the participation of our target audience: **relevance!**

How – not entirely seriously – the new **digital needs pyramid** (loosely based on *Maslow*) is shown in **◘** Fig. 1.11.

In the following, we will discuss the **expectations of prospects and customers** based on this, which they express to companies in words and deeds. The comprehensive consideration of these expectations is indispensable for the successful design of marketing in general, but also of online marketing in particular. These expectations can be characterized with the catchwords "I, everything, immediately and everywhere". **◘** Figure 1.12 shows how these expectations are concretised in individual cases.

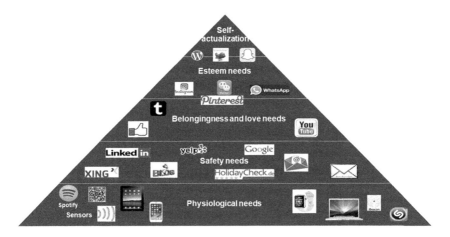

◘ Fig. 1.11   The new digital hierarchy of needs

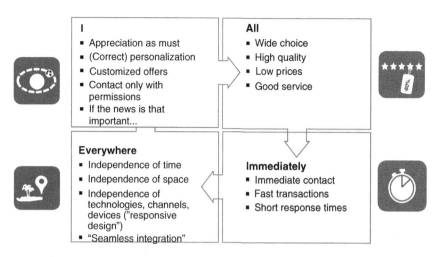

I
- Appreciation as must
- (Correct) personalization
- Customized offers
- Contact only with permissions
- If the news is that important...

All
- Wide choice
- High quality
- Low prices
- Good service

Everywhere
- Independence of time
- Independence of space
- Independence of technologies, channels, devices ("responsive design")
- "Seamless integration"

Immediately
- Immediate contact
- Fast transactions
- Short response times

◘ Fig. 1.12 Concretization of customer expectations

Due to the high intensity of competition in almost all areas, the customer can allow himself under "**I**", among other things, to expect or demand a high level of appreciation in the interaction. If this is denied, there are usually many competitors waiting to win the customer over. The "lived appreciation" includes a **correct personalization**. This refers to addressing the target person correctly by name. At the same time, the expectation of being taken seriously as an individual with specific, possibly even individual wishes increases. This is reflected in whether a person receives individual addresses and offers – or still a mass approach. The **requirements from the perspective of a (prospective) customer** – with which we are confronted – are concretized in the following questions:

- Are the offers tailor-made for me?
- Does the potential business partner speak my language and does it make itself understood to me?
- Am I getting exactly the information I want via e-mail, e-newsletters, mailings, posts, status updates, push notifications, etc.?
- Are my specifications for addressing by mailing, post, telephone, e-mail and fax respected by the advertising companies?
- Can I find the information I need quickly online and offline?
- Can I just order and pay?
- Can I find the help I need?

1

— Can I make desired transactions at a time and place according to my preferences?
— Is the seller giving me the exact information I'm missing?

Ego-orientation culminates in the statement: "**If the news is that important, it will find me.**" This means that people believe that they no longer have to actively search for information and offers because these are brought to them via shares, likes, comments, re-tweets, pins or *WhatsApp* messages – but only if the content is really relevant!

The question of the (lack of) appreciation of the users is also documented in another point: the **handling of the GTC** and other agreements. Here, data protection declarations that are presented to the (prospective) customer are especially to be thought of. *Facebook*'s terms of use – including the explanation of rights and obligations – are laid out on about five pages. Another four or so pages define the data policy. *Google* also publishes comprehensive terms that fill many pages and must be accepted each time you log in.

Here's the thing: The most common **lie on the Internet** is probably, "I've read the GTC."

Companies are well advised not to foist unilateral, unusual or surprising clauses and conditions on users. These may either not be legal and therefore invalid, or they may be validly agreed and interpreted to the customer's disadvantage. If the associated disputes are fought out in social media, lasting damage to the image of the company can be the result (cf. on the legal aspects Blind and Stumpfrock 2021, pp. 607–633).

The expectations regarding **individualization** are concretized in the already mentioned assignment of permissions for contacting. Via these **permissions** a (prospective) customer defines for a company the "permitted" way of contacting him. Such permissions are also necessary if the geographical location ("geo-location") is recorded and/or cookies are set. These permissions can be revoked at any time by the customer. Companies are legally bound to strictly observe these permissions to contact. The customer hereby develops into the **Master of Communication**. He decides when, who, what and via which channels the company is allowed to communicats with him and which data may be accessed in the process.

Different concepts are used to obtain these permissions on the Internet (e.g. for sending newsletters) (cf. ◘ Fig. 1.13). With the so-called **single opt-in** a customer indicates that he is interested in receiving an e-mail newsletter, for example. This is the basis for the transmission. With the **confirmed opt-in** the interested party receives a confirmation that the permission has been received. This allows the person to revoke the interest if necessary. With **dou-**

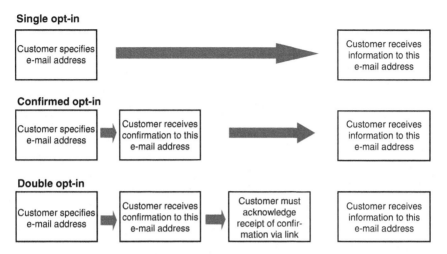

Fig. 1.13 Different concepts for obtaining a permission

ble opt-in – the most demanding type of permission collection – the interested party must send a further confirmation of his expressed interest to the offering company. Only then this address can be used to send an e-mail newsletter. This last type is the only one that provides sufficient legal certainty when obtaining a permission in many countries.

An **offline permission for sending newsletters** requires an explicit declaration of intent with date and signature of the customer. In addition, the customer must be informed here of what content he can expect and with what regularity. These declarations are to be archived by the company and presented in the event of a conflict.

In order for a website to be allowed to use **cookies**, a **permission** must be obtained to **set cookies**. **Cookies** are small files that are stored by the web server on a device's local hard disk to identify it. In the further usage process on other websites or in subsequent visits at a later time, these files can be queried and the computer can thus be clearly identified. This has particular advantages for providers, who can recognise users and provide them with correspondingly individualised support. For the users themselves, cookies often lead to a higher degree of relevance and, in particular, convenience in the handling of websites (cf. in-depth Kreutzer 2021b, pp. 67–70).

The self-centredness of customers documented in ◘ Fig. 1.12 is also reflected in their **demands on the media**. Fewer and fewer people want to watch news, films and documentaries when they are being broadcast on

1

TV. That is one of the reasons why **on-demand** and **streaming services** are booming. In the long term, these services will make CD and DVD players superfluous – as well as linear TV. The classic hardware producers will lose out to the detriment of content distribution platforms (such as *Amazon Music/Video, Netflix, Spotify*), unless they become content marketers themselves (such as *Apple* with *iTunes, Apple TV, Amazon Video*). *Amazon* even acquired the movie studio *Metro-Goldwyn-Mayer (MGM)* in 2021 to become a more important content provider.

At the same time, distribution platforms and service providers will become hardware providers themselves (such as *Amazon* with *kindl* and *Alexa/Amazon Home* and *Google* with its own smartphone *Pixel*). In addition, platform operators themselves are becoming content providers – such as *Facebook* with its *Facebook Watch* offering, which presents its own video offers in order to keep users in the *Facebook* world for longer (cf. on the ecosystems emerging here Kreutzer 2022b).

The strong ego-orientation of customers also leads to **customer loyalty to brands, sales channels and companies** tends to decrease. The group of **variety-seekers** who like to try out new things and change brands and providers to do so, has become even more important in the online age. It often turns out that online shoppers are more likely to switch providers than customers who have personal contact with the company (via branch or telephone).

The **"everything"** expectation (cf. ◘ Fig. 1.12) shows the high level of expectations that customers have in most industries today. Customers have learned that "everything is possible" often applies:

 ▬ Test-winning products be found as the lowest-priced offer.
 ▬ *H&M* offers clothes by designers *Jimmy Choo, Anna Dello Russo* and *Kenzo* at low prices.
 ▬ *Amazon* offers a broad and deep assortment, combined with a highly individualized recommendation of "suitable" additional products – including delivery the next day or even the same day.
 ▬ More and more brands allow individualization of the product – from *Ray-Ban* glasses to *Laura Biagiotti* sweaters to *Prada* bags. With some prestige brands, anyone can now become a self-made designer.
 ▬ The Internet offers an almost inexhaustible supply of information – around the clock, often highly topical or even in real time as a news stream, and mostly free of charge. Whereby "free of charge" is not correct.

> **Notice!**
>
> Wherever we don't have to pay on the Internet, we pay with our data. Here the motto is: "If you are not paying for the product, then you are the product!"

In many areas of the Internet, there are a **"I don't pay"** mentality and a **"main thing is for free"** mentality. As a result, in many areas only a few users are willing to accept a **paywall** set up by the content provider (by analogy with a firewall). The successful introduction of paywalls, in which users are motivated to pay for services, is a vital task, especially for publishers. After all, users have learned that they don't have to pay for great tips. Neither for the information where there are price advantages, nor which hotel offers a particularly good price-performance ratio. Nor for information on which airline offers the cheapest flight from Frankfurt to Delhi. Also for answers to all possible and impossible answers the user does not have to pay anything. Why then should one pay for an editorial message from the *New York Times*? That's what many users wonder.

An the users almost consistently avoid overcoming the paywalls that **content provider** have built or are in the process of building. Time and again, attempts have been and are being made to price content created at great expense on the Internet as well. While few get the idea of not paying for a printed newspaper at the newsstand, free access to the same substance in online format is virtually taken for granted. This leads to existential problems for many companies. So one may be curious how the **paid apps** and **additional paid content** of selected publishers will be received by the user community in the long term.

But it is not only the willingness to pay for content that is decreasing. Users are also putting a stop to the other source of income for content providers – such as placing advertisements on their own websites – by using **ad blockers**. It is easy to understand the financial difficulties business models that finance themselves (primarily) through online advertising can run into. Consequently, users are repeatedly called upon by publishers to refrain from using ad blockers. In some cases, the deactivation of ad blockers is also a prerequisite for accessing certain content from publishers. In my opinion, particularly perfidious are the business models of ad blockers that charge companies for displaying their advertisements despite the fact that an ad blocker is installed. This is a **chargeable whitelisting** by the ad blocker providers.

1

In many cases, companies strive to meet the expectation of **"everywhere/ always"** (cf. ◘ Fig. 1.12). Mobile accessibility – not only as telephony, but also as access to service offerings via the Internet – is now a matter of course in the developed industrial nations and increasingly also in many emerging markets. The expectation results in particular from the **always-on generation** – who are themselves "always available" – and often expect this from companies as well, regardless of whether this takes place in a professional or private environment, or whether they are stationary or mobile. This also increasingly blurs the boundaries between private and public or professional spheres. This is why leads and clients often expect companies to provide access to the customer service center around the clock: every day, 7 days a week, 365 days a year – without thinking about the cost implications on the company side.

Access to corporate offerings is thus increasingly shifting from "classic opening hours" at "specific locations" to a **customer-driven interaction process** that is flexible in terms of time and space. It applies that the (prospective) customers can both receive and send everywhere and around the clock. This challenge places high demands on businesses. In this **instant society** the following motto applies: "any channel, any device, anywhere, anytime". The streaming offers already mentioned are a perfect example of how this expectation can be met.

This challenge has a special significance for online marketing because it leads to high demands on the accessibility of companies. At the same time, e.g. through **location-based services**, completely new business models and promotion approaches are possible. For example, an e-coupon can be sent to a mobile phone if the customer is in the vicinity of a *McDonald's* restaurant and has previously given permission. For this purpose, a "digital fence" is erected around the location. This is why it is called **geo fencing**. When this fence is crossed, a corresponding push notification is then sent. With such offers, the following applies once again: **relevance through proximity!**

In addition, there is the expectation **"immediately"**, which causes acceleration effects in a wide variety of areas (cf. ◘ Fig. 1.12). It is true that companies are given less and less **time to react** by (prospective) customers. If there is no response to an e-mail after 4 hours, many times people follow up. And why should a customer wait a week at another company when an order at *Amazon* is fulfilled within 24–48 hours by default? *Amazon's* experience is used as a benchmark (i.e. a reference value) for evaluating the performance of other companies – even across industry boundaries. Whether this seems appropriate from a vendor's perspective in a particular case is of little interest to the ego-driven prospect or customer. Through **channel hopping**, the user can punish the slow by a mouse click at the competitor – and possibly get lost as a customer forever.

What are the **expectations in terms of response time** that users have in companies is made clear below (cf. Innomega 2021):

- When a company receives questions about **mailings** hardly anyone expects an answer in the same week.
- If an inquiry is made by **e-mail** the answer should reach the questioner at the latest after 48 hours, better still within 24 hours.
- A question on *Facebook* must be answered within a few hours to avoid appearing "uninterested" or "arrogant".
- If *Twitter* or **instant messenger services** are used as support and information channels, users expect a response within minutes.

This "instant" leads to another interesting development, which can be described as a **culture of nowness**. It is no longer only among younger target groups that it is increasingly observed that while watching TV (which now often takes place on a laptop, smartphone or tablet PC), they not only regularly check their *Facebook* account, *WhatsApp* messages and e-mail inbox, but also exchange information on a wide variety of topics via *Twitter*. For employees and managers, **multitasking** leads to the phenomenon that they continuously check their e-mail inbox on *iPhone* & Co. – even and especially during ongoing conferences, meetings or lectures. However, current **studies on multitasking** make it clear that humans are not designed for this and consequently achieve significantly poorer results when concentration is divided between several tasks. It has also been shown that this phenomenon not only occurs in men, but that women are not really capable of multitasking either (cf. DGUV 2010)!

> **Notice!**
>
> What is the big **driver of nowness**? The **FOMO-effect** – fear of missing out! The danger of missing something important (cf. in-depth Kreutzer 2020).

With regard to **time as a critical success factor,** the process shown in ◘ Fig. 1.14 should therefore be taken into account. When dealing with an offer, the **motivation of (prospective) customers** initially increases. At the highest point, a request for further information or an order is often placed. Afterwards the motivation level sinks again, because other offers fight for the attention and the own attention slowly falls into oblivion. The faster, for example, the requested catalogue, the first e-newsletter or the delivery from

1

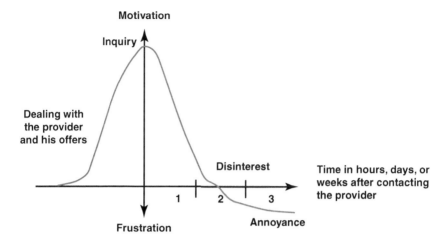

◘ Fig. 1.14   Speed as a critical success factor

Zalando or *Amazon* arrives, the greater the motivation that can still be found, which can have an image- and purchase-promoting effect.

One thing is certain: the later the desired information arrives, the less of the initial motivation remains, because other companies may have already – more quickly – provided further information or interesting offers. This may not be a matter of weeks, but of days and – especially in e-commerce – of hours! It is not for nothing that many companies are working on the concept of "same day delivery". *Amazon Prime Air's* delivery concept aims to use drones to deliver goods within 30 minutes or less of receiving the order.

If the (online) requested information, the requested offer or the ordered goods arrive much later than expected, the delivery may be met with **disinterest** because the interested party or (potential) customer no longer remembers his request or has in the meantime decided on another provider. However, **annoyance** can also arise because the information or products were not available at the expected time and one feels that one is not being taken seriously enough as a person or company. Consequently, information remains unread or goods are returned.

Notice!

Brian Solis (2012) has vividly summarized this development:

"With customers today being increasingly connected, informed, and ultimately empowered, their expectations only escalate. In short, they are more discerning and demanding than ever before."

This makes it understandable why every company should deal with the requirements of "I, everything, everywhere, immediately" before and alongside the use of online marketing. This can be done with the objective of first comparing one's own performance with the expectations of the relevant target groups. At the same time, starting points can be identified in order to achieve **differentiation in the competitive environment** by convincingly fulfilling these expectations.

However, it is clear that in order to meet the expectations outlined above, customer-oriented processes must be designed with a consistent focus on efficiency. The increasing use of online marketing will further increase the pressure on this in the future. Here, it is increasingly important to achieve **digital business excellence** (cf. in-depth Kreutzer 2022b). At the same time, it must be examined how valuable the customer relationships are in order to profitably serve the identified expectations (keyword "**value-oriented customer management**"; see further Kreutzer 2021a, p. 30–43).

1.5 Learning Control

Short and Sweet

Online marketing is a central field of action for all companies. Online marketing has gained in importance decisively. More and more companies and customers – B2B and B2C – are using a wide variety of online channels to prepare for and follow up purchases or to make them. Companies must try to understand the customer journey of their customers in order to be represented at the relevant customer touchpoints with relevant information.

It is crucial not only to understand the possibilities and limitations of the individual online tools, but also to know the motivational landscape of online users. Only then will online concepts achieve the desired effects. The challenge here is to successfully manage the I-all-immediately-everywhere expectations.

Let's Check

1. What is meant by the 10:20:70 rule? Why is this rule so important?
2. What is meant by the DiSoLoMo trend? Which developments are meant by this?
3. What are customer touchpoints? What is their significance?
4. How can the general expectations of online users be described?

1

❓ Networking Tasks

Analyse the online and offline platforms on which *Zalando is* currently represented in terms of communication. Work out which target groups are addressed in each case and which offers are currently highlighted.

ℹ️ Reading and Deepening

- Chaffrey, D./Ellis-Chadwick, F. (2019). *Digital marketing.* 7th Edition. New York.
- Chaffey, D./Smith, P. R. (2018). *Digital marketing excellence.* 5th Edition. London.
- Kingsnorth, S. (2019). *Digital marketing strategy: An integrated approach to online marketing.* 2nd Edition. London.
- Peppers, D., & Rogers, M. (2017). *Managing customer relationships. A strategic framework* (3. Aufl.). Hoboken/New Jersey.
- Stokes, R. (2018). *eMarketing: The essential guide to marketing in a digital world.* 6th Edition. Red & Yellow.

Online Marketing Concept

Contents

© Springer Fachmedien Wiesbaden GmbH, part of Springer Nature 2022
R. T. Kreutzer, *Online Marketing*, https://doi.org/10.1007/978-3-658-35369-8_2

2

Learning Agenda

How does online marketing fit into classic marketing? How should online marketing activities be planned? In this chapter, you will become familiar with the most important terms and forms of online marketing. After reading ...

- ▶ Section 2.1 you understand how online marketing fits into traditional marketing.
- ▶ Section 2.2 you can plan and control online marketing activities in a target-oriented manner.

2.1 Classification of Online Marketing in Classic Marketing

Before showing how the planning process of online marketing works, online marketing should first be positioned in the classical marketing concept. This raises the question of how to define the concept of marketing as a whole.

┌─ **Notice!** ─────────────────────────────────────

Today, **marketing** is mostly referred to as the concept of **market-oriented corporate management**. In this context, market is not to be understood solely as a synonym for sales market. The market is to be understood as all areas in which an exchange – regulated by market mechanisms – takes place with other service providers.

Marketing can be understood as a **guiding principle of management** with regard to ensuring **market-oriented corporate management** as well as a **corporate function** (in addition to procurement, production, human resources, etc.). The goal of market-oriented corporate management is reflected in the philosophy, values and/or vision of a company. If marketing is understood primarily as a corporate function, then marketing is located in terms of processes as part of the corporate value chain and is identified organizationally as an element of the organizational chart of companies.

The **action orientation of marketing** is ensured by the strategies and instruments used, which should contribute to the achievement of the company and marketing goals.

The following concepts belong to the central **marketing strategies** (see in-depth Becker 2018; Kreutzer 2022a):

- **Market field strategy:** With which offers does the company want to be active?
- **Market stimulation strategy:** With which value proposition does it want to convince the market?
- **Market segmentation strategy:** Which market segments should be served?
- **Market area strategy:** In which regions of the world should this take place?

Strategies are characterized by their **long-term orientation**. They are often based on a time horizon of 3 years or more. The entire company or complete strategic business fields (SBFs) or strategic business units (SBUs) are often the focus of strategy development. Strategies often formulate certain **focal points** that define the strategic direction of the company. This includes the question of whether or not a retail company or manufacturer should establish an e-commerce sales channel. This fundamental direction of strategies can also include the decision to offer streaming services and to close stationary bank branches in order to promote online banking. The comprehensive establishment of social media marketing is also part of the strategic decisions.

Strategy also includes the **design of systems** that underlie entrepreneurial activities. This includes the further development of the existing business model and the development of business model innovations (see Kreutzer 2022b). These changes are usually accompanied by a reorganization. This includes the further development of the **organizational structure**, which is reflected in the company's organizational chart. Parallel to this, adjustments to the **process organisation** are often necessary. In addition to the production processes, the process organization also includes the processes of planning, purchasing and controlling. The necessity for a realignment of the operational and organizational structure can also result from the entry into online marketing with its own e-commerce presence. After all, such a step is accompanied by new requirements for internal processes as well as for the allocation of responsibilities in marketing and sales.

Operational planning, which is hierarchically subordinate to strategic planning, is based on a **short- to medium-term orientation**. This covers a time horizon of less than 3 years and usually focuses on 1 year. The marketing mix and the marketing instruments dominate here. These are intended to contribute to the **implementation of the concepts** designed in the strategic planning to create, secure and exploit success potentials. These instruments are usually referred to as the **"4 Ps"** (product, price, promotion, place) of the classic marketing mix. Within the framework of the marketing diamond, they have been supplemented by the **fifth P** for **people**, in order to take into account the increasing importance of the company's own employees for market success (cf. in-depth Kreutzer 2022a). The operational tasks of online marketing include, for example, the planning of online advertising, the tasks of search engine optimization and the development of a content strategy for social media engagement.

2.2 Planning the Online Marketing Deployment

The concrete form of the online marketing commitment must be determined periodically as a part of the **operational marketing planning**. ▢ Figure 2.1 shows how this is integrated into marketing management as a whole. The starting point for online marketing can be a **SWOT analysis** in order to gain key insights for the definition of goals and for the design of the online strategy. "SW" stands for strengths and weaknesses in the sense of advantages or disadvantages of one's own company in a competitive comparison. **SW** covers the **internal perspective** of the analysis. The decisive factor is that these must be determined in comparison with relevant competitors. Only in this way can entrepreneurial strengths and weaknesses be identified. "OT" stands for opportunities and threats. **OT** integrate the **external perspective** into the analysis. An opportunity is, for example, the possibility for stationary retailers to address target groups online that were previously difficult to reach. A risk for bricks-and-mortar retailers can be, that more and more customers

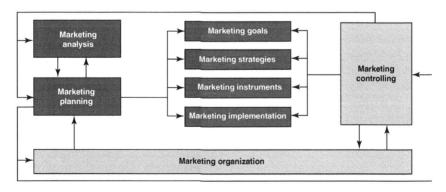

▢ **Fig. 2.1**   Marketing management process

make their purchases online. Strategic conclusions for the design of online marketing can only be drawn from the synthesis of external and internal perspectives (see Kreutzer 2019, pp. 99-114 for a fundamental SWOT analysis).

It is important that online marketing is systematically integrated into the overall marketing planning process at an early stage. This means that already during the development of marketing goals, it is systematically examined to what extent online tools can be used for this purpose. This requires cross-departmental cooperation both in the planning phase and in the implementation phase in order to overcome the silo mentality in companies already described. This is the only way to develop an **integrated overall concept for addressing and supporting customers**.

The further process for designing online marketing can be oriented according to ◘ Fig. 2.2. It becomes clear that the fundamental objectives for the **development of the marketing concept** are derived from the overriding corporate and marketing objectives. The objectives for online marketing are also to be identified in this concept. The possibilities of online marketing are to be systematically evaluated within the marketing planning process with regard to their contributions to the achievement of higher-level marketing goals. The necessary **noline approach** can only be achieved through an integrative planning approach in which online and offline activities are designed together (see ◘ Fig. 2.2).

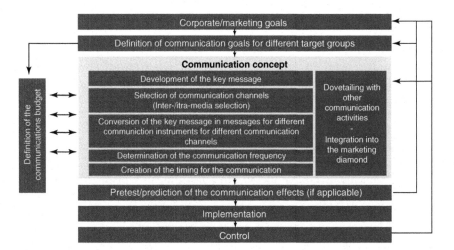

◘ **Fig. 2.2** Process for the design of marketing

2

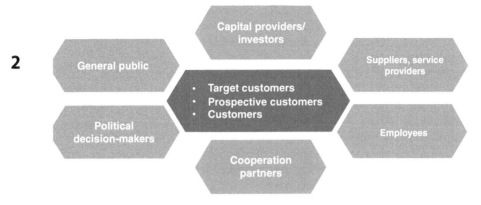

■ **Fig. 2.3**   Important target groups of marketing

Different **target groups** can also be addressed in online marketing. By default, the following target groups are the focus of the company's activities, which in sum describe the "prey scheme" of a company:

- **Desired customers** or **target customers** that a company would like to acquire for itself.
- **Prospective customers**, that is, persons who have already shown a general interest in the services and are addressable (also called prospect or lead).
- **Current customers** to be served and developed after the purchase.
- **Former customers** to win back after the jump.

Furthermore, with regard to the other target groups mentioned in . Fig. 2.3 examined in what way their acquisition and/or support can be carried out using online marketing instruments. These target groups are also referred to as **stakeholders**. The term "stakeholder" refers to persons or groups of persons who – in this case – have an interest in the company and its activities.

With regard to the entrepreneurial core target group of **prospects** and **customers**, it is important to examine, for example, which **business model** should be supported by online marketing. The following options, which can also be implemented in parallel in some cases, must be distinguished:

- **Distribution format for manufacturers**
  - Own online presence for direct sales via own online shop
  - Own online presence to support direct sales via own offline shops
  - Own online presence to support indirect sales through integrated sales partners

- **Stationary retail**
  - Own online presence to support sales via own offline shops (pure retail business without own online shop)
  - Own online presence for direct sales via an own online shop (in addition to the stationary retail store)
- **Mail order**
  - Own online presence to support sales with offline catalogue
  - Own online presence to support sales with online catalogue
  - Own online presence to support sales via own online shop
  - Own online presence to support direct sales via own offline shops
- **Distribution format for additional service providers**
  - Own online presence for direct sales via own online shop
  - Own online presence to support direct sales via own offline shops
  - Own online presence to support indirect sales through integrated sales partners

In marketing as well as in online marketing, a distinction must be made between the goals of **acquisition of information** and the **distribution of information**. In order to ensure goal-oriented **information management**, the goals for both directions must be formulated as precisely as possible.

- **Objectives of the acquisition of information**

Through online activities, information can be obtained about suppliers, service providers, employees, cooperation partners, political decision-makers, capital providers, investors as well as the general public. Of particular importance, however, is the data that can be obtained about prospective customers as well as active, passive and/or former customers. In addition, information gathering can also relate to product/service innovations, to process and business model innovations as well as to the company's competitors and the wider industry-specific or international environment.

For **prospects and customers**, the focus is on capturing address and profile data. These provide the relevant background for action. After all, only these make a person addressable (address data) and allow conclusions to be drawn about the offers relevant to them (profile data). The important **address data** of the target persons include – depending on the business model – postal address, e-mail address, telephone number (stationary/mobile), fax number as well as the address of an own homepage. In addition to the communication data, the corresponding permissions for their use must be recorded. Even if a company is only active online and does not deliver any physical products, the postal address has important functions. On the one hand, the

2

creditworthiness of a person can only be checked using a postal address. In addition, a date of birth helps to uniquely identify persons. The creditworthiness check is in turn the prerequisite for being able to offer a payment method "against invoice" securely. Only a postal address enables access to further databases, for example, to enrich one's own addresses with information from microgeographic segmentation (see Kreutzer 2021a, pp. 71-81).

Profile data about the target persons, in turn, provide interesting clues for determining needs. In addition to age and gender, this also includes the living situation and current needs. By using *Facebook* data to target advertising, companies can integrate the best-maintained and most comprehensive preference database in the world.

In the course of interaction with consumers or with employees/companies, **action data** and **reaction data** must also be continuously recorded. Among other things, this involves the question of how and where the target persons obtain information and carry out transactions. Attention should first be focused on the **company's own touchpoints**:

- Visit of retail stores and/or usage of the online shop?
- Direct contact with the manufacturer and/or the dealer?
- Use of a customer service center?
- Reading your own articles and advertisements in the traditional media, your own mailings, e-mails and/or e-newsletters?
- Visiting your own online presence (corporate website and/or social media channels)?
- Use of an online product configurator?
- Participation in your own blogs, forums, communities and/or in the course of company-owned engagements in the social networks?

In addition to the information needs of a company that are directly geared towards prospects and customers, there are further fields in which information can be obtained. The **touchpoints outside the company** are of great importance, too (see ◘ Fig. 1.7). As already described, these are outside the sphere that can be directly influenced by the company. Nevertheless, these touchpoints can have an important influence on purchasing decisions.

The task for companies is to systematically check the information and opinions found there for their relevance. In view of the abundance of information available here on the one hand and its very different quality and relevance on the other, however, this requires special instruments in order to distil the really important content from the multitude of sources and data. Such information gathering and aggregation is the aim of so-called **web monitoring** (see in-depth Kreutzer 2021b, pp. 87–90). This is sometimes also called **web scouting** or **buzz tracking**. Buzz stands for the "hum and buzz" or also for the buzz of voices that needs to be monitored. The relevance for this comes from the following insight.

> In a nutshell: **markets are conversations** – and conversations are increasingly taking place on the web. And these conversations are happening there, whether companies are listening or not. But better they listen!

A special form of web monitoring is **online trend monitoring**. The use of the free service *Google Trends* makes it possible to differentiate the relevance of topics, people, products and companies regionally and temporally. This allows a quick overview of emerging trends to be gained.

Social media monitoring is when social media like social networks, forums and blogs, are the focus of monitoring. Here, it can be determined how intensively topics relevant to a company are discussed. These can be questions of data protection as well as possibilities for the protection of the own house against burglars, if a company offers corresponding solutions. In this way, it can be determined in which environments which topics are "hot" and possibly have advertising relevance. It can also be determined who is currently talking about one's own brand and where – in order to enter into a dialogue if necessary. Social media monitoring should pay special attention to the posts that are placed. Due to their viral spreading potential, such messages often trigger shitstorms.

A **shitstorm** is a phenomenon of social media and refers to the mass emergence (hence "storm") of critical statements (hence "shit") towards companies, certain offers and/or persons. Social media creates the possibility of viral spread through likes, re-tweets, blog posts, etc. The achievable momentum often leads to factual criticism being mixed with unobjective comments and a goal-oriented discussion is no longer possible. The counterpart of a shitstorm, when positive messages are spread virally, can be called a **roseshower**.

> To the point: In sum, it is indispensable for most companies to systematically search not only social media, but the entire Internet for company-relevant entries through web monitoring.

The information to be searched for can be opinions, trends and feedback on own or third-party offers, product and service reviews, but also impulses for innovations. A first and free option for web monitoring is the use of *Google Alerts*. After defining important search terms at *Google Alerts, Google* auto-

2

matically generates e-mails when online contributions to the defined search terms appear. In this way, it is possible, to receive news from certain areas in a timely manner and to monitor competitors or industry trends. It can also be determined whether entries appear about one's own person, one's own offers and brands or one's own company.

Companies can additionally install **blog monitoring** to monitor the so-called **blogosphere** and to make use of this source of information. After all, there are many examples of product weaknesses first being reported in blogs. In some cases, such complaints have become a mass phenomenon and have caused not only a drop in sales for the companies concerned, but also, in some cases, a decline in their share prices. Blog search engines can make an important contribution to finding the relevant blogs. This Internet monitoring should also include *Twitter* monitoring, as information relevant to the company may be available here in real time – with both positive and negative effects on the company.

The big challenge is to determine not only the **number of statements**, but also their **tonality**. This is the field of application of so-called **sentiment analyses** (e.g., by ▶ cirticalmention.com). Their task is to separate positive from negative posts. Ideally, this also works for posts that carry an ambiguous message. This is the case with the following statement: "That was really a GREAT service??!!!!??" Is this now a praise or a criticism with an ironic undertone? When classifying such posts, many professional service providers rely on **semi-automatic sentiment recognition**. In plain language, this means that a human eye (in cases of doubt) makes the classification. The information obtained is often classified according to the categories "positive", "neutral" and "negative", and examples are provided in corresponding result reports. The great challenge in the evaluation and assessment of messages on the Internet and especially in social media is the distinction between fact, opinion and populism!

Another key question is: **What is the intention of the sender?**

Consequently, it is important for every company that not only an intern sporadically googles the company or product name to find out what is being reported about the company, its brands and offers. This is where the **installation of a continuously running Internet monitoring system** is required. Such a system is required at least when the company has reached a critical size. The information obtained in different ways forms the background for the design of the (online) marketing.

■ **Objectives of the distribution of information**

Corporate communication is intended to convey information about the company, its culture and values, service program, position in the market, etc. to various target groups in order to trigger certain reactions. **Making** the company and/or its services **known** is the first priority in order to build up a desired image and to support the demand for one's own services.

The acquisition and distribution of information is not an end in itself, but in turn serves the achievement of overriding corporate goals. In the case of profit-oriented companies, long-term profit generation dominates here. These companies focus on one essential goal: the **acquisition and retention of valuable customers**. Within the framework of the development of a coherent **marketing concept**, the goals of providing information via the classic communication instruments as well as those of dialogue and online marketing must be coordinated. Therefore, the exploitation of synergetic effects should already be considered in the planning phase in order to create the basis for **integrated marketing**.

Brand building – whether as a corporate brand and/or product/service brand – is often the starting point. The brand makes a decisive contribution to the purchase decision. Due to the increasing shift of communication budgets to online instruments, **online-based brand building** is of particular importance. It should be examined in what form online engagement can contribute to the fields of brand building shown in ◘ Fig. 2.4 (cf. Esch et al. 2005, p. 121).

In the digital age, further fields of influence of the brand image must be taken into account in the course of operational brand management. These include **user-generated content** and the further **interactions of third parties with the brand**. These two areas have gained dramatically in importance for brand management in recent years. Online communication and especially the dissemination of information via social media (often in real time) have achieved an unprecedented speed and impact.

Against this background, companies are called upon to also influence the areas of user-generated content and third-party interactions with the brand through their own brand communication in their brand management. In this way, the brand experience of the users ("external stakeholders") should correspond as closely as possible to the defined brand identity of the "internal stakeholders". However, it must be taken into account that companies cannot exert any direct influence on the user brand experience. The significantly more complex task of **brand management in the digital age is** shown in ◘ Fig. 2.5 (see in-depth Kilian and Kreutzer 2022).

2

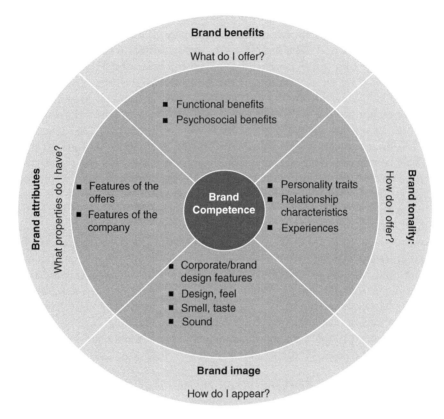

Brand benefits

What do I offer?

- Functional benefits
- Psychosocial benefits

Brand attributes

What properties do I have?

- Features of the offers
- Features of the company

Brand Competence

- Personality traits
- Relationship characteristics
- Experiences

Brand tonality:

How do I offer?

- Corporate/brand design features
- Design, feel
- Smell, taste
- Sound

Brand image

How do I appear?

○ **Fig. 2.4**   Brand identity approach

❯ To put it in a nutshell: **The experience is the product!**

A combination of all online and offline marketing activities geared towards (prospective) customers takes place within the framework of the **customer relationship lifecycle** as the content of customer relationship management (CRM; see ○ Fig. 2.6; cf. Stauss 2000, p. 16). The tasks of **prospect management** initially include the generation of contact data of prospects and customers; task: **"Get"** in the sense of acquisition. This can be done, for example, through online coupon ads, advertising banners or through the placement of paid advertising in the context of search engine hit lists or through engagement in social media.

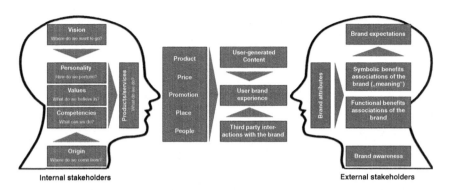

Internal stakeholders   External stakeholders

◘ **Fig. 2.5** Holistic brand management in the digital age

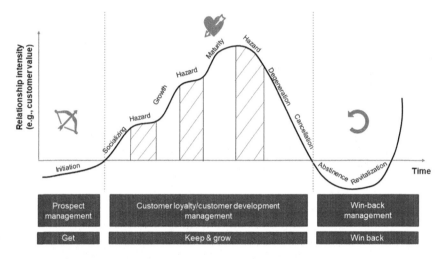

◘ **Fig. 2.6** Customer relationship lifecycle

Customer loyalty/customer development management is intended to bind particularly valuable customers to the company; task: **"Keep & grow"** in terms of customer loyalty and development. This can be done through relevant content ("content marketing"), which is provided through high-quality e-newsletters in the form of white papers or through videos on *YouTube*. E-coupons with a price advantage can also be sent out – to be

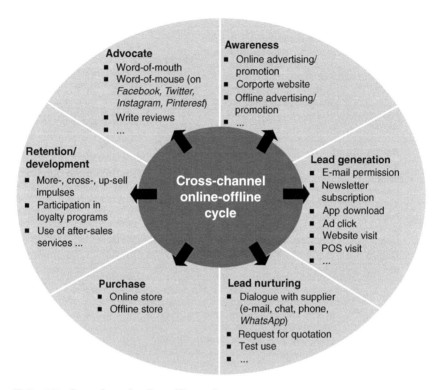

Fig. 2.7 Cross-channel online–offline cycle

redeemed with the next (online) purchase. In addition, it is important to exploit the cross-sell and up-sell potential of customers – for example, through individual recommendations. The various instruments of social media marketing can also contribute to customer loyalty by regularly communicating with customers via *Facebook*, *Instagram*, *Twitter* and/or *WhatsApp*.

In the course of **win-back or churn management**, it is important to reactivate inactive customers, for example, through telephone calls, field service visits, e-mails, e-coupons, mailings or *WhatsApp* messages. The task is: **"Win back"** in the sense of winning back (profitable) customers. Another task is to address terminators, for example, through telephone marketing, field service or e-mails or mailings, and to motivate them to stay with attractive offers – as long as these consumers or companies have an attractive customer value.

The **cross-channel online–offline cycle** described in Fig. 2.7 can provide important orientation here. After the **awareness phase**, in the course of **lead**

acquisition, it is a matter of acquiring further data about the prospect online and offline. In the course of **lead nurturing**, the aim is to develop the leads gained with the aim of further preparing the **act of purchase** – online and/or offline. The term "nurturing" stands for "care" or "breeding". This is followed by the phase of **customer retention and development**. This cycle can be crowned in the **advocate** phase, when the customer acts as an advocate for the brand and/or the company.

Due to the dovetailing of online and offline activities that has become visible here, it becomes clear in my opinion that there should be no differentiation between **CRM** and **e-CRM**. After all, one and the same person cannot be divided into an online and an offline user. Consequently, every form of CRM must be holistically oriented to the individual prospect or customer across all media and channels. Only then can a **comprehensive customer centricity** be achieved and a CRM successfully implemented (see fundamentally Kreutzer 2021a).

The support of each individual person requires the already mentioned **transparency of the prospects and customers**. Without such transparency, no further targeted measures for customer acquisition in the sense of increasing the number of target customers can be implemented. Only by creating the appropriate transparency in the company does it become clear which are the actual "desired" target customers of a company. For example, these customers generate particularly high contribution margins for the company or have an important multiplier or opinion leader function for the conquest of further markets. At the same time, it is important to record how these people behave online and offline in order to further optimize one's own approach.

Moreover, only comprehensive transparency with regard to one's own customer structure will reveal starting points for **increasing customer value**. On the one hand, this can be achieved by **focusing on the "right" customers** who have a particularly high (prospective, in the sense of future) customer value. On the other hand, the **triad of customer care** contributes to increasing customer value through the following thrusts:

- **More-sell**
- Here, the customer is supposed **to buy more of the same**. This can be achieved by means of e-newsletters that regularly draw attention to the range of offers and motivate him to buy.
- **Cross-sell**
- The customer should also **generate sales in other product areas of the company**. Therefore, reference is made to services or parts of the product or serive range that a customer does not yet use. The aim is to generate a

2

higher turnover – or more precisely – a higher contribution margin from a customer address.

= **Up-sell**

= This motivates the customer **to use higher-value offers**. For most companies, these also bring higher contribution margins. This is achieved by pointing out luxury editions or limited editions of products, through which higher margins can be achieved. Online platforms that use a freemium pricing model (e.g., *Spotify*) regularly try to motivate users of the free or ad-financed basic services to use the paid premium version.

Here, it becomes clear that a company cannot be solely concerned with retaining customers longer if this is not simultaneously accompanied by the development of more-sell, cross-sell and/or up-sell potential and thus higher contribution margins. Only a combination of all these factors underlines why increasing the **length of time** a customer stays with one's own company is a very central goal of (online) marketing. Importantly, online tools can help achieve all of these goals without requiring a purchase to be made online.

When **selling physical products**, the online purchase triggers a classic shipping transaction. The ordered goods are sent to the desired delivery address through the company's own services and/or the involvement of a logistics service provider. When **selling non-physical products** (e.g., e-books, music/video content or software), the online purchase no longer triggers a traditional shipping transaction. Instead, the possibility of **downloading, using online** or **streaming** music and films is created. When **selling services** (e.g., insurance, but also when booking flights, trains, buses and hotels), the entire sales process can often be handled online. This ranges from online selection and booking to online delivery of the confirmation or the online tickets themselves, which are often also read out online during access control. In some cases, however, there is still a media break here, for example when tickets or other booking documents are sent by post and/or have to be printed out.

The online activities used can also be limited to **supporting stationary sales** and/or **building a (positive) corporate reputation**. In this case, a sale is merely prepared online, but not processed online.

► **Example: Automobile Trade**

One example of this is the automobile trade, the majority of which – at least for new cars – is currently not (yet) handled completely via the Internet. The possibility for this would exist through the connection between a car configurator, a link to the manufacturer or to a dealer, and even electronic payment. Even delivery could take place – without the involvement of a dealer – directly at the customer's place of residence through a "delivery service" of the manufacturer. In this way, the classic distribution stage of the automobile retail trade would be completely bypassed. The first automotive groups have now launched online sales on a trial basis. *Tesla* in particular is a pioneer here.

In the market for used cars, *AUTO1,* a start-up from Berlin, has now become the largest online B2B marketplace for used cars in Europe. More than 60,000 retail partners in over 30 European countries use ► AUTO1.com to buy and sell used cars (see Auto1 2021). ◄

After the formulation of the online marketing goals, the **online strategies** are developed. Within this framework, it is decided, for example, whether a company's own online shop should be installed, a corporate blog launched and/or a company's own online community built up. Here it is also to be examined whether a company would like to set up its own online platform or enter into a partnership with already existing platforms. Business model innovations can also be developed in this field (cf. in-depth Kreutzer 2022b).

These strategies find their concretization in the **online instruments**, which can be directly implemented operationally. The operational decision fields addressed here refer, for example, to the questions:
- What forms of online advertising should be used?
- How should search engine optimization be implemented?
- Is affiliate marketing set up – alone or as part of affiliate networks?
- Is there any engagement in social networks? If so, in which ones? And what does the corresponding content strategy look like?
- Is there a *Twitter* engagement to be designed out?
- Should the business be on *Instagram, Pinterest, TikTok* and/or *YouTube*?
- Is the integration of messenger services such as *Facebook Messenger* and/or *WhatsApp* useful?
- Should web monitoring and/or social media monitoring be set up?
- Should an influencer marketing concept be implemented?
- Is there content marketing to be developed?

It is generally recommended that the use of individual online instruments be preceded by a **test phase** (pretest) to determine and forecast the achievable effects of the intended measures (cf. ◘ Fig. 2.2). Online marketing should generally be guided by the guideline "test, test, test". Because it is less and less guaranteed that the successful concepts from the past will still be valid tomorrow.

The **flexibility of the online measures in terms of content and time** allows for a very differentiated design of the individual instruments. These should

2

be based on the insights gained through analyses of completed or ongoing campaigns. For example, different e-newsletters, conversation guides for telephone marketing, *Facebook* posts, *YouTube* videos, advertising banners, etc. can be developed and tested for their effects on different target groups. In some cases, this testing can even be done in real time, so that insights from a just-completed phone call can be used to optimize the selection of the next person to call. Similarly, the insights from an ongoing banner advertising campaign can be used to optimize it immediately. The **variation possibilities of online instruments** are much greater here and also much more cost-effective than with TV spots, ads or poster campaigns. The latter often not only require a much longer lead time, but also incur significantly higher adaptation costs.

The **planning of the implementation of online measures** is of particular importance. In contrast to classic advertisements and TV or radio spots, which are often not intended to trigger an immediate reaction from the target persons, online instruments often demand an immediate reaction. For this purpose, the already mentioned calls-to-action are used. All **customer touchpoints** for which the company is responsible must be prepared for the response triggered by this. This applies to the sales force as well as to a customer service center, which will see an increase in telephone, e-mail, fax and/or mailings after the appropriate measures have been implemented. Likewise, the company may receive more chat requests and *WhatsApp* messages. Feedback from users can also be received via social media (especially *Twitter* and *Facebook*) as well as through posts in blogs and online communities.

In order to manage this volume of communication, the **employees** required to follow up on the resulting contacts must first be **scheduled** and provided with an appropriate **briefing** regarding the campaign. If prospective customers encounter poorly prepared employees or if the customer service center is constantly busy, the success of the entire campaign is jeopardized. In addition, the materials offered for advertising must be kept in sufficient quantity in order to be able to react quickly.

Studies repeatedly make it clear that many companies still have major **deficits in the execution of measures**. These are not only manifested in a **late response to inquiries**, but also in some cases in a **non-response**. Such a phenomenon can be found equally in online and offline inquiries. As a result, requests for information and/or product samples as well as orders are not processed. In this way, companies lose interesting potential for success – and the company's image may be damaged forever. In addition, a campaign may be considered a failure simply because the company did not do its homework.

An important part of implementation planning is to **"think ahead" to the controllability of actions**. This can be achieved by assigning **action codes** to all the instruments used. Then it is possible to trace the reactions of people back to specific impulses and thus to determine their efficiency. In the **offline area**, different mailboxes are printed on reply envelopes (envelopes for a response), reaction media in classic media (such as coupons or reply cards) are provided with an advertising code and different telephone numbers are given for contacting by telephone. In the **online area**, different landing pages or offers can be prepared or special telephone numbers can be given. In addition, cookies can be used to record from which sites an online user switches to one's own website. A site from which a user has come to the current site by clicking on a link is called a referrer. If the corresponding characteristics are not defined in the conception phase or the processes for recording the relevant success criteria are not set up, no differentiated success evaluations can be carried out.

In the course of **implementation planning**, the question of **make-or-buy arises**. Decisions must be made here about the extent to which certain services should be provided by the company itself or by external online service providers. This involves the following questions:

- Should **web space**, i.e. storage space on a server that is to be accessed via the Internet on a long-term basis, be rented or built up yourself?
- Is the **web design** created by your own employees or by a relevant agency?
- Are own employees to be provided for **social media communication** or is this function delegated to appropriate service partners?
- Is **search engine optimization** done in-house or outsourced to service providers?
- Are **addresses** rented for the construction of an e-mail distribution list and/or obtained independently?
- Are **online PR** tasks developed independently or outsourced?
- Is content for **content marketing** created in-house or acquired from relevant content agencies?
- Should influencers be recruited and managed independently for **influencer marketing** – or should appropriate service providers be used for this purpose?
- Is the further development of the **user experience** carried out by your own employees, or are the capacities for this purchased externally?

All of the above steps must be accompanied by the **establishment of an efficient controlling system**. In the corporate environment as a whole, **controlling** is understood as a comprehensive **control and coordination concept**

2

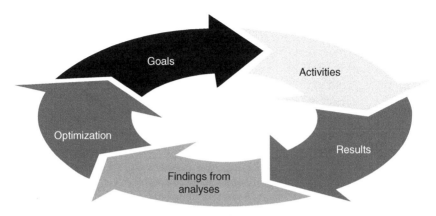

■ **Fig. 2.8**   Closed loop of online marketing

which supports the management or the heads of individual divisions and departments (e.g. marketing) in their work by providing information, instruments, processes and systems. In essence, the aim is to ensure the economic efficiency and target orientation of the use of resources in the company. In this way, controlling should also contribute to the achievement of corporate goals.

With regard to the tests mentioned as well as for comprehensive **online controlling**, it is important that separate goals are formulated for each online tool. Only then can the **closed loop of online marketing** shown in ■ Fig.2.8 be implemented. Then – based on precise goals for each individual online tool – the corresponding measures must be worked out and the results achieved through them recorded. Based on their analysis, measures for optimization are to be derived, which in turn are to flow into the goals of online marketing. The result is a **learning organization** that draws its conclusions from the successes and failures of the past and acts accordingly in the future.

Online controlling focuses on the target-oriented use of resources for online marketing and its instruments and is part of the overall marketing controlling. The focus here is on two central questions:

- How **effective** is the use of the various online measures?
- How **efficient** is the use of the various online measures?

In order to carry out online controlling, relevant measurement and evaluation criteria as well as the relevant questions for determining them must be defined at an early stage. The **effectiveness of the online marketing deployment** (question: "Are we doing the right things?") is about the target orientation of the corresponding deployment. This can be determined using the following questions:

- Is there a large enough number of prospective customers and customers who are interested in reading a **corporate blog** and learning about companies and brands here?
- Does a click on an **advertising banner** lead to a prospect or a customer feeling well informed by the company and ideally buying right away or at least coming back?
- Does the user who subscribes to an **e-newsletter** gain a real information and service advantage in order to remain loyal to the company in the long term?
- Do your own prospective customers and customers actually become fans and followers through your **social media activities**, and do they purchase the services you offer?
- Are the company's fans on *Facebook, Instagram, YouTube* & Co. so well looked after in terms of information that they ideally become **brand ambassadors**?
- Are **followers on** *Twitter* or **fans on** *Facebook* gaining a real information advantage and receiving benefits to engage with the company on an ongoing basis – and ideally generate sales there on a regular basis?
- Can content be presented on key **media sharing platforms** to help build image and/or support sales?
- Is it worth integrating **messenger services** to improve customer communication?
- Does **content marketing** actually result in not only improving corporate reputation, but also increasing sales in the long run?
- Does **influencer marketing** actually have a positive impact on company, product and/or service image and also lead to additional sales?

The **efficiency of online marketing** is about the input-output ratio of the engagement (question: "Are we doing the things right?"). The following questions are to be analysed:

- What does it cost to attract **prospective customers** to your offer through the various online channels?
- Which costs for the acquisition of **new customers** are associated with which online measures?
- Which online measures lead to particularly **loyal customers** and at what cost?
- Which online tools for reactivating **inactive customers** are particularly cost-effective?

2

- Which online measures can be particularly successful in **turning prospective customers into customers**?
- Which online stimuli are best suited to exploit **more-, cross- and up-sell potential** with specific customer groups?
- Which online activities pay particularly sustainable dividends in terms of **positive branding**?
- What does it cost to gain a **fan on** *Facebook* or a **follower on** *Instagram, Pinterest* or *Twitter*?

In order to be able to assess the value of online results, the **values of target achievement** must also be determined:

- What importance is attached to a fan on *Facebook* and a follower on *Instagram, Pinterest* or *Twitter*? What value does a fan or a follower embody?
- What is the value of an interaction, e.g. clicking on a banner, subscribing to an e-newsletter, requesting an information package?
- What is the value of a recommendation by a customer?

Only if such values are defined at an early stage can the expenses for an online engagement also be compared with the results or **value contributions** achieved. In addition, the **functionality** and **performance of the online engagement** itself must be monitored. The goals mentioned cannot be achieved if, for example, the loading times of online applications are too long (end-to-end response times), the availability is insufficient, the bandwidth provided is not sufficient or important content cannot be accessed in a legible form on mobile devices (keyword "responsive design").

A great advantage of many online marketing instruments is the possibility to carry out a very precise success control. On the one hand, a lot of **data is available for controlling** during the process and can be evaluated accordingly. If these evaluations are carried out anonymously, there is usually no need to consider any further data protection aspects. However, if success rates and usage patterns are to be determined on a person-by-person basis, it is necessary to obtain the appropriate permissions. On the other hand, many **tools for controlling** are available on the Internet (partly free of charge) and often allow a very differentiated analysis. In addition, **service providers for online controlling** have established themselves that can provide companies with important assistance in distilling essential insights from the flood of data. Nevertheless, many companies only partially exploit the learning potential of their online marketing activities.

At the level of the individual online instruments, the relevant **key performance indicators** (KPIs) are defined in ▶ Chap. 3. These are to be summarized across instruments in an **online cockpit** or an **online dashboard**. In contrast to traditional communication, reactions triggered online or occurring online can often be directly traced back to specific triggers and thus also more easily assigned to the associated costs. This is because most of the data required to determine the key figures defined below is available after the campaign has been completed and may "only" need to be merged from different systems. However, one challenge that remains is that there are still hardly any comparable "currencies" to record the effects achieved online and offline that are upstream of the purchasing process.

> In a nutshell, you often only get what you measure. That is even very likely. What you do not measure or cannot measure is therefore often lost.

> According to *H. Thomas Johnson*

In any case, it is crucial that the results achieved through the use of online tools, whether these are contribution margins, sales and/or newly acquired prospective customers and customers, are compared with the results of other measures. To this end, the relevant KPIs must be brought together by the **triad of profitability analysis** in order to evaluate individual campaigns and compare their results with each other (cf. ◘ Fig. 2.9). This triad combines the three decisive parameters of **product/service**, **target group** and **channel** within the framework of a campaign.

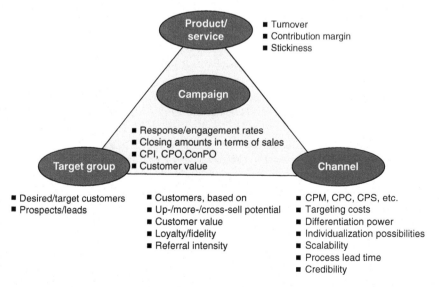

◘ **Fig. 2.9** Triad of economic analysis

2

The **product or service to be advertised** can be selected depending on the targeted **sales** or **contribution margins**. The selection can also be based on the **stickiness of the offer**. This is, for example, much higher for a subscription offer with a term of several months than for a single product sale. Here, for example, a *Netflix* subscription or membership of *Amazon Prime* comes to mind.

The **target group** can be recruited from **desired/target customers**, existing **leads** or from **customers** already acquired. Customers can be selected according to their more-, cross-sell or up-sell potential. Or customers are addressed who have a particularly high churn probability, but should be retained by the company. Or the persons are addressed who show a particularly high intention to recommend the company to others. The previous or predicted customer value can also be an important orientation parameter for the target group to be addressed.

The selection of the **online or offline channels** to be included can be based on the **cost parameters** CPM (Cost per Mille), CPC (Cost per Click) or CPA (Cost per Acquisition). In addition, it is necessary to check which **targeting options** exist for the different channels and which costs are associated with them. Finally, the question also arises as to what **differentiation power** and what **individualization possibilities** the various channels have. These criteria must be evaluated with regard to the goals of the campaign.

The **scalability of the respective channel** is of additional importance. We speak of high scalability when software can also be used for other tasks or for a larger amount of data without incurring disproportionate costs. In the context of advertising, scalability refers to the phenomenon that a multiplication of online advertisements does not itself cause (large) additional expenses. Additional costs only arise from the click costs incurred, which are, however, also associated with a desired advertising effect. In contrast, a convincing telephone campaign can only be expanded to a very limited extent. Often the necessary permissions for contacting or qualified call agents are missing. Other important aspects in the selection of a channel are the required **time or procedural lead time for an advertising campaign** as well as the **credibility of the channel** for the own service offer.

The **campaign** itself, which results from the combination of product/service, target group and channel, can be evaluated on the basis of criteria such as **response rates**, **redemption rates** and the **closing amounts** achieved. In addition, it is necessary to determine how high the **costs** are for CPI (Cost per Interest), CPL (Cost per Lead) and CPO (Cost per Order) and how many **contacts** were necessary to **close the deal** (ConPO – Contacts per Order).

In view of the frequently encountered **euphoria about the dominantly higher profitability of many online activities**, it should be noted: Many successes that are now measured online in clicks, requests, subscriptions and/or purchases would not have been achieved without image building – often ongoing for years in offline media. It is important to note that this does not speak against online engagement, but rather shows that success is to be sought in synergetic interaction – between **performance marketing** on the one hand and **brand building** on the other. However, this interaction must also be systematically monitored in order to identify the most successful concepts.

> **Notice!**
>
> In online controlling, the majority of companies have a dramatic need to catch up. Here, many learning areas remain unprocessed – because by not using consistent controlling, neither mistakes nor successes can be learned from.

2.3 Learning Control

☺ Short and Sweet

The **development of an online marketing concept** follows the procedure of classic marketing. Online marketing must be comprehensively integrated into classic marketing so that it can unfold its full effect. It is to be avoided that further – not integrated – fields are built up next to "classic marketing" to implement online marketing. In order to achieve holistically convincing communication (called noline approach), both fields must be closely interlinked – also organizationally. The planning of online activities can make use of the proven processes and concepts of classic marketing. Care must be taken to exploit the comprehensive possibilities that online marketing in particular offers for monitoring success. There is still room for improvement in many companies!

❓ Let's Check

1. Which target groups are distinguished in online marketing?
2. What are the key objectives of information acquisition?
3. What are the key phases and contents of the customer relationship lifecycle?
4. Characterize the approach and relevance of the closed loop of online marketing!

2

🕜 Networking Tasks

Try to determine the organisational anchoring of online marketing via online research or within companies with which you have a good contact. Where is the responsibility for which areas of online marketing located? How do the processes work, for example, to coordinate online/offline campaigns or to carry out social media activities? How systematically is success monitored?

🛈 Reading and Deepening

- Chaffrey, D./Ellis-Chadwick, F. (2019). *Digital marketing.* 7th Edition. New York.
- Chaffey, D./Smith, P. R. (2018). *Digital marketing excellence.* 5th Edition. London.
- Kingsnorth, S. (2019). *Digital marketing strategy: An integrated approach to online marketing.* 2nd Edition. London.
- Stokes, R. (2018). *eMarketing: The essential guide to marketing in a digital world.* 6th Edition. Red & Yellow.

Instruments of Online Marketing

Contents

© Springer Fachmedien Wiesbaden GmbH, part of Springer Nature 2022
R. T. Kreutzer, *Online Marketing*, https://doi.org/10.1007/978-3-658-35369-8_3

3.1 Introductory Remarks on Online Marketing Tools

Learning Agenda
After working through this section, you will be able to distinguish between push and pull communication. You will be able to distinguish between multi-channel and omni-channel engagements.

All the instruments presented in this chapter contribute in different ways to shaping online marketing. Many instruments initially focus on **online communication**. This communication can be direct in a way, that a company develops a corporate website, establishes a presence in social media, sends e-mails or places advertising banners. But it can also be implemented indirectly through search engine optimization in order to be found more easily on *Google* & Co.

When integrating online media into a company's communication, a distinction must be made between the communication goals that a company is aiming for. If the aim is to integrate online media into a company's overall communications presence, the term **online communication** is used. If the aim is to achieve PR goals through online media, the term **online PR** is appropriate. If the focus is on advertising objectives or direct sales promotion, the terms **online advertising** or **online sales promotion** are appropriate. Unfortunately, these meaningful differentiations are often dispensed with in everyday language use.

In online communication, different **types of user involvement** can be distinguished. On the one hand, there are information offers that require an **actively searching user**. Users search for companies and products on *Google, Yahoo!* or *Bing*. The corporate website, for example, is called up by entering the corresponding web address. The term "homepage" is often used for the corporate website, although strictly speaking the term "homepage" only refers to the start page of the respective online presence. In content marketing studies, white papers and other material are offered with the aim of motivating the user to actively demand them. This is therefore referred to as **pull communication**.

Advertising banners, keyword ads, e-mails and e-newsletters, on the other hand, are based on **push communication**. This is also the case with messages that are already called "push notifications" and often go hand in hand with the use of apps. In these cases, the user is presented with certain information – without being asked. In the case of promotional e-mails and

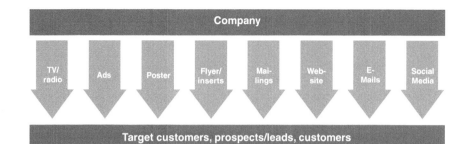

◻ **Fig. 3.1**   Basic concept of multi-channel communication

e-newsletters, however, permission to send them must have been granted in advance. Here, the user is not actively searching – the **user is directly confronted with different kinds of advertising content**.

If different online and offline instruments and channels are used in parallel – but largely unconnected – on the way to addressing, acquiring, supporting and retaining customers, we speak of **multi-channel concepts.** In **communicative multi-channel approaches,** different communication channels are used to reach the target groups. The term **cross media** is often used here because different media forms and media types are used within a campaign in a combined and/or staggered form. This is to be distinguished from a **distributive multi-channel concept** (also multi-channel distribution), in which different distribution channels are used to reach the target groups. In this concept, however, these different channels stand unconnected next to each other. ◻ Figure 3.1 shows this approach.

Today, companies are increasingly striving to develop **omni-channel concepts.** Instead of a "juxtaposition" of different channels, an "integrated overall concept" is strived for. The necessity for this results from the goal of leaving a **consistent overall impression** on the target group even when using different channels and additionally achieving synergetic advantages.

The necessity for communicative coordination also results from the fact that media use by the target persons is always also an **intermedia use.** This means that a target person uses different media in parallel and/or one after the other. From the company's point of view, however, a convincing overall impression should be created. If the focus is on the interested party or the customer, this is referred to as **customer centricity.** ◻ Figure 3.2 shows how an exemplary allocation of channels to the individual phases of a purchase and usage cycle can take place in the omni-channel concept.

◘ Fig. 3.2 Allocation of channels to the individual phases of a purchase and usage cycle in the omni-channel concept

Through an **integrated use of media,** a potential interested party can be made aware of a certain offer online. To trigger a purchase, a coupon can be offered – for online or offline purchase. In the case of online use, further communication can then be supported by e-mail. In the case of offline use, depending on the distribution channel preferred by the company, incentives for further online or offline purchases can be conveyed by (personalised) coupons.

Why such omni-channel concepts are relevant is shown by a look at the daily **usage time of various media** in Germany (cf. ◘ Fig. 3.3). This data was collected by surveying 8613 people in Germany in the age group from 14 to 69 years (cf. Statista 2021a). The most important media today – viewed across all age groups – is still **television**, with an average of **237 minutes per day per person. Internet use** is already in second place with **133 minutes. Radio** follows in third place with **103 minutes.** An analysis over time shows that the time spent on Internet use in the overall population has doubled since 2014 by 2020.

It should be noted that there is a high degree of **parallel use of different media.** These phenomena are referred to as **"second screen"** or **"multi-screen usage"** in the sense of parallel use of different screens. It should also be taken

3

* Content Internet inclues online videos, online shopping, social networking, reading articles/posts, blogs/forums, online navigation, e-learning, online banking.
** Music includes streamig music and CD and mp3 use.

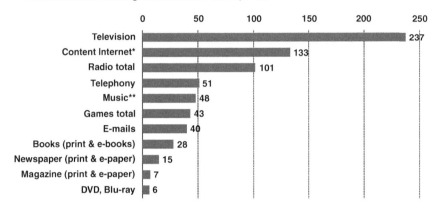

□ **Fig. 3.3** Average daily usage time of selected media in Germany 2020 – in minutes. (Source: Statista 2021a)

into account that media usage behaviour differs significantly depending on the age group. This must be taken into account when selecting suitable communication channels for different target groups.

The challenge is therefore to develop **cross-media campaigns** that take this development into account. To this end, it is necessary to optimize the selection of advertising media and instruments with regard to function, timing and advertising pressure in order to achieve the highest possible **campaign quality**. The **integration of communication** requires corresponding internal organizational structures and/or coordination processes, as the responsibilities for different media genres or forms of communication are often still to be found in different corporate divisions (cf. on the newsroom concept Kreutzer 2021a, pp. 381-384).

In the distribution sector, it is also very exciting to replace multi-channel concepts with omni-channel concepts. A retailer can offer interesting services through a **distributive omni-channel approach** in which the various channels are linked together (cf. ► Sect. 4.2). This shows the advantages of further developing existing multi-channel concepts in the direction of "omni-channel".

3.2 Corporate Website

> **Learning Agenda**
>
> What is the importance of the corporate website for the online and offline engagement of a company? Which requirements have to be considered when building a corporate website? Which methods can be used to determine the usability of a corporate website? Which tools can be used to build up the frequency of the corporate website? Which tools can be used to control the website performance? After reading ...
> - ▶ Section 3.2.1 you understand how to build a corporate website.
> - ▶ Section 3.2.2 you can ensure the usability of a corporate website.
> - ▶ Section 3.2.3 you know how to build up frequency for a corporate website.

3.2.1 Development of a Corporate Website

The most important step in online marketing is to establish your **own online presence** through a **corporate website.** Compared to other forms of advertising on the Internet, this not only has the greatest reach because it can usually be accessed worldwide. It also represents the **nucleus of a company's entire online communication** and is often integrated in communicative omni-channel campaigns.

> ┌─ **Notice!** ─────────────────────────────────────
> The **corporate website** is the online presence of a company. It is also called web presence or web offer.

As a virtual space on the Internet, the **corporate website** comprises the documents/files and other resources that are grouped together and accessible via a uniform navigation. It is therefore important to note that "website" must not be mistakenly translated as "web page", because the website describes the entire online presence and not just one or a few web pages. In addition to providing information of all kinds, components of a corporate

3

website can include the ability to request information, an e-commerce platform for direct orders, a product configurator, a store finder, and closed user areas for particularly important customers or members. Links to the social media activities of a company can also be found here.

▶ In a nutshell: The **corporate website** represents the **online business card of a company**. If it is not convincing, the user may already lose interest in the company and its offers at the first contact. And here applies:

▶ **You'll never have a second chance to make a first impression!**

In addition, all companies building a corporate website should be aware of one thing.

▶ In a nutshell: The development of a corporate website is not a project with a defined beginning and end, but rather a process that is never finished or should never be finished.

The **homepage of a corporate website** serves as the entry point to a company's web presence and can be the central **hub of all offline and online activities** (cf. ◘ Fig. 3.4). Thus, many offline activities refer to a company's online presence. The central importance of the **website** for online measures results from the fact that the links found in banners, in search engines or in price and quality rating portals often lead to this pages of the corporate website. However, it is more targeted when marketing campaigns link to campaign-specific **microsites** (micro-websites) or corresponding **landing pages** (pages where you "land") by clicking on an ad or hyperlink to extend the campaigns online. For more complex applications, the landing page can in turn be designed like a microsite itself – but it doesn't have to be. In contrast, the introductory page of microsites often serves as a landing page itself. Links that lead to such "deeper" content on the corporate website are also referred to as **deep links.**

Notice!

Imagine your website as a digital sales force. Can it convince in all dimensions? Where do you see the greatest potential for optimization?

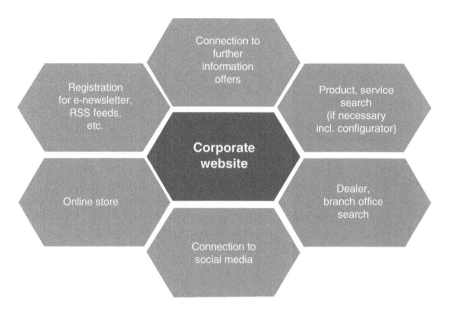

□ Fig. 3.4 Corporate website as the linchpin of offline and online engagement

A **microsite** is a lean website that usually has only a few subpages and a low navigation depth within a larger online presence. The microsites represent a thematically and formally independent small online presence. An automobile manufacturer may have a microsite dedicated to a specific model. Such microsites make it possible – in addition to the superordinate web presence – to inform (prospective) customers in a very targeted manner, e.g. within the framework of advertising campaigns. For this purpose, the microsite can not only be designed in a particularly entertaining and interactive way, but may also contain campaign-specific response elements. These can be used to obtain further information or place orders directly.

The so-called **landing page** is to be distinguished from the microsite. This is often specifically advertised as part of a campaign in order to ideally facilitate the user's entry into a website. This landing page can either be the homepage of a company itself – often less effective – or any sub-page of the entire website. However, it is more effective if the user "lands" on a web page specifically prepared for the user's particular origin by activating a hyperlink.

When designing the landing page, it is therefore important to ensure the greatest possible match between the expectations of the users built up by the

3

preliminary information on the one hand and the content provided on the landing page on the other. Consequently, the information offers to be found there should cover exactly the topic areas that were "promised" by the respective trigger (banner, post, tweet, photo, video, etc.). This can be further detailed information, sources of supply, downloads, photos, videos, reference statements, etc., which in turn can be accessed via a hyperlink. Calls-to-action for ordering or requesting further information can also be presented.

It is also important that **key visuals** used in ads, banners, flyers, photos, videos, etc. (such as the exact product advertised, a brochure touted, a testimonial included) are reflected on landing pages to build trust. Generally, the following should be avoided: A user searches for "tuxedo." Clicking on a link in the hit list on *Google* links to a landing page on which the products searched for are not visible or not clearly visible because the provider presents its entire range of services or completely different products. This often leads to frustration on the part of the user, who has to restart the search process. Often he leaves the website again immediately!

If there is a high degree of **coherence** between the built-up expectations and the landing page through the content shown there, the probability increases that the user will show the desired reactions (e.g. place an order directly or subscribe to a newsletter). To **optimize the landing page,** the following aspects should be considered:

- **Definition of the goals of a landing page**
  - The target can be downloads, newsletter subscriptions, offer requests or direct sales.
- **Definition of the target groups of the landing page**
  - For which target groups or for which personas is the landing page intended? The benefit argumentation and the wording of the offer should be aligned with their expectations.
- **Ensuring recognisability**
  - Users must immediately recognize that they have landed on the right page. For this purpose, the key visuals as well as relevant keywords of the page of origin are to be included.
- **No distractions**
  - The visitor of the landing page should not be distracted from the goal of the campaign by any other offers. Such distractions can be caused by animated banners or other promotional activities. For this, it is necessary to clarify what the dominant goal of the campaign is.
- **Convincing calls-to-action**
  - Short and concise – with consistent benefit argumentation – the visitor is to be conveyed what he now has to do concretely. These calls-to-action can be designed as follows:

- Order here!
- Redeem the coupon here!
- Sign up for the newsletter now and get a € 10 coupon!
- Request further information here!
- Arrange a test drive immediately!
- Request a callback here!
- Search for more products here!
- Make a rating now!
- Request catalogue now!
- The fewer clicks necessary to achieve the desired result, the better. At the same time, answer all relevant unspoken user questions, which are presented below.

■ **Integration of trust anchors**
- The user should recognize that he is in good company as a customer. Either because many other customers were very satisfied with the offer (for example by integrating review results), or because *Stiftung Warentest, TÜV, Trusted Shops* or others have checked the quality. Clarity about the delivery conditions, the use of the data provided and encrypted data transmission can build further trust.

■ **Consistent follow-up**
- Although the planning of the follow-up steps is no longer part of the design of the landing page, it is very much part of the overall process. Therefore, these steps must also be considered in the course of designing the landing page. The necessary resources must be planned for this at an early stage.

To encourage users to engage intensively with their own (advertising) content, companies are increasingly using **rich media**. This refers to online content that is visually or acoustically enriched by the integration of video, audio or animation elements. This is intended to increase attention to website content and intensify engagement with it.

In order to lead an online process to a successful conclusion, an orientation towards the **unspoken reader questions** known from dialogue marketing is helpful (cf. Vögele 2005, pp. 76-78, 176-181). The use of the following questions contributes sustainably to the responsible managers achieving the necessary "receiver orientation" in communication. Through a dialogue with the target group, these questions can be answered systematically. For this purpose parts of this target group are to be called upon to evaluate their own website or to be involved in a personal dialogue (for example, in the form of a customer workshop or through a personal survey).

- Is it worth it for me to read the content?
- What benefits are offered to me?
- What unique advantage (from a company perspective this is the USP/ Unique Selling Proposition) does the company or the specific offer provide me with – or colloquially: What do I get out of following this offer?
- Who can "prove" these performance advantages of the offer to me (e.g. through customer reviews, test results, certificates)?
- Who has already bought what I want and can give me information about it (references from customers, customer reviews)?
- Can I find more information about the company, for example on *Facebook, Instagram, YouTube* or in blogs and communities?
- Is the company trustworthy (presence of test seals, e.g. *"Trusted Shops"*)?
- How many customers has the company already acquired – or would I be the first?
- Who can I contact with questions, complaints, etc.?
- Does the company have an address and/or contact person in my country?
- Is communication limited to e-mail, or can I also contact the company by phone or chat?
- What should I do specifically to request information or subscribe to an e-newsletter?
- How many e-mails can I expect to receive per day or per week if I opt-in?
- How many e-newsletters will the company send me if I opt-in?
- Can I unsubscribe from an e-newsletter quickly?
- Can I get more information from the company via *Twitter* or an RSS feed?
- How quickly do I have to react in order to achieve the advantages presented?
- What should I specifically do to place an order?
- How could I cancel an order?
- Is the product or service I ordered available?
- When can I expect delivery?
- Will I be offered trustworthy payment methods?
- What warranty and/or exchange options do I have?
- How transparent and understandable are the terms and conditions for me?
- Will my address data be passed on?
- How is data protection ensured?

These **unspoken questions** must be answered before a website is created in order to generate content and organize processes which are relevant from the user's point of view. These are then to be presented in an easily understandable way – oriented to the typical procedure of a website visitor.

An online presence in the form of a **corporate website** is already used by the majority of companies to draw (potential) customers' attention to their own offerings. An indispensable prerequisite for setting up one's own web presence is to first register a **domain name**. The domain name must not yet be occupied and should ideally be identical or at least related to one's own company, offer or brand name. For companies, it is important that the company itself is registered as the domain owner and also as the administrative contact – and not the online agency looking after it! Such an error is usually only noticed when there is a change of agency.

When a company is setting up an online presence for the first time or revising an existing presence, the desired **functions of the corporate website** must be defined. The functions described below are often used in combination by companies:

- **Point of information**
  - The **provision of information** dominates here. For this purpose, companies present themselves, their products or their services. In addition, reference can be made to branches, stationary shops and the responsible sales representatives. In addition, possibilities can be offered to subscribe to e-newsletters or RSS feeds or to become a fan on *Facebook* or a follower on *Twitter, Instagram or Pinterest*. Such a form of online presence dominates with media companies or branded goods companies that do not have an online shop themselves.
- **Point of interaction**
  - With a website designed as point of interaction, the aim is an **exchange of information between the company and (prospective) customers and/ or other stakeholders.** The possibility of requesting specific offers, initiating a callback or arranging an appointment for a visit serves this purpose. Through offers such as forums, communities or blogs on the company's website, an exchange of information between (prospective) customers themselves can also be stimulated. Such an orientation is given by many B2B companies, but also by B2C platforms.
- **Point of Sale (POS) or Point of Purchase (POP)**
  - A central content of the online presence here is the offer to carry out online transactions. In addition to classic service providers such as banks, insurance companies, hotels, airlines and car rental companies, a wide variety of online shops dominate here.

3

When **building a corporate website,** there are always **two target groups** to consider at the same time. The first target group is the **target persons** themselves, whom you ultimately want to address. This includes (prospective) customers, suppliers, applicants, investors, etc. The second target group are the **reading robots of the search engines,** which must not be neglected. These reading robots (also called spiders, robots/bots or crawlers) are used by search engines. These reading robots are computer programs that search websites (worldwide) and index them for databases and thus make them findable.

However, both target groups – the target persons and the reading robots – place different demands on the corporate website, which must be taken into account in the website design. While the target persons would like to find the most relevant content possible on the website, the reading robots must first of all be able to read the content at all and prepare it for the algorithms of the search engines.

The **design of the corporate website** can be based on various concepts. Here, the following **anchors of the web presence** are to be distinguished:

- **Corporate brand for manufacturers**
  - Here, the corporate brand stands above the individual brands (e.g. at
    ▶ *audi.com*).
- **Service mark**
  - In many companies, the service brand coincides with the corporate brand (e.g. ▶ *zalando.com*).
- **Product brand**
  - This brand presents itself (relatively) independently of the company (e.g. ▶ *nutella.com*).
- **Target group**
  - Here, information is often provided across companies and/or offers, oriented towards specific target groups (e.g. ▶ *tinder.com*).

The aforementioned central functions of a company's website – **Point of Information, Point of Interaction** as well as **Point of Sale (POS)** or **Point of Purchase (POP)** – can be used for the various anchors of the web presence.

If companies want to provide interested target groups with new content on a regular basis, this information can be sent to users via **RSS.** RSS is used to store content from a website and/or changes to it and make it available in a standardized, machine-readable form. The messages that can be subscribed to via RSS often consist of a headline, a short text excerpt and a link to the respective original page. These so-called **RSS feeds** can also include the complete content (full-text RSS).

Another way to make a corporate website interesting is to provide **podcasts**. This refers to audio and video contributions that can be distributed via the Internet and subscribed to there. There are various feed formats (usually RSS) for **subscribing to audio and video podcasts**. **Podcasting** refers to the production and offering of (subscribable) media files via the Internet. In order to provide interested users with easier access to such information, podcast portals have been established in which podcasts – sorted by topic and tagged with appropriate keywords – can be entered. *Apple, Google* and *Spotify* offer a wide variety of podcasts.

The integration of **audio and video content** into the website can be done either on own IT resources or on a media sharing platform. This content can be accessed online via streaming and/or download. **Streaming** refers to a data transmission in which audio or video content is received from a computer network and played back the moment it is received. The content itself is referred to as a **livestream**. In contrast to live streaming, **downloading** involves downloading the data to the user's computer. They can then be played and/or archived regardless of time and place and without an Internet connection. The described functions enable an **on-demand offer**, where the user can decide for himself when he accesses certain content.

For companies, the **presentation of videos** (e.g. on *YouTube*) can be interesting to explain the use of a product or the application of a service. Brands can also be comprehensively staged and fashion shows as well as product demonstrations can be made accessible to everyone at any time. Similarly, current radio or TV commercials can be offered. On-demand offerings can also be found on many media industry sites. Companies such as *Redbull* offer a whole range of audio and video podcasts to provide information about activities of the players they support.

Video messages in particular can convey much more emotion than text, sound and still images alone. For companies, the particular challenge is to prepare information (with an advertising background) in such a way that the largest possible number of listeners and viewers subscribe to the content and ideally forward it to their circle of friends. For this, more than "pure advertising" must be offered on a regular basis. These offers are part of the content marketing approach.

In order to enrich the corporate website with further content, a **corporate blog, links to social media** or a **wiki** can be integrated there. A wiki is a hypertext system of websites whose content can not only be read online by users, but can also be changed. In this way, a corporate website can become a contact point for interested users who, for example, build up a common dictionary. If target groups have a high affinity to a company, an offer and/or a brand, the development of an **online community** can be target-oriented. **Online forums** are a special form of online community.

3 | **3.2.2 Ensuring the Performance of a Corporate Website**

To ensure the performance of a website, it is essential to be guided by the following **performance criteria, the** consideration of which has a lasting effect on the **user experience** (UX):

▬ **Findability**
  – A website can only achieve its goals if it can be found by users in the online environment. In particular, achieving a good **position in the organic hit lists of search engines** is essential. This is the task of search engine optimization (cf. ▶ Sect. 3.4).
▬ **Accessibility**
  – This refers to the **ease of access of a website.** This includes first of all the functionality of the website when accessed via mobile devices. Furthermore, a high stability of access should be guaranteed even with a slow Internet connection. In addition, accessibility also means the barrier-free nature of the website. Moreover, a social log-in can be used for easier access to the content of a website. Accessibility also improves when no additional software needs to be installed for optimal use of the website.
▬ **Scannability**
  – This term is used to describe how easy it is to **recognize central content when skimming the website** ("scanning"). Is important information clearly highlighted? This applies first of all to the various **headings** that convey important content. **Highlighting** in the text itself can also convey important content to the quick viewer (e.g. by using bold print). **Lists of lines** additionally increase the scannability of the content. The following applies here: People like lists! **Short paragraphs** invite reading. **Calls-to-action** should also be quick to find and easy to understand.
  – Scannability is therefore on the one hand about the type of preparation of online content for the quick reader, since online content often does not have the full attention (especially with mobile users). Therefore, the most important information should be presented "**above the fold**". If, at first glance, the website only shows a large photo without text and without further information about the content of the page, the bounce rate will tend to be high.

- On the other hand, **readability** is also addressed here – as a subset of scannability, so to speak. For in addition to the question of easy access to the content through the formal preparation, it is also about the good **readability or comprehensibility of the content offered.** Are these texts designed in a reader-friendly way (e.g. no light grey font on a white background; no capital letters in longer texts)? Are the texts easy to read on the screen – large or small? Are terms used that the average user can understand? Or are the texts written by specialists who cannot understand that other users do not have the same profound knowledge?
- **Active language** is also important – it shortens sentences and makes the message much clearer. It is better to say "Download the white paper here" instead of "The white paper can be downloaded here ".
- Taking these requirements into account is even more important when **accessing** a website on the **move.** Here it is important to get to the point quickly and leave out distracting information. Key information (especially contact and address data) as well as important calls-to-action should be presented first.

Notice!

Compaction is the order of the day here!

— **Usability**
- This performance criterion is about the **usability of a website or an application.** How easy is it to use? Is it intuitive to use – or do you have to work through a thousand-page manual to understand how to navigate the website? How easy is it to access tools for easier usability (e.g. search masks)?
- All in all, the contents are to be presented in such a way that the user intuitively understands the contents as well as the process of access. For this purpose, it is important to support the user's reading flow learned online. Since the competitor online is always only one or two mouse clicks away, a **low frustration tolerance of the user** must be assumed in the conception of the web design. This means that there is only a low willingness to "suffer" when operating a website.
- For example, the question arises as to how easy it is for a user to successfully complete tasks on the website the first time. Here, it is advisable to follow the success formula "**KISS**" for "Keep it short and simple", which ensures simple and easily recognizable user guidance.

- This is also about the question of the **efficiency of a website:** How quickly can users repeatedly master tasks once they have been learned in order to achieve the desired results? The stability of the learning results contributes to a high efficiency. It is necessary to examine how easy it is for users to regain high efficiency in processing after a certain period of non-use of a website.
- Contributing to the cross-website **stability of learning outcomes,** links are often colored and underlined, site navigation starts at the top left, and log-ins are found at the top right. Search screens are also often found in the upper right. Website designers should be guided by these user experiences.
- "Crisp" **calls-to-action** also contribute to the efficiency of the website. It should always be made clear to the user at the relevant points what he should do – and what benefits are associated with it. Such calls-to-action can be "Click here to learn more," "Subscribe for free here," or "Buy now and save 20%." Generally, active verbs contribute to achieving the desired conversion.

— **Trustability/credibility**
- At its core, this criterion is about **trust in the website.** This begins with the question of whether the company or the corresponding brand is actually behind the website. This question is very significant in view of the large number of fake shops. Additionally, it is about the trustworthiness of the content presented there. When establishing the trustworthiness of a website, the trust anchors mentioned in ▶ Sect. 3.2.1 can provide important orientation.

— **Usefulness**
- The question here is the **usefulness of the content offered.** Do they create added value for the user? Does the user benefit (in the short or long term) from having engaged with the website and the information presented there? How enjoyable is it to engage with the website and the content presented there? Does the user enjoy the engagement? This is essentially about the content of the website and the way it is presented. These must be geared to the expectations of the different users and oriented towards the success factors discussed in ▶ Sect. 1.3.
- The relevance of the content required there is concretised in the web presence, in particular, in a high degree of topicality of the information presented and an easily accessible presentation. Furthermore, it is always important to make clear to the user the **advantages of concrete offers** (keyword "**benefit selling**") as well as the presented calls-to-

action. Therefore, instead of "Tips for text creation on the website", it would be better to say: "Ten steps to online texts that sell".

- The **individualization of the content presented on the website** (mass customization of content), which is oriented towards the customer relationship, also increases the value of the website for the user. In this sense, usefulness represents a success criterion that is superior to the other criteria. Here we can also speak of **desirability** in the sense of a **desirability of the website** itself – always from the user's perspective.

▬ **Shareability**
- In order to facilitate further dissemination of your own content – possibly even in viral processes – it should be equipped with share, like, retweet, pin, social bookmarking buttons, etc. in order to achieve (viral) dissemination on the various social platforms.

▬ **Speed**
- The load time (also page speed) refers to the speed at which a website is loaded. The loading time comprises the period between the submission of a request and the complete delivery of the requested content. This load time has a huge impact on the user experience. No user wants to wait longer to open a website. The loading time also affects the ranking of the respective website within the organic hit list.

▬ **Traceability**
- In all measures, companies should try to trace the results achieved (both positive and negative) back to the respective causes. This is essentially what is meant by the term traceability. This possibility of determining the causes of the communication results must already be planned for in the conception of the corresponding measures.

To remember these **performance criteria**, the following made-up word, which is made up of the first letters of the criteria, can help: **FAUUSSSTT**.

If these performance criteria are not taken into account, **users leave the website** because:

▬ it is difficult to operate.
▬ it is not clear what a company's offer really is and how it can be taken up.
▬ users get lost on the site.
▬ information provided is difficult to understand and/or does not answer users' questions.
▬ the desired content cannot be found easily and quickly.
▬ the company's request for information is not balanced in relation to the service offered.

— the navigation on a website differs significantly from the learned navigation – and the extra effort is not "rewarded" by exciting content.
— payment information is requested for a free service.
— information is collected that is not necessary for the provision of the service.

It becomes clear: companies should not only invest in the content of their website, but also in the form of its preparation in order to achieve a good overall website performance. To achieve this, it can be helpful to **integrate representatives of the target group into the design process**. For this purpose, these persons have to process typical tasks: e.g. placing an order or requesting a customer card or e-newsletter. This form of **target group participation** should take place in the course of the initial development of a web presence, but also flanking its use for ongoing optimization.

> ▶ **Example:** *Google*
>
> *Google* supports the development of a website through a variety of **tools** (▶ *www. google.com/intl/de_de/webmasters/#?modal_active=none*). These allow **testing and optimization of the content and the structure of websites** without incurring any costs. Through these tools, the following goals can be achieved:
> — **Increasing conversion rates** on the website (CRO/Conversion Rate Optimization)
> — **Reduction of the bounce rate** of visitors
> — **Increasing the stickiness of the website** ("stickiness" expresses how well a website succeeds in retaining the visitor)
> — **Increase the satisfaction** of website visitors
> — **Achievement of a stringent and easy to learn user guidance**
>
> Whether a consistent consideration of the defined requirements could be achieved is to be checked regularly by controlling methods. ◀

3.2.3 Frequency Building for a Corporate Website

A central task for a company is to achieve a sustainable increase in **frequency for the corporate website**. To this end, classic **offline response instruments** can initially be used, which are also of great importance in dialogue marketing (cf. ◨ Fig. 3.5; cf. Kreutzer 2021a, pp. 171–206). These include **inserts** in parcels as well as in newspapers and magazines. Parcel inserts with a reference to the corporate website are regularly used by many online shops. The advantage of such an insert, which should not be underestimated, is that all the receivers of parcels are active online shoppers and have made recent purchases. This ensures that a behavioural characteristic that is indispensable for

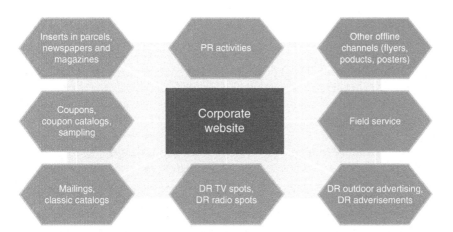

◘ Fig. 3.5 Offline instruments for building up the frequency of a corporate website

an online provider is fulfilled in the target persons addressed: the affinity for online purchasing.

Additionally, incentives to visit the website can be provided through **newspaper and magazine inserts.** Another possibility is the distribution of **coupons.** These can be aimed at visitors in the retail store to encourage them to visit the company's own online shop. This is also referred to as an **e-coupon,** which is an electronically redeemable coupon or online coupon. Coupons can also be distributed as package inserts.

In addition to these measures, coupons can be placed in **coupon catalogues** distributed regionally or nationally, or **sampling** (i.e. the distribution of product samples with a response medium, e.g. a card or an online coupon) can be used as an incentive to visit a particular website or online shop. **Classic catalogues** can also be used as a trigger to visit the corporate website. E-coupons can be used for this purpose in order to overcome any hurdles that may exist when making contact to the website. An incentive to visit the website can also be provided by **mailings** in which e-coupons are delivered.

In addition, **DR TV and DR radio spots** as well as corresponding **DR ads** in newspapers and magazines can be used to point to the target address of the corporate website. DR stands for **Direct Response** (in the sense of a "direct answer"). DR expresses the fact that the viewer, listener or reader should be encouraged to take direct action and call up a website, for example. A **DR outdoor advertisement** can also provide an online address, as can the company's own sales force. This can encourage prospective customers to call up more detailed information via reference reports, product videos, product descriptions, etc. via the website.

3

Posters and **flyers** as well as the **products** themselves can also provide references to the company's website. Finally, the various methods of classic **PR** also make an important contribution to frequency building. When specifying web addresses, it is important to ensure that they are "speaking domain names" that are easy to remember and simple to enter into the browser. **Short links** also contribute to this. For this purpose, the often long URLs are shortened by certain methods (so-called URL shorteners) to make them easier to use.

An alternative to naming a URL to be entered is the **QR code**. QR stands for quick response. It consists of a square matrix and contains data that can be read by software. This is available for mobile phones (often apps) and other reading devices and is sometimes even integrated into the camera function of smartphones. If the reader is pointed at the code and scanned, the software decodes the code and the user is redirected to the corresponding website. To generate the QR code, a **QR code writer** is required, which is available online free of charge (e.g. through ▶ *qr-code-generator.com*).

The **QR code** can be used in all print media to encode a web address and provide the user with **further information** or **specific offers**. After scanning and reading the code, the user may only need to press send to trigger an order. The code can also contain telephone number, address or other textual information. To distribute the code, it is often used in advertisements, flyers, mailings or on posters and even on beer mats. The QR code is also used in magazines and newspapers to offer further information.

The **advantage of the QR** code is that it eliminates the need for error-prone and time-consuming typing of a web address, thus providing a real user benefit. However, it is noticeable that QR codes are often found without clearly highlighting what the user can expect after scanning them. But the reading of QR codes must also be "sold"! A QR code without a reference to the offer accessible through it is like a door without a reference to what can be found behind it! Who then wants to open it?

The next stage of evolution is already foreseeable: "**addressable TV**". This refers to the possibility of selectively broadcasting TV advertising. This means that during an advertising break, advertising can no longer be shown in a "one-to-mass" format, but in a "one-to-many" format, and in the future possibly even in a "one-to-one" format. Based on individual characteristics of the viewer, different spots are broadcast in the same slot. By combining the large TV reach with the precise playout as with many online contents, the relevance of TV advertising is to be increased. Connected TV represents the necessary technological platform for this and is developing classic, linear TV from an offline medium into an online medium (cf. Pilot 2021).

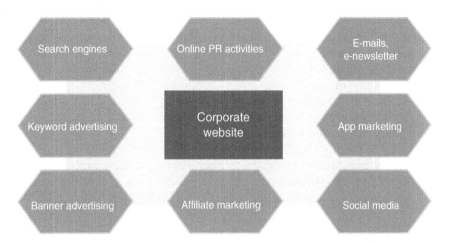

◐ Fig. 3.6 Online instruments for building up the frequency of a corporate website

---

Notice!

Thus, despite all the prophecies of doom, TV remains a relevant mass medium.

In addition to these offline instruments, many of the online marketing instruments already mentioned or still to be discussed can aim to systematically attract users to one's own website (cf. ◐ Fig. 3.6). These include, first and foremost, **search engines** to lead searchers to the website via the hit list of the organic search. The various forms of online advertising are also very important. These include **keyword advertising** and **banner advertising**. Their distribution can be achieved through special **affiliate marketing.** The links placed via these forms of advertising often lead directly to the homepage, special microsites or landing pages. Additionally, corporate engagement on **social media** can help drive traffic to the corporate website. The use of own apps as well as engagement in apps of business partners can and should generate traffic for the website (**app marketing**). An important function of **e-mail marketing** as well as **online PR** is also the generation of visitors on the own website.

The multitude of instruments to be used makes it clear that **building website traffic** must be done just as professionally as the design of the website itself. After all, corporate websites are only found if they are specifically searched for and/or if references to the website are communicated to the

relevant target persons. Consequently, building a compelling website and promoting it must go hand in hand. In order to check whether a corporate website contributes to the achievement of the defined goals, the following methods can be used (cf. in-depth Kreutzer 2021b, pp. 167-192):
- Web analytics
- Analysis of the user experience
- Eye tracking
- On-site survey and mystery surfing

Important insights can be gained through the use of these methods. These must be taken into account – on an ongoing basis – in further optimization.

3.3 Online Advertising

Learning Agenda

What is the importance of different forms of online advertising? On the basis of which criteria can online marketing be evaluated? How does search engine advertising (SEA) work? What is affiliate marketing and how can it be used? After reading …
- ▶ Section 3.3.1 you will be able to distinguish between different formats of online advertising and use relevant key figures to evaluate online advertising.
- ▶ Section 3.3.2 you can use search engine advertising in a targeted manner.
- ▶ Section 3.3.3 you know how affiliate marketing works.
- ▶ Section 3.3.4 you know what else to look out for in online advertising.

3.3.1 Formats and Measurement Criteria of Online Advertising

Online advertising includes all advertising formats and advertising concepts that make use of the Internet to disseminate advertising information. Various questions need to be answered when using online advertising:
- **Why?**
- Here, the **goal of the advertising approach** must be defined.
- **Who?**

- In addition, it must be clarified which **target persons** or **target companies** are to be addressed. The answers to this question can be based on certain criteria, such as the regional origin of the online user or their previous or expected behaviour.
- **How?**
- For online advertising, various **formats of online advertising media** are available (such as banner or video advertising).
- **Where?**
- Closely related to the question of the target group is the question of on which websites and thus in which environments the defined target group should be addressed. On the one hand, **search engine advertising** (keyword advertising) can be used here. On the other hand, **advertising** can be played out in **social media** (social media ads), but also on **third-party websites**. **Affiliate marketing** can be used for this purpose.
- **How much?**
- Here it must be determined which **budgets** are to be used to achieve the objectives.

A look at the development of **expenditure on online advertising in Germany** shows that investments in **search engine advertising** dominate (cf. ◘ Fig. 3.7). **Social media advertising** follows in second place – already at a clear distance. In third place comes **banner advertising**. In 2019, social media advertising had already displaced banner advertising in this third place. **Video advertising** and **classified ads** follow in fourth and fifth place (cf. Statista 2020e).

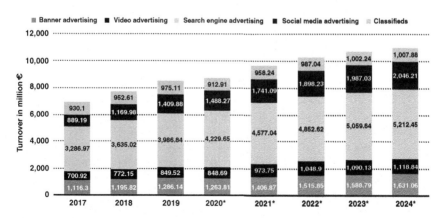

◘ **Fig. 3.7** Forecast of expenditure in the market for online advertising in Germany until 2024 – in € million

3

Not only the willingness to pay for content with money is decreasing. Users are also putting a stop to the other source of income for content providers – placing advertisements on their own websites – by using ad blockers. **Ad blockers** are filter programs that block advertisements on Internet pages. This means that a large proportion of advertising banners are no longer displayed to users.

Online advertising includes a **wide variety of advertising formats.** It should be noted that – even if online advertising formats are referred to in the following – advertising objectives do not necessarily always have to be the focus. Promotion or PR goals can also be targeted with an online engagement. Even if the basic functionality of the different formats remains largely unaffected by the respective communicative goal, the various formats are differently suited to achieving the desired goals. The specific **characteristics of online advertising** include:

- **High reach**
  - The Internet has a **global reach** as long as country-specific filtering programs (such as in China) or lack of Internet connections do not restrict access.
- **High availability**
  - The Internet is available around the clock, 365 days a year.
- **Low entry costs**
  - Many of the online advertising formats described below can already be created with **little effort** and placed at **low cost.**
- **High flexibility**
  - Online advertising media can generally be changed at short notice and thus achieve a **high degree of topicality.** The reactions of online users to advertising content can thus be recorded promptly or even in real time and optimization measures can be derived.
- **Offers for immediate interaction**
  - The majority of online advertising is geared towards a direct response from the user through the use of calls-to-action.
- **Target group and target person specific content**
  - On the one hand, advertising content can be provided online by **addressing specific target groups.** This can be achieved by placing ads on ▶ *washingtonpost.com* or ▶ *playboy.com* and by advertising on the online portal ▶ *parents.com.* On the other hand, it is possible to **address specific target groups** if users are clearly identified via a log-in or through the use of cookies. **Personalisation** is then possible by address-

ing the target person by name, which can also be continued in the advertising address on the website itself. The provider achieves **individualisation** when offers are geared to the specific needs of the user. Here, too, the Internet offers a multitude of fields of action.

– Many of the forms of advertising described below are grouped together under the term **display ads** or **display advertising.** The term is derived from the word "display" for "monitor". The central aspect of display advertising is the use of advertising space for own offers on non-own websites (i.e. outside the own corporate website). This includes the various forms of banner advertising. However, depending on the business model, the company's own website can also be the delivery location of display advertising for third parties. In the case of display advertising, advertising information is integrated into a **third-party website** as an **interactive advertising space.** This can also be the websites of social networks. The advertising medium refers to the advertising company with a hyperlink. This is activated by the user clicking on it (e.g. an advertising banner, button or link).

The various **advertising formats** can be classified in more detail with regard to the following criteria, which, however, partly overlap (cf. in-depth Kreutzer 2021b, pp. 199-213):

- **Size and shape** (e.g. super banner, skyscraper and wallpaper)
- **Degree of animation** (static or animated banners)
- **Position on the website** (e.g. delivery within or outside the editorial section)
- **Time of insertion** (interstitials, prestitials)

Due to the intensive placement of online banners and the associated habituation effects among users, **banner blindness** occurs. This describes the phenomenon that users virtually "automatically" hide the advertising banners from their field of vision. Against this background, it is understandable why the **click-through rates (CTR)** on online banners have fallen continuously worldwide in recent years and have reached 0.05% as an average for all formats (cf. Smart Insights 2020).

The **CTR** is determined as the percentage relation between the clicked and seen banners. It thus says something about the efficiency of the advertising media placed. A CTR of 0.05% means that out of 10,000 banners seen (e.g. more precisely: "placed in the viewer's field of vision"), only five banners are clicked on.

$$\text{Click-through rate} = \frac{\text{Number of ad clicks}}{\text{Number of ad impressions}} \times 100$$

3

The **overloading of websites** with advertising messages that are often irrelevant from the user's point of view and the rapid **rotation of the advertising media** presented have contributed to this low advertising efficiency. This has led to an **explosion of brand and message diversity,** which has had a negative impact on click-through rates. This development has been further exacerbated by the fact that almost all industries and product ranges are now advertised online.

The low click-through rates illustrate why banner advertising is often used to **increase brand awareness** and **build brand image** rather than to generate an immediate response. However, if banners are placed on many websites with a correspondingly high volume of ad impressions, even a click-through rate of 0.05% can lead to significant frequency on the linked website.

❯ To the point: In sum, the **low advertising effectiveness of online banners** underscores the need to develop innovative forms of banner advertising to overcome banner blindness and achieve user attention.

In order to achieve **branding effects** and to **trigger purchasing processes,** advertisers define the number of targeted **ad impressions** and the number of **unique impressions** to be achieved by the advertising partners. The target of "unique impressions" comes closest to the "net reach" figure familiar from traditional advertising. This is the question of how many people have seen the advertisement at least once. Multiple contacts with the same person are therefore not counted. With regard to uniqueness in the online sector, it must be pointed out that this refers to a delivery with regard to an IP address and not necessarily to the actual user. The same computer can be used by several people, and an identical user can use different devices (e.g. a smartphone and a tablet PC in addition to a stationary PC).

In the long term, only **cross-device identification** (CDI) or **cross-device tracking** will be able to provide a remedy. This should enable users to be clearly identified along the customer journey – irrespective of the used device. Cross-device identification describes the ability to track customer activities across multiple devices (desktop, tablet, phone, etc.) and to merge them into a **single customer view**.

With *Attribution* in *Google Analytics,* the company *Google* aims to master this challenge (cf. Google 2021). Then it should no longer apply: Last cookie wins! Until now, this meant that the transaction (conversion) achieved was automatically assigned to the last corresponding advertising medium for which a cookie was set. With *Attribution,* a free data-driven attribution for several channels is available to all customers. *Google Attribution* aims to determine the influence of each touchpoint along the customer journey and weight it according to its relevance. All channels should be captured: display, keyword or video ads, corporate website, social media platforms and apps. By integrating the *Google services Google Ads* and *Google Analytics*, the company can make an important contribution to this – and at the same time further expand its eco-system for companies.

The restriction of advertising material deliveries to an IP address is ensured by so-called **frequency capping.** This refers to the limitation of the frequency of the display of (identical) advertising media at an IP address. Frequency capping can be used to ensure that, for example, only five identical ads are displayed per computer and day or that only ten contacts are made in the course of a particular campaign. Frequency capping is primarily carried out by the marketers, as their sites request the advertising from the ad servers. Frequency capping is intended to avoid **banner burnout** or **ad fatique.** This refers to the diminishing advertising effect of a banner, which can occur if it is repeated too often or displayed for too long to the same user.

In order to **avoid scattering losses,** the delivery of online advertising must be carried out as specifically as possible. For this purpose, **targeting** is based on personal and/or computer-related criteria, which are sometimes also used in combination. The most important **types of targeting** are presented below as an overview (cf. in more detail Kreutzer 2021b, pp. 219-226):

- **Sociodemographic targeting**
  - Starting point: personal characteristics of the online user
- **Geo-targeting/IP-targeting**
  - Starting point: regional origin of the online user
- **Technical targeting**
  - Starting point: technical specifications of the hardware/software used by the online user
- **Context targeting/content targeting/semantic targeting**
  - Starting point: websites visited by the online user
- **Behavioural targeting**
  - Starting point: surfing and search behaviour of the online user in the past
- **Predictive behavioral targeting/lookalike targeting**
  - Starting point: surfing and search behaviour of online users

— **Keyword targeting/searchword targeting**
  – Starting point: search terms used by the online user
— **Social media targeting**
  – Starting point: profile and preference data of social network users

3

The different types of targeting that can form the basis of a delivery are often used in a combined form. This is the case with a regionally oriented delivery of advertising in search engines. However, it must be taken into account that **targeting** is also associated with **higher costs** and therefore its **optimization contribution** must be consistently recorded. When using targeting variants, it must therefore be continuously checked whether the higher costs are more than compensated for in each individual case by the targeted higher success rates.

It must be noted that the different **targeting approaches** cannot be used or are not available for **all forms of advertising**. In addition, the **achievable reach** is reduced by narrowly defined targeting grids. Consequently, the use of targeting variants reduces the achievable volume of page impressions and thus the visibility of online advertising.

Various partners can be integrated for the **delivery of online advertising media**. These include search engine providers and affiliates or affiliate networks. Today, online bookings are increasingly being made through so-called **real-time advertising/realtime bidding (RTB)**. The terms **programmatic advertising** or **programmatic ad buying** are also used for this concept. RTB is the process of automated and data-driven media planning to acquire advertising inventory in real time based on auctions and to automatically target predefined audiences. In this concept, advertisers buy advertising space via a so-called demand side platforms (DSPs). Advertising space ist offered by the publishers on so-called supply side platforms (SSPs). On the so-called data management platforms (DMPs), relevant data on the user profiles as well as on the websites visited are provided in order to support the advertiser's purchase decision. The basic concept of RTB shows ◘ Fig. 3.8. In Germany, about 75% of display ads were booked automatically in 2020. For 2025, this share is expected to increase to 78% (cf. Statista 2021b).

Online advertising is essentially billed on the basis of the **thousand-contact price (TCP)** principle familiar from traditional advertising. It indicates the amount to be paid for addressing 1000 contacts each. In the online context, we speak of page impressions or ad impressions instead of contacts. Specifically, this is the number of times an online advertisement is displayed on a website. The insertion of an advertisement is equated with its perception in the sense of an impression.

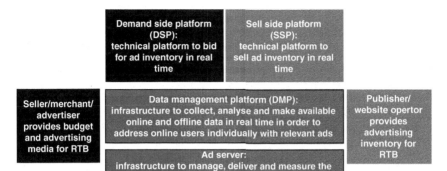

□ Fig. 3.8   Basic concept of real-time bidding (programmatic advertising)

The billing method itself is called **Cost per Mille (CPM)** in online marketing and describes the **costs per 1000 impressions**. With this billing model, the advertiser must pay € 20, for example, to reach 1000 people per ad impression. Other billing methods are based on **ad clicks** or on the **duration of the advertising presence** on a website (e.g. 1 week or 1 month). Advertisers are increasingly trying to implement a payment method for online advertising that is based on concrete actions by online users (so-called "actions" or "conversions"). As already reported, this is referred to as performance marketing. In addition, the costs of **targeting**, possible **frequency capping** and the **creation of the online advertising media** themselves must be taken into account in the **calculation of online marketing campaigns**.

As part of the **controlling of online advertising** and other online activities, various key figures of online marketing are used (also called online KPIs). The following **key performance indicators of online advertising** initially express the different kinds of the **contact quality** achieved or the **type of results** achieved.

- **Page impressions/page views**
    - These key figures indicate how many hits a website has received from users. This is also referred to as the **reach of a website.**
- **Ad impressions/ad views**
    - This key figure is intended to indicate whether there was **visual contact** with the respective advertising medium. De facto, however, this parameter is not the recording of a real visual contact. This is because, depending on the recording method used, the **request for the advertising medium** can also be counted, regardless of whether the user is still on the site at the time of delivery or not.

3

- **Ad clicks**
  - This records how many users were motivated by a communicative impulse to click on a certain content of a website (e.g. an online advertisement).
- **Click-through rate (CTR)**
  - The CTR is determined as the percentage ratio between the ad clicks (e.g. 50) and the ad impressions (e.g. 50,000) and says something about the efficiency of the advertising media placed. In this example, the CTR is 0.1%.
- **Bounce rate**
  - The bounce rate quantifies the number of visitors (in percent) who have only visited a single page of the website. It is an important indicator of whether the expectations of the user built up, for example, by banners or links in the organic hit list of the search engine are also fulfilled.
- **Site stickiness/duration**
  - Site stickiness indicates how long a user stays on a specific website on average. However, a high dwell time alone should not be considered "good". Whether a high dwell time is to be welcomed can only be determined if one also recognizes that the desired "conversions" have taken place – that is, whether the website has reached its goal.
- **Sign-up – generation of leads/prospective customers**
  - Sign-up is understood to mean, in particular, the **entry in an e-mail list** for regular receipt of a newsletter. But also the **request for a callback,** the **request for information material** or similar expresses an interest of the user. During the sign-up process, it is possible to record the user's data. This user is then referred to as a lead, prospect or interested party who can be further supported.
- **Sales/revenue – generation of buyers**
  - If, after the presentation of an advertising medium, a **purchase** is made by clicking on it and the further guidance of the user, this is referred to as a **sale** (in the sense of turnover). Here, the number of buyers is recorded first. If, for example, coupons or special codes are issued online for a subsequent purchase, even offline sales can be attributed to an online advertising medium.
- **Turnover per purchase act**
  - This key figure shows the turnover generated by persons during a purchase act. If an e-coupon is used, the key figure can be shown as sales per coupon.

■ **Redemption rate**
  - The redemption rate shows the number of people in percent who redeemed a coupon out of the total number of coupons distributed.
■ **Conversion rates**
  - The conversion rate expresses in percentage terms how many online visitors have completed a desired action. The content of conversions can be clicks, inquiries, registrations, orders or similar.

The **cost indicators of online marketing** on which the measurement of success is based are defined by the following criteria. If there is no fixed remuneration for the service providers or partners involved, but payment based on the KPIs mentioned, this is referred to as **performance marketing.** There are different success- or performance-based billing models for various forms of advertising. The costs in online marketing are referred to with the following terms (more detailed information on the billing models can be found in the glossary).

■ Cost per Mille (CPM)/Thousand-Contact-Price (TCP)/Cost per 1000 Impressions
■ Cost per Click (CPC)/Pay per Click (PPC)
■ Cost per View (CPV)
■ Cost per Lead (CPL)/Cost per Interest (CPI)
■ Cost per Order (CPO)/Pay per Order (CPO)/Pay per Sale (PPS)
■ Cost per Conversion/Cost per Acquisition (CPA)
■ Cost per time interval
■ Targeting costs
■ Costs for Frequency Capping

By means of an integrated evaluation of the usage and cost indicators of online marketing, the following **efficiency and effectiveness indicators of online marketing** can be determined. In some cases, the key figures described below – as shown – are also used to remunerate the online advertising partners involved (more information on these key figures can be found in the glossary):

■ Cost per Lead (CPL)/Cost per Interest (CPI) – overall view
■ Cost per Order (CPO)/Pay per Order (CPO)/Pay per Sale (PPS) – overall view
■ Cost per Coupon (CPCoup)
■ Cost per Redemption (CPR)
■ Contacts per Order (ConPO)
■ Break even point
■ Return on Investment (ROI)

3

The aforementioned **success indicators, costs** and **efficiency** or **effectiveness indicators of online marketing** can be used to evaluate current campaigns. They also allow comparisons between different online measures as well as between online and offline measures. Finally, they can also be used for comparison with past results and/or those of competitors. For this purpose, these parameters must be determined and evaluated on an ongoing basis in order to ensure continuous optimization of online advertising. The values achieved for the various criteria must be compared with the target or forecast values. It is important that the results achieved are evaluated in the light of qualitative aspects. For example, a high conversion rate alone is not sufficient for further occupancy of an online channel if a higher return rate and/or poorer payment behaviour can be observed among the corresponding responders.

3.3.2 Search Engine Advertising (SEA)

Two concepts are classically distinguished for finding online content when using search engines: SEO and SEA. **Search engine optimization** (also **SEO**) subsumes all measures that aim to ensure that one's own offer, i.e. one's own online presence, appears in the first places of the organic hit lists of the search engines (cf. ► Sect. 3.4). These **organic hit lists** comprise the results of a search process initiated by the online user and determined by an algorithm of the search engine. These results are not shown there due to a payment to the search engine operator. The ranking on the organic hit lists results from a match – determined by the search engine operator – between the search terms used by a user and the content available online from various providers.

   Search engine advertising (SEA) refers to measures that result in the company's own online advertising formats appearing on the first pages of search engines under advertising or similar when certain search terms are entered in return for payment. This process is also referred to as **keyword advertising.** There is also talk of **paid search** and – not quite precisely – **pay per click**. The latter term also applies to many online banners and is therefore should not be applied to search engine advertising.

   Search engine advertising results are called **keyword ads** (also **sponsored links**). The ads of the main search engine *Google* are called *Google Ads.* SEA is also offered by the *Microsoft Search Network* under the name *Microsoft Advertising.* Previously, this advertising option was marketed under the name *Yahoo! Bing Network* or *Bing Ads.*

For the advertiser, the use of keyword advertising has the advantage that the ads are presented at the moment when the online user deals with pre-defined keywords and thus signals a basic interest in corresponding offers. Therefore, keyword ads are generally superior to classic online banners – measured by the achievable click-through rate.

The **click-through rate for search engine ads** is on average around 2%. It is thus considerably higher than the average value of 0.05% for display ads. The significantly better click-through rates of keyword ads are also an important explanation for the fact that search engine advertising ranks first in online advertising in Germany (cf. ◘ Fig. 3.7). An exception to the less convincing CTR values for banner advertising can be banners, which are used on the basis of the targeting variants described in ► Sect. 3.3.1 or are targeted to very precisely defined target groups in the course of affiliate marketing and enjoy great relevance here.

The entirety of marketing activities geared towards search engines – i.e. search engine optimization and search engine advertising – are referred to collectively as **search engine marketing (SEM)**. Just for the sake of completeness, it should be noted that some companies speak of "search engine marketing" when actually "search engine advertising" is meant. Therefore, it is always advisable to ask what exactly an interlocutor understands by search engine marketing!

How the results turn out for the search term "praxisorientiertes online marketing" is shown ◘ Fig. 3.9. First of all, it is exciting to see that *Google* achieves 460,000 hits for this book title! If ten organic hits are listed per page, the offers for this keyword are spread over 46,000 pages. This example illustrates the **challenge for search engine marketing.** Since the first page of the hit lists receives the most attention from the searchers, all corresponding providers want to be present here. In order to appear there or at least still on the second or third page, many of the **search engine optimization** activities shown in ► Sect. 3.4 must be used. With **search engine advertising,** however, there is the possibility of buying a place – ideally on the first hit pages of the search engines – because these places are awarded via auction processes.

The search engine results shown in extracts in ◘ Fig. 3.9, which include both the organic hit list and the keyword ads and the so-called info box, are called **search engine result rages** – **SERPs** for short. Such a conflating term is appropriate because search engine users also perceive the search result – consisting of these different parts – as a **holistic search result.** The **search engine advertising results** as paid placements are marked with a dashed line in ◘ Fig. 3.9. Marked with "1" here are **advertisements of relevant agencies** that use the title of a reference book to draw attention to their online con-

3

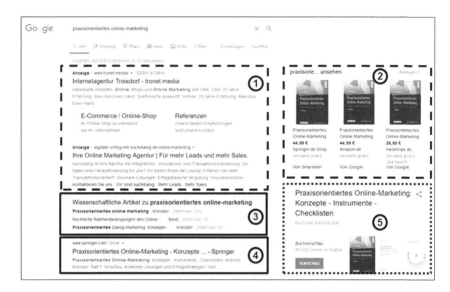

◘ Fig. 3.9   SERPs – keyword ads, scientific reception, organic hit list, info box at *Google* for the search term "praxisorientiertes online marketing"

sulting services. **E-commerce offers** are found under "2". By clicking on these ads, you usually end up in an online shop and can order the presented product directly. Under "3", the **scientific reception of a textbook** is shown in terms of citations by third parties. Under "4" the **results of the organic search** are presented. The ranking achieved here shows how well *Springer Gabler's* search engine optimization has succeeded. "5" indicates a search result that is particularly relevant for voice search, the so-called **info box** (also known as the *Google Knowledge Graph*).

The ***Google Knowledge Graph*** is a **knowledge database** created by *Google* to supplement the results of its search engine with information from various sources. The information is presented to users in the so-called info box next to the search results. This is also referred to as **position zero,** because this info box is presented above (for mobile searches) or next to the results of the organic hit list. *Google* accesses sources such as *Factbook*, *Wikidata* and *Wikipedia to* create this info box, but without naming these sources in detail. It is not known which algorithms *Google* uses to create the info box.

Getting into this info box with their own information is exciting for companies for two reasons. On the one hand, the info box promotes the trend towards **zero click search**. This refers to the fact that search queries are increasingly answered just by looking at the info box – and no further clicks are made on ads and/or results in the organic hit list. As a result, businesses must try to get in the info box themselves with content. On the other hand, information from the *Google Knowledge Graph* (equivalent to the info box) is used by *Google* as part of **Voice Search** to answer directly spoken questions in *Google Assistant* and *Google Home.*

The following **goals of earch engine advertising** can be targeted by companies:

- **Achievement of branding effects** through the placement of ads in the environment of product and/or service-relevant search queries (e.g. for new product launches) in order to increase brand awareness.
- **Increase of traffic** on your own website or on specific landing pages/ micropages (e.g. to generate applications)
- **Attracting prospective customers/leads** (measured, for example, by requesting informational materials, signing up for an e-mail or e-newsletter distribution list, and/or downloading content offered).
- **Acquisition of customers** (direct purchase, insofar as this supports the business model, or lead to stationary purchase in the sense of a push to store; also O2O – Online to Offline)

The **advantage of keyword ads** and thus of search engine advertising is that, with regard to the desired traffic, the acquisition of leads or customers, very specific **quantitative goals** can be defined, the achievement of which can be verified during the ongoing campaign. If the figures determined are compared with the costs incurred to achieve the objectives, an **efficiency analysis** becomes possible. The combination of these goals of search engine advertising takes place within the framework of a **conversion funnel** (cf. ❏ Fig. 3.10). In this funnel, not only the different conversion steps become visible (from awareness to consideration to purchase and binding), but also the different communicative approaches to this. This provides a holistic view of the entire online and offline marketing.

Within the scope of SEA, this **conversion funnel** can be used to first determine what percentage of searchers have registered as prospective customers or have actually initiated or completed an order process or purchase as a result of a keyword ad. In a detailed analysis, it is important to determine the **melting rates from stage to stage** along the conversion funnel in order to identify any areas for optimization in the online process. For example, it is necessary to check how many potential customers drop out on the way to purchase, e.g. when entering the billing address, selecting the payment methods, the order overview or when displaying the transport costs. If products and/or services have already been placed in the "shopping cart" without the

3

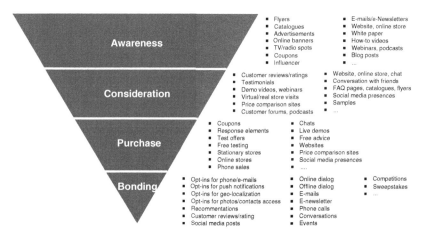

Awareness
- Flyers
- Catalogues
- Advertisements
- Online banners
- TV/radio spots
- Coupons
- Influencer

- E-mails/e-Newsletters
- Website, online store
- White paper
- How-to videos
- Webinars, podcasts
- Blog posts
- ...

Consideration
- Customer reviews/ratings
- Testimonials
- Demo videos, webinars
- Virtual/real store visits
- Price comparison sites
- Customer forums, podcasts

- Website, online store, chat
- Conversation with friends
- FAQ pages, catalogues, flyers
- Social media presences
- Samples
- ...

Purchase
- Coupons
- Response elements
- Test offers
- Free testing
- Stationary stores
- Online stores
- Phone sales

- Chats
- Live demos
- Free advice
- Websites
- Price comparison sites
- Social media presences
- ....

Bonding
- Opt-ins for phone/e-mails
- Opt-ins for push notifications
- Opt-ins for geo-localization
- Opt-ins for photos/contacts access
- Recommentations
- Customer reviews/rating
- Social media posts

- Online dialog
- Offline dialog
- E-mails
- E-newsletter
- Phone calls
- Conversations
- Events

- Competitions
- Sweepstakes
- ...

■ **Fig. 3.10** Conversion funnel

check-out with payment having been carried out, this is referred to as **shopping cart abandoners**. These are the ones to pay special attention to because – from the company's point of view – they have given up shortly before reaching their destination. Re-targeting often takes place with these people in order to motivate them to complete the purchase process after all. Re-targeting measures are used to specifically address such target persons again.

Notice!

The **conversion funnel** can be used to analyse the success of all advertising measures of a company!

An important task is to determine which **customer qualities** are achieved in terms of **return and payment behaviour** via different channels. For the overall evaluation of a campaign, it is important to know whether the customers thus acquired return an above-average number of goods and/or do not pay their bills (cf. in-depth on customer value Kreutzer 2021a, pp. 28-43).

In order to achieve the most convincing conversion rates possible, the company has to deal with the following **tasks of search engine advertising**:

- **Development of a convincing campaign idea**
- **Precise definition of campaign objectives** (incl. quantitative advertising target, duration, spatial focus, language)
- **Definition of the relevant search terms** (keywords) for linking with ads as well as **definition of the excluding keywords**

- **Determination of the maximum amount of money for booking the ad space** (in total or for a certain period of time, e.g. per day/week/month)
- **Decision on the search engines to be used**
- **Development of online advertising media** (including ad extensions, if necessary)
- **Controlling the results**

▶ **Example:** *Google Ads*

The further **process of search engine advertising** is shown here on the basis of *Google Ads,* the corresponding offer from *Google,* because *Google* is the most important search engine in many regions of the world. The tool for *Google Ads* guides the user systematically through the various steps. Step by step, the relevant settings can be made. These include the following steps for creating a campaign (cf. in-depth Kreutzer 2021b, pp. 248-255):

- Definition of the campaign goals
- Determination of the type of campaign
- Selection of the communication channels to be used
- Installation of a tracking code on the website
- Definition of the locations to be targeted by a campaign
- Determination of the language
- Booking *Google Audiences*
- Determination of the bidding strategy (CPC bids and daily budgets)
- Adding ad extensions
- Creation of the ad group and selection of the keywords
- Definition of the keywords to be excluded
- Entry of the ad text
- Recording of the payment modalities
- Launch of the campaign ◀

The **advantages of search engine advertising** can be summarized as follows:
- Keyword ads are developed easily and can go live very quickly.
- Advertising effects can be determined within a few hours and used to optimize the campaign
- Keyword campaigns scale well as long as there is a sufficiently attractive search environment.
- The keyword ad placement is based on a success-oriented payment on a click basis. As a rule, payment does not have to be made for the pure insertions in the form of ad impressions
- The advertiser can control whether a keyword ad is visible to the searcher by setting the cost-per-click bid.

3

Since the advertising environment is very dynamic and the estimates determined by *Google* are based on real-time data, the specifications regarding the keywords used, the ad design, etc. require continuous review by the advertiser. Therefore, an **efficient controlling** is indispensable for search engine advertising. This is the only way to check the **advertising impact** of the different formats, timing, content, etc. with regard to the most diverse target groups.

The search engine operators as well as the providers specialized in online marketing provide a variety of **conversion tracking tools** to analyse the behavior of visitors on their own website. Because often it is not only the build-up of traffic that is desired, but the highest possible conversion rates are aimed for. In order to check this conversion, *Google's* services also include **conversion tracking**. *Google* generates a code for this, which is to be integrated into the own web presence in order to record the conversion that has taken place. Through this, the effectiveness of *Google Ads* as well as that of the selected keywords can be determined.

> ❯ To the point: The highest-clicking keywords don't always produce the most and/or the most valuable prospective customers or customers. We have to find out what is best for our company!

For controlling, the criteria listed in ▶ Sect. 3.3.1 are applied in total. **Page impressions** indicate the number of impressions by the search engine. **Cost per Click** (CPC) or **Cost per View** (CPV) refers to the average costs incurred per click or per video viewed. These can deviate from the maximum CPC or CPV given, as the search engines aim to optimise within the defined limits. In addition, the **rank in the hit list** indicates which position the ad achieved on average. Furthermore, the **conversion rate** is to be determined.

Here is a small calculation: If five users perform the desired actions (e.g. purchase in an online shop) with 200 clicks per day, a conversion rate of 2.5% is achieved. If € 1.50 has to be paid for each click, this results in **total costs of € 300 per day**. **The Cost per Buyer** (Cost per Order or Cost per Acquisition or Cost per Conversion) is calculated by dividing this total cost (€ 300) by the number of customers acquired (5). The value of the **CPO** for this promotion is € 60.

Such evaluations are to be carried out for the different keywords or for groups of keywords. In addition, it can be determined whether regional concentrations can be identified, which are to be taken into account in further optimization work. A **holistic conversion tracking** is indispensable, which does not stop at the one-time evaluation. Because here, as with online advertising in general, the success variables such as conversion rates, sign-ups, leads and buyers must be evaluated in the light of the further behaviour of the leads and customers thus acquired. Only in this way can the quality dimension of the contacts gained be taken into account. In order to be able to assign further actions to the contacts acquired via the search engines, the **origin of the prospective customers and customers** must be recorded in a meaningful way in the customer history in a CRM database (cf. in-depth Kreutzer 2021a, pp. 43–59).

3.3.3 Affiliate Marketing

In **affiliate marketing,** advertising space is integrated on the websites of partner companies in order to draw the attention of online users to the company's own offering. The **advertising company** (also known as provider, advertiser or merchant) places links or banners that lead to its own offers on the websites of **partner companies.** These partners are called website operators, publishers or affiliates. Affiliate marketing is thus a specific form of **placing advertising on the online presence of third parties**. The basis of the cooperation is usually a contract between the provider and the affiliate, which often provides for remuneration of the partner in the form of a commission based on the measured actions (e.g. clicks) and/or transactions (such as purchases). A merchant often concludes corresponding agreements in parallel with a large number of affiliates in order to achieve a high visibility of its offers as an important prerequisite for gaining customers on the net. In order to know to which affiliate an interaction of the user can be traced back, the corresponding advertising material is provided with a **partner code. ◘** Figure 3.11 illustrates the basic concept of affiliate marketing.

Affiliate marketing is also referred to as **partner program** or **online-based sales cooperation** and uses the affiliate in its **feeder function for the provider**. Mostly, **affiliate networks** are involved, which perform an interface function between many merchants and many affiliates.

The primary **objective of affiliate marketing for the merchant** is to expand its own online presence and thus its own online reach through visibility on the affiliates' websites. On the one hand, it is necessary to **win over prospective customers** and to guide them through the conversion funnel. On the other hand, depending on the offer, the aim is to **trigger immediate online purchases** or to **prepare offline purchases** (keyword "push to store"). Depending on the respective goals of the merchant, different response enhancers can be used to trigger an immediate reaction from the online user.

3

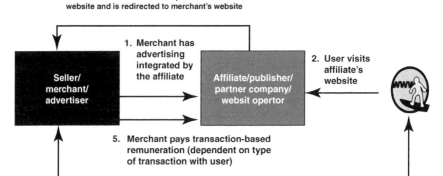

▢ Fig. 3.11   Basic concept of affiliate marketing

Increasing awareness and **building an image** for the company, its brands and/ or specific offers are often only secondary goals of affiliate marketing.

The **objective of affiliate marketing for the affiliate** itself is to generate **advertising revenue** through ads from the merchants. In addition, the **affiliate's image** can be positively or negatively influenced by the integration of advertising partners. Ideally, the affiliate succeeds in increasing the attractiveness of its own website for online users. This can be improved by presenting information offers or accompanying services to the own offers.

Often, however, the opposite is more likely to be the case: unattractive and "shouty" offers distract from the content of the website and impair its impact. Publishers should bear this in mind before integrating advertising on their own website. Therefore, it is important to check in advance what the **core task of one's own website** is. Is it about generating advertising revenue or about communication and/or the sale of own offers?

In order to enable cooperation between a merchant and sometimes many thousands of affiliates on the one hand and between an affiliate and many thousands of merchants on the other, **affiliate networks** are integrated. These take on the function of a hub between merchants and affiliates (cf. ▢ Fig. 3.12). More and more frequently, they are also integrated in parallel with the establishment of their own advertising partnerships.

Some of the best known and largest **affiliate networks** include:

— *Awin (▶ awin.com/en)*
— *Belboon (▶ belboon.com/en)*
— *Commission Junction (▶ en.cj.com)*

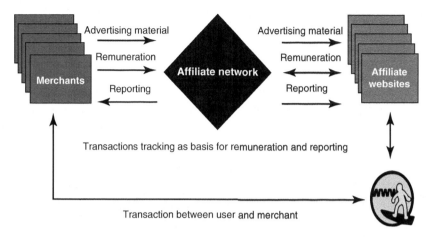

O Fig. 3.12 Implementation of affiliate marketing with the integration of an affiliate network

— *Digistore24 (▶ digistore24.com)*
— *Rakuten Advertising (▶ rakutenadvertising.com)*
— *TradeDoubler (▶ tradedoubler.com/en)*

These **affiliate network operators** usually perform the following functions, which in their entirety are also called **affiliate program:**
— Contractual **initiation of the cooperation** between merchants and affiliates
— Enabling **access to a large number of affiliate sites** for the merchant or **access to many merchants for an affiliate** through one **contractual partner**
— **Transmission of the merchant's advertising material** for the websites of the connected affiliates
— **Provision of a tracking system** as the basis for billing between merchant and affiliate
— **Execution of payments** and possible cancellations of commission payments to the affiliates as well as to the operator of the affiliate network
— **Evaluation of the results** achieved for the assessment of the cooperation (with regard to the speed of integration as well as the updating of advertising media, the possibility of a targeted placement as well as a performance-oriented evaluation, e.g. for the measurement of the effectiveness of advertising media as well as of commission models)
— **Accompanying support** for merchants and affiliates

3

The **central criteria** for **evaluating** affiliate marketing are the following KPIs, which have already been defined in ▶ Sect. 3.3.1:
- Ad impressions/ad views
- Ad clicks/clicks
- Click-through rate (CTR)
- Sign-up – generation of leads
- Sales/revenue – generation of buyers

In addition, the cancellation rate (i.e. return rate) is also taken into account as a measurement criterion in some cases.

A particular advantage of affiliate marketing is the predominantly **performance-based remuneration of the affiliates' services**. This means that the pure communication performance of the affiliates is not to be paid via a Pay per View (Cost per View). The following performance-based remuneration variants are used – sometimes in combination:

- **Pay per Sale (Cost per Sale/Cost per Order)**
  - A commission is linked to a specific purchase. This can be the **first sale**, but the commission payment can also be based on **sales within a certain period** or on **all subsequent purchases by the customer**.
- **Sign-up (Cost per Sign-up) – Pay per Lead (Cost per Lead)**
  - A fee is paid when online users leave their data by filling out contact forms. This can be done by subscribing to an e-newsletter or in the course of downloading information. Since in this case only one interested party is recruited, we can also speak of pay per lead.
- **Pay per Click (Cost per Click)**
  - The commission is already due here when the integrated advertising material is clicked on.
- **Pay per Click-out (Cost per Click-out)**
  - The commission is only due when the user clicks on an advertising medium on the merchant's site – often from a third-party partner.
- **Pay per Install (Cost per Install)**
  - A commission is due when the user installs software on his computer for the first time.
- **Pay per Print-out (Cost per Print-out)**
  - Payment is made if the user initiates the output of advertising information via a print interface.
- **Postview procedure**
  - At the moment a banner is displayed, a cookie is set without the banner having to be clicked on. If the online user visits the advertised online shop at a later time, this visit is traced back to the banner and remunerated accordingly.

- **Pay per Action (Cost per Action)**
  - In this billing method, different actions of the user are defined as a prerequisite for payment. In some cases, the terms pay per action or cost per action are also used.
- **Set-up Fee**
  - A set-up fee can additionally be charged by the affiliate independent of performance. The basis of the remuneration is the initiation of a cooperation between the affiliate and the merchant with the establishment of the necessary interfaces.

In practice, **hybrid billing models** are sometimes used. These combine the affiliate's frequency performance (Pay per Click) with the merchant's target achievement (such as Pay per Sign-up, Pay per Lead or Pay per Sale). In this way, the affiliate receives payment even if he achieves a high level of traffic on the merchant's site when the merchant is unable to convert the user into a prospect or customer.

In order to be able to ensure precise **remuneration of the affiliate**, each advertising material is connected to a link that contains the code of the affiliate. This makes it possible to record which affiliate has led to a contact on the merchant's sites. Various **tracking concepts** form the basis for **determining the billing-relevant key figures** (cf. in-depth Kreutzer 2021b, p. 272 f.; Lammenett 2019, pp. 64–68).

After entering affiliate marketing, the activities of one's own affiliates and/or the affiliate networks must be continuously monitored critically in order to be able to take countermeasures at an early stage in the event of possible undesirable developments. In addition, the behavioural patterns of users and competitors are constantly changing, making it necessary to **adapt one's own affiliate measures.** It is important that the merchants first try to direct the target customers or target companies to their own online presence – and not to that of the affiliates. This is because the latter may also include competitor offers.

> In a nutshell: The challenge is to identify the most important affiliates and/or affiliate networks in order to use them for your own messages. This also includes continuously optimizing the merchant's advertising media, developing attractive offers and especially optimizing the merchant's website or shop in such a way that high conversion rates are achieved. In summary, affiliate marketing allows a wide range of online channels to be integrated for advertising purposes. The advantage for the merchant in such an approach is that the build-up of traffic on his own website is partially shifted to the affiliates. The achievement of such traffic is the core of the remuneration concept.

3

3.3.4 Other Aspects of Online Advertising

In addition to the operators of search engines and the integration of affiliates, other important **advertising partners for the delivery of online advertising** must be taken into account (cf. ◘ Fig. 3.13). These include **social networks, media sharing platforms** as well as **messenger services,** which allow different forms of advertising integration. In addition to the options discussed in the context of online advertising, banners can also be distributed via **banner exchange platforms.** This option is sometimes offered as a free service by various online platforms and is often aimed at smaller companies. In addition, special **online advertising marketplaces** (such as *adjug, doubleclick/Google Ad Manager* and *AdScale* from *Ströer*) offer their services for placing online advertising. Furthermore, special **online marketers** or **online advertising networks** offer access to a large number of online platforms.

Finally, **content networks** (from publishing houses) and **service providers** also enable direct advertising access to the users of their websites. In turn, some of the partners use specialized service providers to market their advertising space. As already mentioned, *Google* offers a comprehensive **display network.** *Google* works together with private websites and portals so that ads for defined keywords also appear on these sites if there is corresponding con-

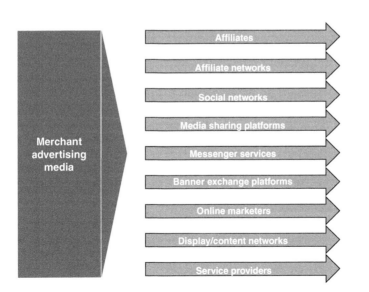

◘ **Fig. 3.13**   Ways to deliver online advertising

tent on these sites. The corresponding *Google* program is called *AdSense* and matches the delivery of ads to the content of a website. The website operators get the opportunity to earn as an online publisher by placing ads provided by *Google*. To do this, the corresponding website must be added to the search engine as a potential advertising partner. A variety of **publisher tools** are offered to support the search for potential advertising partners.

3.4 Search Engine Optimization (SEO)

Learning Agenda

What is the importance of search engine optimization? Why is it at the heart of online marketing? What is the difference between on-site and off-site search engine optimization measures? Which "optimization measures" are forbidden? After reading …

- ▶ Section 3.4.1 you will master the basics of search engine optimization.
- ▶ Section 3.4.2 you can design various measures for on-site and off-site optimization.

3.4.1 Basics of Search Engine Optimization

The term **search engine optimization** is used to describe all activities that lead to a better placement of one's own online offers in the organic or editorial hit lists of the search engines. The organic hit lists contain the results of a search process, which appear as a research result due to an algorithm of the search engine and not due to paid advertising. Consequently, this is not about advertising for online content, but about the **findability of the content** made available online itself. The organic hits of the search engines compete for the user's attention with the keyword ads and represent the overall result of the search process. This are – as already mentioned – the called **search engine result pages** (SERPs).

❯ To the point: A common misunderstanding should be cleared up at this point: **SEO is not free!**

3

❯ Even though SEO does not directly involve paying money for a high position in the organic hit list of search engines, companies must invest – often continuously and possibly higher amounts – in the optimization of the corporate website in order to achieve such a position. Whether the specialists required for this work are within the company or outside: Costs are associated with their activities in any case!

When **optimising online findability** on *Google,* the effects of the development towards the ***Google Knowledge Graph*** already mentioned in ► Sect. 3.2.2 must be taken into account. With the *Google Knowledge Graph* (previously referred to as **Universal Search**), *Google* integrates various information categories in an info box. Here, not only is central information brought together compactly, but – in the case of books – reference is also made to sources of supply (including *Google Play*). Who clicks on the further thumbnails to be found in the info boxes, does not land however with the appropriate books or enterprises, but on the *Google* hit sides to the corresponding search inquiries. Here *Google* keeps the user in its own ecosystem as long as possible!

It would be exciting for companies to be represented in this info box with their own information. After all, the information presented here is the basis for playing out hit results via a **voice interface** (cf. in-depth Kreutzer and Vousoghi 2020; Kilian and Kreutzer 2022).

In all search engine optimization efforts, we need to keep one thing in mind:

❯ In a nutshell: The specific algorithms used by the various search engines are neither universally known nor static. Therefore, SEO is a process that is never finished – and not a project with a defined end!

Consequently, all the measures described below can only point to one **direction for optimization**. Their successes must be continuously monitored using appropriate tools. However, a general **recommendation for the preparation of online content** can already be made here:

Notice!

If you want to achieve a good ranking in the SERPs of the search engines in the long run, you should provide relevant, up-to-date and preferably unique content!

Search engine optimization is a **must for every business.** Regardless of whether it sells online or offline, it must be easy to **find on the web.** The search engines have the key position in online findability. This is because, increasingly, not only online but also offline purchases are prepared through the use of search engines. With regard to search results on *Google, Microsoft Search Network* & Co. the following guiding principle applies:

⌐ Notice! ───

Relevant for the searcher is what appears on the first hit page of the search engine. And every company wants to appear at this position for the relevant search terms!

A **study of five million searches** on *Google* showed the following results (see Dean 2019):

- The **first position** in *Google's* organic hit list achieves an average CTR of 31.7%.
- The **#1 organic search result** is ten times more likely to be clicked than the #10 search result.
- The CTR for **positions 7 to 10** on the organic hit list is practically the same. Therefore, moving up a few places at the bottom of the first page may not result in more organic traffic.

The **aim of search engine optimization** is to increase the quality of search engine hits independently of keyword ads in such a way that one's own offers are ideally to be found among the **top 10 hit results.** However, competitors also strive to achieve an equally good ranking. Since this competitive environment is very dynamic, no company can rest on a once achieved high hit rank. A top position in the hit list can be achieve by **designing one's own web presence** in a specific way, and by **incorporating important search terms** into one's own presence. In addition, **relevant content should be provided on other platforms with a corresponding link** (e.g. on *Facebook, Instagram, Pinterest, YouTube*). On top further **accompanying measures** (e.g. gaining backlinks) are needed.

> ❯ In a nutshell: The **individualization of search results** – based on the preferences of the respective searcher – leads to the fact that uniform placements in the hit lists can no longer be achieved for the entirety of searchers. This makes it much more difficult to check the performance of SEO!

3

An intensification of the competitive situation in search engine optimization arises from the **keyword advertising** of the search engine providers themselves as well as from the multitude of **affiliate programs.** In order to profit from the revenues that can be generated here, providers develop websites or web portals with the sole aim of directing traffic to their own online presence without offering (larger) content of their own. These websites and web portals pass on the traffic generated on their own site to merchants with corresponding content and are paid for their advertising services.

When it comes to **search engine optimization measures,** a distinction must be made between on-site optimization and off-site optimization. **On-site optimization** includes all measures that are carried out on the website to be optimized itself. This includes, among other things, a reader-friendly design and structuring of the content – also from the point of view of the crawlers. **Off-site optimization** includes all measures taken on other websites to improve the own ranking in search results. On-site optimization is considered more important than off-site optimization because of the results it can achieve. Off-site optimization is considered less reliable, but can still have a great impact on the position in the SERPs. The entire process of on-site and off-site search engine optimization can either be performed **in-house** or delegated to specialised **service providers.**

An improvement of the position in the SERPs can be achieved by legal measures. These are also referred to as **white-hat techniques** and are explained below. The illegal **black-hat techniques** will be named later so that no company (unintentionally) uses such measures. In between there is an intermediate area of so-called **grey-hat techniques.**

3.4.2   On-Site and Off-Site Search Engine Optimization

■ On-site search engine optimization

The **process of on-site search engine optimization** can be guided by the following process flow (see further Kreutzer 2021b, pp. 302-320):

━ **Decision for the relevant search engine(s)**
- For both desktops and mobile, *Google* dominates the search market worldwide (with the exception of China, where *Baidu* is the market leader). Therefore, it makes sense for most companies to base their optimization on *Google.*

━ Selection of relevant search terms and combinations of search terms

━ Optimization of relevant search terms and combinations of search terms

- It is necessary to continuously check the **traffic intensity of the website** as well as the **number of desired transactions** generated by the keywords used. The following questions arise here:
  - Which keywords lead to the **desired transactions** on the website to a greater extent than others?
  - Which keywords are therefore the **traffic bringers with a particularly high closing potential** (e.g. as an immediate purchase)?
- Editing of online texts oriented to the defined search terms and combinations of search terms
  - The text should be written in such a way that a high **search word density** or **keyword density** is achieved. This key figure describes the ratio of relevant search terms in relation to all words of the texts of a website in percent. This value has an influence on the ranking in the search engine hit lists. The **target corridor for keyword density** is between 3% and 5%. Values above 9% can give rise to suspicion of manipulation, which leads to devaluations by search engine operators. Despite the increased placement of relevant search terms in the text, its readability from the perspective of online users must not suffer.

Notice!

When designing a website, we should always keep in mind that we are primarily writing for the users – and not primarily for the search engine robots!

- Optimization of website content
  - A general **guiding principle for text optimization** is that each website can only be optimized for a specific topic and thus for a limited number of search terms. Placing a large number of search terms within a website in the top 10 search results is at the expense of readability. Nevertheless, the website should have a high **text content** with a corresponding density of relevant keywords. The relevant search terms should therefore be placed in particular in the following places on the website:
    - Hostnames (domain and subdomains)
    - File names
    - Home page/title tag
    - Headlines
    - Start of text
    - Alternative texts to pictures
    - Text (multiple)

3

- Such a positioning of the keywords within the online presence signals a high relevance of the respective keywords to the search engines. In addition, the **uniqueness of the content** (keyword "unique content") and a **consistency with the defined search terms** are necessary. If the search engine operators notice that searchers return to the search engine after clicking on a hit result after a short time and search for the same term, this can be evaluated as a lack of relevance of the content and have a negative effect on a future ranking in the hit results. The **relevance of website content** – from the user's point of view – is still crucial for a good position on search engine hit lists. That's why "relevant content" for human readers – and not for search engine crawlers – should be the focus of search engine optimization. Perhaps it is therefore better to speak of **content optimization** instead of search engine optimization.

— **Alignment of the website with the standards of the W3C**
  - In order to prevent companies from manipulating their findings or assumptions about the search engine algorithms, the worldwide consortium *W3C (World Wide Web Consortium)* was founded. The tasks of this consortium are the **standardization of techniques affecting the Web** and the **development of specifications and guidelines** to achieve a high technical and editorial quality of Web content. At ► w3.org, the ► validator.w3.org itself can be used to determine free of charge whether websites meet *W3C* requirements.

— **Checking the website using *Google Search Console***
  - By logging into *Google Search Console,* the confirmed website owner gets the opportunity to first determine how *Google* crawls and indexes the website. Furthermore, it can be analysed where *Google* sees possible problems when accessing the website. Additionally, internal and external links can be analyzed and mobile usability can be checked. Furthermore, it can be determined how many users found the website in the search results and from where the users reached the website (keyword "search analytics").

— **Regionalization of website content**
  - *Google* has recognized that regional content is of particular importance for online users in many cases. Therefore, every regionally active company is called upon to make the regionality of its offers and its business clear through its web presence. In concrete terms, this means that several local pages should be set up and maintained for several locations. Companies operating nationwide should develop local landing pages that include the relevant city names. The latter should also

appear in the title tag and description. Depending on the business model, regionally relevant content can also be prepared in order to continue to be present in the first hit positions. This can improve the position in the SERPs – if the general guidelines for SEO are taken into account. At the same time, nationally operating companies must strive to create the – digital – impression that they also have something to offer regionally.

- **Website programming**
  - In addition, there are many other aspects to consider when developing the website (cf. in-depth Kreutzer 2021b, pp. 309-316).

Since 2021, the requirements for the creation of online content by *Google* have been geared even more strongly towards the **page experience.** Here, *Google* expects a positive user experience as the basis for a good ranking in the organic hit list even more than before. For the **evaluation of the page experience,** the previously valid requirements will continue to be taken into account. These include the following factors (cf. Beilharz 2020):

- **Mobile friendliness**
  - Since 2015, *Google* has been analysing whether a website is designed for mobile use (keyword "responsive design"). The check of the mobile friendliness can be checked by the tool ▶ https://search.google.com/test/mobile-friendly.
- **Safe browsing**
  - Sites with harmful content will continue to be punished. This includes websites that install malware on users' computers or spy out sensitive information about users (keyword "social engineering"). Hacked pages that involuntarily contain spam code or other malicious code will also be punished. This tool can be used to determine whether a website has security problems: ▶ https://search.google.com/search-console/security-issues.
- **HTTPS encryption**
  - Every website should still be SSL-encrypted, because the presence of HTTPS encryption is an important factor in *Google's* algorithms. The relevance of this encryption is independent of whether user data is transmitted via a contact form or not.
- **Aggressive advertising**
  - Furthermore, *Google* checks whether a website uses aggressive advertising formats that worsen the user experience. This primarily refers to banners or layer ads that overlay the content and obscure it. Irrespective of this, legally required layers can be used which contain an opt-in for cookie use or an age confirmation.

3

From 2021 onwards, the factors described below and referred to by *Google* as **Core Web Vitals** will additionally be used to **evaluate the page experience**, measuring loading time, interactivity and stability of the page (cf. Beilharz 2020):

- **Largest contentful paint (LCP)**
  - "Largest contentful paint" describes the time at which the majority of a page is loaded. This means that the "paint" can be viewed as a result. LCP takes into account the "perceived" loading time, which is important for the user experience. A user wants to be able to operate a website – regardless of whether it is already fully loaded. *Google* advises an LCP of less than 2.5 seconds.
- **First input delay (FID)**
  - The FID metric measures how long a website takes to respond to a user interaction (e.g. a click on a button or a link). *Google* expects an FID of less than 100 milliseconds.
- **Cumulative layout shift (CLS)**
  - When the reloading of an element on a website causes the layout to shift unexpectedly, it degrades the user experience. After all, a user may want to click on a link that is suddenly in a different place due to a subsequently uploaded element. Such degradation of user experience affects *Google* ranking. *Google* measures such instabilities in the layout through the CLS and recommends a score below 0.1.

The **criteria of the Core Web Vital** (LCP, FID, CLS) described here can be determined for one's own website – but also for those of competitors – by means of the following tools:

- ► https://www.webpagetest.org
- ► https://developers.google.com/speed/pagespeed/insights/?hl=de

In ◘ Fig. 3.14, the Core Web Vitals are summarized once again (cf. Ranganath 2020). The *Google Search Console,* which has already been mentioned several times, also provides helpful tools for checking these important criteria.

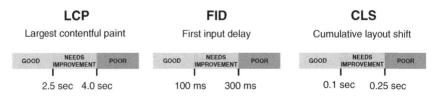

LCP	FID	CLS
Largest contentful paint	First input delay	Cumulative layout shift

◘ **Fig. 3.14**   Core Web Vitals

Across the board, the following **guiding ideas of search engine optimization** should be considered:
- **Be honest and direct!**
  - There should be no attempt to mislead search engines or website visitors. The keywords used should match the actual content presented.
- **Be well organized!**
  - Clear priorities in the presentation of content and options for action should be apparent on the website. The fewer clicks required, the better.
- **Repeat what is relevant!**
  - The use of a synonym dictionary to present content in a varied form should be avoided. Terms should be used that are also used by the users. The terms should be placed where they are searched for (for example, in tables of contents) to give readers a quick overview.
- **Be precise!**
  - The content should be presented as concisely as possible. In addition, images, lists and bulleted lists should be used whenever possible, as these also contribute to a reduction of the content and at the same time to an overview and thus ensure the aforementioned scannability.

■ **Off-site search engine optimization**

In order to determine the importance of a website, the search engines not only access the content available there, but also obtain **references to the website from third parties**. In this way, the relevance determined "on site" is to be validated by external references. The core of **off-site optimization** activities has so far been the **creation of backlinks.** However, the **engagement of companies in social media** is also of central importance, because here positive ratings are gained through "Like" and "Pin It" buttons, which are relevant as **"social signals"** for SEO. In addition, it is recommended to all companies with stationary branches to create a significantly better visibility through the *Google My Business,* which will be presented later.

Off-site optimization includes the measures that are carried out on external websites to improve search rankings. These include, on the one hand, links that refer to one's own website from other websites. These are referred to as **backlinks.** Search engines view websites that are referenced more frequently as more relevant. **Link popularity** refers solely to the number of backlinks pointing to a particular website. For example, in a blog about smartphones, there are 100 different posts that contain links to a vendor's website. In this case, a total of 100 backlinks would count. Link popularity used to be an

3

important criteria for search engines. Nowadays, many search engines have switched to focusing on **domain popularity**, which provides information about the quality of the backlinks in addition to quantity. The domain popularity of a website is determined by the number and quality of the backlinks it achieves. For this reason, it is important to get as many quality backlinks as possible. Consequently, it is important that the websites that are referred from have a greater importance themselves; this importance is in turn measured by the domain popularity.

Backlinks can also be achieved through **registration in member registers, trade fair catalogues, regional platforms** or **(regional) article directories.** If service providers are involved in the **backlink building process**, then a service contract should ensure that backlinks are only set on valuable pages and that dishonest measures are avoided. This is because *Google* also monitors here whether link building takes place "organically". A company that has 100 new backlinks "overnight" is viewed critically. A **natural link building,** in which a few backlinks are gained week after week, is "normal" from the point of view of the crawlers of the search engines. In addition, the client of an SEO agency should make sure that the backlinks gained are retained once the agency relationship is terminated.

Additional backlinks can be gained by referring to one's own website on **media sharing platforms.** Further backlinks are gained – to a limited extent – by referring to one's own content in **online forums and communities.** Finally, **social bookmarks** are also used by the search engines in the evaluation. Therefore, every company should strive to do well in the allocation of these bookmarks as well, since the search engines use such directories to determine which websites are particularly popular among users.

An **analysis of one's own backlinks** shows how many backlinks are present and what value they have in each case. In addition, it can be determined how many backlinks originate from a website. For this purpose, the following tools can be used, among others, which often also provide answers to many other SEO-related questions:

- ▶ *backlinkwatch.com*
- ▶ *linkdiagnosis.com.websiteoutlook.com/*
- ▶ *seorch.com*
- ▶ *sistrix.com*

One *Google* service should be mentioned separately, which can be counted among the off-site measures and – beyond SEO – is an **indispensable part of the online presence** for every company: ***Google My Business.*** With *Google My*

Business it can be achieved that potential customers come across relevant providers in the regional environment when searching with the *Google* search engine or especially on *Google Maps* – and especially regional offers are often of great relevance for the searchers.

This only requires an entry in *Google My Business,* which is offered free of charge – consequently to be paid with data to *Google!* The interesting thing is that this **display service** does not even require a website of its own. Anyone who wants to register their company with *Google My Business* simply calls up ▶ *google.com/business/.* Through a simple dialogue, all relevant data and additional content (photos, videos, etc.) are requested.

If an online user searches for providers of "marketing and management consulting" via *Google* or on *Google Maps* (marked "1" in ❏ Fig. 3.15), the registered companies from the relevant catchment area are displayed with address, opening hours and possibly even company, owner and/or product photos (marked "2"). At the same time, the *Google* search result also points to the ▶ *yelp.com* rating platform, where the company is also listed. In addi-

❏ **Fig. 3.15** Organic hits when searching for "marketing and management consulting" in Bonn – based on *Google My Business*

3

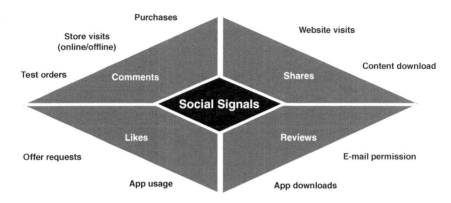

Fig. 3.16   Social signals – factors influencing SEO and more

tion, *Google* presents various books by the author in the organic hit list on the first rank positions (on ► books.google.de!) – all driven for the engagement with *Google My Business*. This service must – as already mentioned – "only" be paid for with data.

Off-site SEO measures also include the field of action **social SEO**. Here, various influencing factors must be taken into account, which are collectively referred to as **social signals** (cf. ■ Fig. 3.16). **Likes** from users – for example by clicking on "Like", "Pin-It" or "Retweet" buttons – are rated positively by *Google* because it points to new and/or interesting content. **Sharing** content is also interpreted as an indicator of its relevance. Finally, user **comments** are also an important indicator of interest in certain content. The more **social buzz** generated, the higher *Google* tends to rank the corresponding content. Furthermore, ■ Fig. 3.16 shows that social signals also have a positive effect on many other online marketing objectives.

In addition – lying on another logical level – the **backlinks** spread in the social media are also important. Here we also speak of **social backlinks**. Such backlinks are created through content sharing on other pages or through re-blogging or retweeting. The great advantage of these activities is that backlinks in the form of recommendations can also be generated by users who do not have a website themselves.

■ **Black-hat techniques – forbidden measures of search engine optimization**
Google works systematically to ensure that relevant content is presented to searchers – and that no pages are supported that were only developed for the search engines' crawlers. Therefore, *Google* pursues the goal of recognizing and penalizing the measures for the "artificial" improvement of the position in the search results, which are referred to as **webspam,** since they do not generate any added value for the users. **Illicit search engine optimization measures** include the following activities, through which a better rank in the search engine results is sought (more detailed information on illicit search engine optimization measures can be found in the glossary):

— **Cloaking**
— **Keyword stuffing**
— **Linkfarm**
— **Doorway pages**
— **Duplication of content**
— **Integration of foreign brand names in the meta tag**
  – The integration of third-party brand names into one's own website violates trademark law and is therefore prohibited, even if the corresponding brand names are not visible to the user. The integration could take place (possibly not visible to the user) on the website itself or in the meta tags.

There is a **self-regulatory mechanism for these illegal black-hat techniques.** Anyone who recognises such behaviour – e.g. on the part of competitors – can report it to *Google.* If the accusations are confirmed – whether the black-hat techniques are used by the website operator or its service provider – this can lead to the website being **banned from the search engine indices.** Depending on the severity of the offence, this can be for a month or several months. *Google* defines important **guidelines for webmasters** via *Google Search Central* so that website operators can work successfully and with few errors. On the one hand, an orientation towards these guidelines should enable better hit positioning. On the other hand, by taking them into account, sanctions from *Google* – such as the (temporary) exclusion from the index – can be avoided.

3.5 E-Mail Marketing

3

Learning Agenda
What is the importance of e-mail marketing? Which fields of action are to be distinguished? How can the success of e-mail marketing be determined? What is A/B testing in this environment? After reading …
- ▶ Section 3.5.1 you will master the basics of e-mail marketing.
- ▶ Section 3.5.2 you can consider the success factors of e-mail marketing when designing measures.

3.5.1 Basics of e-Mail Marketing

E-mail marketing comprises the systematic transmission of marketing-related information by e-mail or by e-newsletter (hereinafter also referred to as **e-communication**) to achieve marketing objectives in both the B2B and B2C markets. Before going into the various aspects of e-mail marketing, an important statement must first be made:

The **relevance of e-mail** continues to grow steadily.

Even the triumph of social media as well as messenger services cannot change the dominant position of e-mails and e-mail marketing. While *Facebook* will "only" expand its user numbers to over 2.8 billion in 2021, around 4 billion e-mail users will be active in the same year – and the number of e-mail users is still growing. And the good thing about e-mail communication – compared to social media – is that e-mail can, should and may sell!

The **importance of e-mail marketing** is also reflected in the fact that it can be used as part of the entire **customer relationship lifecycle**. E-mails are suitable …

- to **address potential customers** (through rented e-mail addresses),
- to **contact prospective customers** (who, for example, have left their e-mail address on a website with permission for further use),
- to **carry out transactions** (such as e-commerce),
- for the **provision of various services** (in the pre-sales, sales and post-sales phases),
- for the **delivery of digital products and services** (e.g. information, e-books and other types of files), and
- to **deepen the customer relationship**.

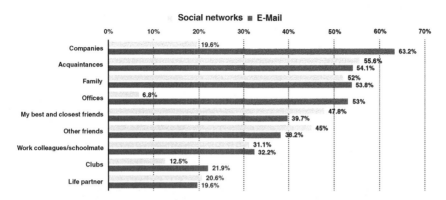

⬛ Fig. 3.17 Survey on the use of communication tools by interlocutors – in %

This assessment on the part of companies is confirmed by the actual use of various communication channels. To determine this, 1008 Internet users were surveyed on their **use of e-mails and social networks for communication by interlocutor** in Germany (cf. Statista 2020a, p. 24). ⬛ Figure 3.17 shows that e-mails are primarily used for communication with "official bodies" (companies, offices). However, e-mail is also still in first place for communication with family, work colleagues/schoolmates and in clubs. In private communication with family, friends and life partner social networks dominate.

Although e-mail marketing often focuses on communicative or advertising objectives and should therefore be referred to more precisely as **e-mail communication** or **e-mail advertising**, the more vague but more familiar term e-mail marketing will be used below unless very specific aspects are to be highlighted.

In e-mail marketing, four **types of e-communication** can be distinguished:
1. Trigger e-mails
2. Transaction e-mails
3. After-sales e-mails
4. E-newsletter

Trigger e-mails can be used as part of **stand-alone campaigns** that aim to achieve communication goals with a single e-mail. Goals here can be the sale of certain products/services or the announcement of a new collection with an invitation to visit a stationary retail store or an online shop. However, trigger e-mails are much more frequently the starting point for **longer-**

3

term **campaigns** in which complex communication chains are used. For example, several triggers can be applied to motivate a target person to take out insurance or buy a new car. Finally, trigger e-mails are often also a component of **cross-media campaigns** in order to address the target person via different communication channels. Here, the initial trigger can be a poster that invites people to visit the website. If the company succeeds in gaining the e-mail address for further communication, additional e-mail impulses can follow. Automated **e-mail steps** make it possible to address different target groups in a continuous and differentiated manner. This is also referred to as **dialogue programs**. The entry into such programs can be very simple: For example, the customer is invited to fill out a card displayed in the stationary store.

If such invitations are made, a **content strategy** must be developed for this. As in an **editorial plan** or a **conversation plan** or a **content calendar**, the content to be communicated should be defined for different target groups in a time-phased manner. In this way, prospective customers can be successfully developed into buyers through automated e-mails. For this purpose, the own services are to be presented and attractive introductory offers are to be made. Customers can be motivated to make further purchases through automated more-, cross- and up-sell impulses. At the same time, it is important to continuously obtain further information about the profile of prospects and customers in order to be able to communicate relevant content.

Transaction e-mails accompany the business transactions between the company and its leads and prospective customers. These e-mails can contain the confirmation of receipt of an inquiry or order, inform about the status of processing, announce the delivery, present the invoice, issue a payment reminder and survey the satisfaction with the service after completion of the transaction. They are an important companion to many transactions in order to build up a feeling of trust among online users throughout the entire process towards the – often only virtually experienced – business partner.

After-sales e-mails are positioned at the interface between transaction and trigger e-mails. On the one hand, they contribute to the successful completion of a purchase process by, for example, providing important information about the use and care of the purchased products. On the other hand, interesting additional offers can be pointed out, whereby such a mail has a trigger character for new purchases. The general guiding idea of after-sales mails is not to break off contact with the customer, but to successfully conclude a purchase, especially "emotionally", in order to ideally prepare a further purchase.

The **e-newsletter** is of particular importance in the context of e-mail marketing in order to inform both leads and customers as well as other stakeholders (e.g. employees or press representatives). The dominant objective is to establish regular communication, especially with prospects and customers, in order to achieve the highest possible level of loyalty and thus a high purchase intensity among recipients. For this purpose, corresponding newsletters are sometimes sent several times a day, weekly or at intervals of several weeks. The e-newsletter as a communication channel is of particular importance in the already mentioned field of content marketing, if not only directly purchase-relevant information is presented here.

An important goal of **e-communication** here is also to trigger **direct impulses for action** or to direct the recipient to the company's own online presence in order to carry out certain activities there. To this end, e-mails and e-newsletters contain links which, when clicked, establish a **direct connection** to other online offers of the company. Such links can be presented as text links or as classified ads embedded in the text. They lead either to the **website** of the relevant company or to a specific **landing page**. The following applies: The expectations built up by such newsletters are to be fulfilled with regard to offer, ambience, service orientation, price worthiness – both online and offline. In order to strengthen the effect of the e-communication, **rich media content** is incorporated into the communication.

Trigger, transaction and after-sales e-mails as well as the dispatch of e-newsletters are an important field of application for **marketing automation**. This refers to the use of software that initiates certain measures by synchronizing various processes and information based on certain indicators or triggers. In this way, even complex, multi-level marketing campaigns can be implemented. For this purpose, the individual dialogue steps – depending on the achievement of certain values – are predefined. In this way, personalization and individualization of the approach can take place with the optimal times for addressing via the appropriate channels – with an automated follow-up depending on the results achieved in each case (cf. ◨ Fig. 3.18).

In the course of the **content marketing** already mentioned, many companies – especially in the B2B market – offer white papers, webinars and studies. These offers are intended to direct the recipients of e-communication to the company's website. There, an attempt is almost always made to obtain further address and profile information (with permission for further addressing) before the possibility of downloading or using content, in order to continue the dialogue with the interested persons.

3

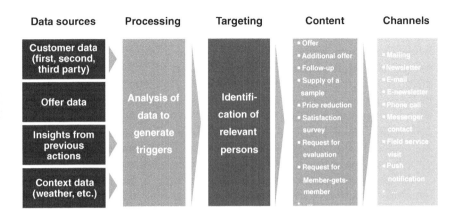

| Data sources | Processing | Targeting | Content | Channels |

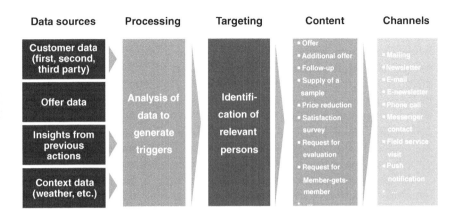

☐ Fig. 3.18   Core processes of marketing automation

The following **guiding ideas for successful dialogues** have already proven their worth in a large number of campaigns:

- Enable **cross-media communication** (on- and offline integrated; the customer can use the channels he prefers)
- Ensure **personalization** and **individualization**
- Demonstrate **willingness to engage in dialogue**
- Ensure **emotionalization of communication**
- Use dialogue steps to **obtain further information**

This makes it clear that e-mail marketing is not only about **quantitative list building**, but also about **qualified list building**. Indications of the content relevant to the user – which can of course also be recorded in a CRM database – are also provided by the pages visited on one's own website where a newsletter was ordered. Ideally, this content should be taken up again in further communication steps. In addition, **calls-to-action** should be regularly integrated into the e-communication in order to achieve the targeted conversions.

> **Notice!**
>
> **E-mail** is considered by many companies to be a particularly **efficient medium of communication** because target persons can be addressed directly – often personalised and/or individualised. And in e-communication we can also actively sell!

It remains a core task of the company to regularly collect e-mail addresses (with permission) in order to use them in dialogue programs. Companies can apply various methods to **obtain e-mail addresses** independently:

- **Gain when visiting your own website**
  - In order to collect the e-mail address here, the registration for an e-newsletter is to be presented as prominently and "salesy" as possible on the start page as well as on the sub-pages of online shops. Overlays can also be used for this purpose, which invite to register and possibly reward with a value coupon. Above all, however, the benefit of a newsletter for the potential recipient should be highlighted.
- **Extraction in the context of orders and surveys**
  - In such transactions, users are often willing to provide their e-mail address for promotional communication.
- **Winning in the stationary business**
  - The e-mail address can also be gained in direct contact with the customer. However, gaining permission for e-mail contact is an additional "sales process". Here, the sales staff must have good arguments to obtain the customer's consent. This can be learned, for example, via role plays!
- **Winning by telephone contact**
  - Telephone calls also offer the possibility of gaining permission for e-mail contact. However, this telephone "permission granting" must also be proven. This can be done either by a written confirmation or a voice file of the telephone call. However, permission must also be obtained in advance of recording the telephone call.
- **Winning in the social media**
  - Social media also offers several ways to win an e-mail permission.

Every company is well advised to use different ways to acquire e-mail addresses, as far as concepts for e-mail communication exist or are to be established or expanded. In general, it is recommended to use **every dialogue with prospects and customers** to **acquire the e-mail address** as well as to **collect further profile data.** It should be a matter of course that once the e-mail address has been obtained, no further attempts are made to obtain it. However, this requires that all relevant data is recorded in one place, preferably in a powerful CRM system.

3

3.5.2 Success Factors of e-Mail Marketing

The data obtained in the various ways can be used in the context of e-communication. The success factors described below for the use of e-mail marketing must be consistently taken into account (cf. in-depth Kreutzer 2021b, pp. 347-363):

- **Personalization of e-mails and e-newsletters**
  - When analyzing e-mails and e-newsletters, it can be seen time and again that established standards and defined norms are violated when it comes to **personalization**. Correct personalization starts with the correct spelling of the name. It should not be "Dear Angela Meffert", but correctly "Dear Ms. Meffert". Only bad e-mail programs include the first name in the salutation. Additional attention can be gained by **personalizing the subject line.** Then the subject line reads, for example: "Exclusive offer for you, Ms. Roscher!"
- **Individualization of the content of e-mails and e-newsletters**
  - A continuous analysis of e-mails and e-newsletters shows that many companies neither carry out the correct personalization nor a convincing **individualization** or at least a **target group-specific orientation of the content.** Thus, leads, new customers and long-term customers of a company are often addressed with the same newsletter, although their information needs are quite different. To "delight" all target groups with the same content often does not lead to an enthusiasm of the recipients. If a male newsletter recipient of *Procter & Gamble* is offered the product *Gillette Venus*, one cannot speak of a convincing individualization – at least in most cases.
- **Integration of rich media content in e-mails and e-newsletters**
  - E-communication providers should systematically check whether they can integrate **rich media content** – especially video material. Short videos are becoming increasingly popular – especially if they are not classic commercials. By integrating moving images, sound and text, a generally higher learning performance can be achieved.

❯ In a nutshell: e-mails and e-newsletters partially become websites when more and more dynamic elements (such as videos) are integrated into e-communication!

- **Frequency and timing of e-mails and e-newsletters**
  - The question of the frequency and timing of an e-mail or e-newsletter mailing can only be answered in close coordination with the expectations of the target group. Consistent **fine-tuning of the frequency of**

addressing is required in order to achieve the appropriate timing for each target group based on the intensity of use of the information and the number of unsubscribes to be registered.

— **Prompt acknowledgement of receipt and provision of e-newsletters – collection of feedback**
  - In e-mail communication, it is recommended that the receipt of orders, complaints, inquiries, etc. is confirmed promptly – and if necessary also automatically – by transaction e-mails. This way, the sender knows that his message has arrived at the right place. Failure to provide such confirmation may result in time-consuming and costly follow-up inquiries.

— **Reference to the possibility of terminating e-communication**
  - The companies are obliged to point out the **possibility of unsubscribing** in every advertising approach via e-mail or e-newsletter. Against this background, the challenge is to balance the **desired communication density of the company** on the one hand and the **interests of the recipients** on the other hand in the case of e-communication. In order to avoid "overfeeding" recipients with uninteresting information, it is recommended to follow the **golden rule of e-communication:**

Notice!

Don't be ashamed to be silent when you have nothing to say!

— **Relevance of e-communication**
  - The relevance that newsletters can have for prospects and customers is shown by the many millions of subscribers to **consumer newsletters** and the large user base of **business newsletters**. In order to motivate the target persons, who are often wooed by many providers to subscribe to a newsletter, incentives are offered. These can be mainly exclusive news, but also classic competitions, limited and/or particularly attractive price offers as well as coupons. These measures should ensure a continuous inflow of new subscribers. Ideally, this should more than compensate for the loss of existing subscribers.
  - To convey the relevance of the content to the recipient, the **subject line of e-mails and e-newsletters** is of particular importance. In this, the benefits of engaging with the content are to be presented "crisply". This also applies to the initial content, which is visible in the **preview window** or in the upper part of these means of communication. If the address here cannot convince, the e-mail or the e-newsletter is often deleted immediately.

3

- **"Responsive design" in e-communications delivery**
  - E-mail processing represents an increasingly important focus of mobile online usage. Therefore, all companies are called upon to use the concept of **"responsive design"** in e-communication as well. Through this, a positive user experience can be technically supported. The task here is: Representation and content are to be adapted to the usage situation.
- **Design aspects in e-communication**
  - The header of a **dialogue-oriented newsletter** should start with the corresponding logo in the **header** of the e-communication – followed by the personal address. The content could consist of product reviews, coupon offers and information on general topics. Calls-to-action should motive the user to engage with the content. In the **footer** called lower part of the newsletter more "technical" information is provided. The company can motivate the user to save the sender of the newsletter in personal address book so that it is not incorrectly classified as spam. In addition, the privacy policy can be accessed. Furthermore, the use of cookies is pointed out.
  - It is expedient to question proven **address concepts** and to consistently search for **optimization possibilities.** Ways should be tested again and again in order to find new and more convincing forms of address. The experience gained from the various test concepts can be incorporated into the further development of the **templates.** Such a template can be found in ◘ Fig. 3.19.
- **Invitation to interact**
  - E-mails and e-newsletters can offer a **variety of interaction options**, as shown in ◘ Fig. 3.19. Here, it should be made clear to the user whether he can, for example, write directly to the address from which an e-mail or e-newsletter was sent. If this is not the case, this sender address should be clearly marked as "Do-Not-Reply@". If a user nevertheless uses this address, there should in any case be an indication that the message has not reached the recipient. Letting a sender's e-mail address that appears to be usable run off into "digital nirvana" – as can be observed time and again – should be avoided in any case.
- **Bounce Management**
  - Not all e-mails and e-newsletters can be delivered. In the event of **undeliverability,** a so-called **bounce message** is generated by the relevant mail server and sent to the sender's e-mail address as an error message. Since undeliverability can be caused by various reasons, a distinction is made between hard and soft bounces. **Hard bounces** are caused by permanent errors, for example, because the recipient's e-mail

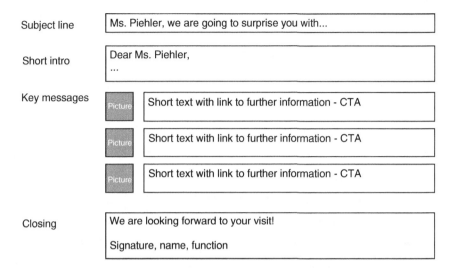

| Subject line | Ms. Piehler, we are going to surprise you with... |

| Short intro | Dear Ms. Piehler,
... |

Key messages

Picture	Short text with link to further information - CTA
Picture	Short text with link to further information - CTA
Picture	Short text with link to further information - CTA

| Closing | We are looking forward to your visit!

Signature, name, function |

◻ Fig. 3.19 Template for visualizing the schematic structure of an e-newsletter

address no longer exists. **Soft bounces** occur when the undeliverability is due to temporary causes. For example, the mailbox may be overfilled or there may be an out-of-office note.

- The question arises whether every hard bounce should immediately lead to a deletion of the corresponding e-mail address. This may also be due to technical problems in the communication. Therefore, this address should be addressed again at a later time as a test. The same applies to softbounces. In this case, appropriate **work instructions for bounce management** must be drawn up. Companies should be concerned about the extent of the bounces, because many bounces are regarded by service providers as an indicator of spam, which can lead to the respective sender being blocked.
- **Integration of e-communication into the overall communication of the company**
  - The sending of e-newsletters should be comprehensively integrated into corporate communications. This allows offline campaigns – for example in print or on TV – to be extended into the online sphere. E-communication can also provide impetus to trigger further activity in social media. Despite the social media hype, e-mail communication is still the most important means of communication between companies and their prospects and customers.

3

In addition to these overarching success factors for e-communication, every company is called upon to determine the specific requirements of its own various target groups for the successful design of e-mails and e-newsletters on a target group and customer-specific basis. The **learning relationships** built on these results can contribute to sustainable competitive advantages in the prospect and customer relationship.

As has been pointed out on various occasions, the rule for online marketing in general and also for e-communication is:

Notice!

Testing, testing, testing!

Even for specialists, it is not always easy to predict the behavior of the target persons. Therefore, **A/B testing** is of particular importance in order to derive further optimizations from the insights gained. In this form of testing, a variant B is added to the previous design A. The variant B may only differ from the original version A in one single component. Only then can differences in response behaviour be clearly attributed to this change. A/B testing can be used in numerous areas. These include testing different calls-to-action, different price advantages for coupons or e-mails with or without a picture of the signer.

In the case of an e-mail, variant B to be tested is sent to a test group, while the original variant A is sent to the control group. Since the original variant has often proven to be particularly successful in previous tests, it is sent to the larger number of people. The distribution is often as follows:

- **Variant A**, control group: 80%
- **Variant B**, test group: 20%

If variant B should turn out much worse, the associated damage is not so great – because it was only sent to 20% of the addressees. The allocation to the test and control group must be done randomly.

In an **A/B test for a corporate website,** online visitors are randomly directed to two different versions of the website, which may also only differ in exactly one single component. Afterwards, the relevant KPIs can be used for analysis. Then, for example, differences between the conversion rates achieved with the two website versions can be determined. The variant with the better conversion results would then be implemented.

In ◘ Fig. 3.20, the **design for an A/B test for the acquisition of newsletter subscribers** is shown. The relevant success variable here is the subscription

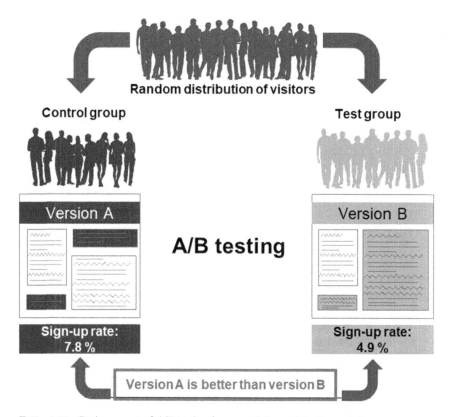

◘ **Fig. 3.20** Basic concept of A/B testing for a newsletter registration website

rate. Through the corresponding A/B test, it was determined that the previous version A with a sign-up rate of 7.8% was superior to the new version B with a sign-up rate of 4.9% and should therefore be retained.

Before the main mailing of an e-mail or e-newsletter, an A/B test can again be used to determine which **subject line** works best. This is done by sending e-mails or e-newsletters with different subject lines to a subset of the target group in a **pre-send.** After 12 or 24 hours, it can be determined which type of subject line achieved the highest read and/or conversion rates. This can then be used for the **main mailing.** In this process, it is important to ensure that a sufficiently large number of target persons are addressed for the preliminary mailing per variant. The lower the expected response rate, the higher the number of test persons required to achieve reliable results. Before optimizations are made based on the test results, it must first be checked whether the result occurred "by chance" or is "statistically significant" (i.e. "overrandom").

Every company should ask itself whether the entire process of e-communication should be carried out in-house or outsourced to service providers. The decision depends on how comprehensively **e-communication** is integrated as a **driver in the value chain**. The more pronounced this is the case, the more there is to be said for an in-house solution, provided the necessary experts are available.

Various key figures can be used to **control** e-mail marketing. A decisive advantage is that the reactions at the recipient level can usually be recorded in real time. The following applies here: Even every non-reaction is a reaction that can be analysed.

Powerful **e-mail software** can answer the following questions:
- **How many e-mails could be delivered or not delivered?**
  - The **delivery rate** and the **bounce rate** are indicators of **the quality of the e-mail addresses used.**
- **How many of the e-mails or e-newsletters were opened or not opened?**
  - The **open rate** (total and mobile) and the **open factor** are **indicators of the relevance of the sender from the recipient's perspective.**
- **How many recipients clicked on something in an e-mail or e-newsletter?**
  - The **click-through rate** as well as the **click-to-open rate** (gross and net in each case), the **clicks per individual link** as well as the average **click rates,** the achieved **reading time,** the **unsubscribe rate** and the **forwarding rate** are indicators of the **relevance of the content from the recipient's perspective.**
- **How many recipients have completed a request for information or a purchase transaction as a result of the e-communication?**
  - The **response rate,** the **request rate,** the **order rate** and the **sales achieved** are indicators of the **relevance of e-communication for action.**
- **How many buyers successfully complete the entire purchase process?**
  - **Payment behaviour, return rates** and **customer-related contribution margins** are indicators of customer **quality from the company's perspective.**
- **How many buyers stay connected to the company?**
  - The **revisit rates,** the **repurchase rates** and the **recommendation rates** are further indicators of **customer quality.** The **engagement rate** is also an indicator of this.

The metrics for **evaluating e-communication** are summarised in ◘ Fig. 3.21.

	Delivery of e-mails and e-newsletters	Pre-sales activities	Sales activities	After-sales activities

Performance metrics	• Delivery rate
	• Bounce rate
	  ▪ Rate of hard bounces
	  ▪ Rate of soft bounces
		▪ Total open rate
		▪ Mobile open rate
		▪ Click-through rate
		▪ Click-to-open rate
		▪ Clicks pro single link
		▪ Click rate (Ø number of clicks per mailing)
		▪ Reading time
		▪ Unsubscribe rate
		▪ Forewarding rate
		▪ Response rate
		▪ Information request rate
			• Order rate
			• Ø turnover rate
				• Payment behavior
				• Return behavior
				• Revisit rate
				• Repurchase rate
				• Recommendation rate
				• Engagement rate (across all phases)

◻ Fig. 3.21 Metrics for the evaluation of e-communication – I

	Delivery of e-mails and e-newsletters	Pre-sales activities	Sales activities	After-sales activities
Costs/ efficiency and effectiveness metrics	▪ Rental costs of external e-mail addresses ▪ Costs for designing the e-mail or e-newsletter ▪ Costs of incentives offered ▪ Costs of follow-up material	▪ Cost per view (an opening does not have to have taken place here) ▪ Costs per opened e-mail ▪ Cost per click ▪ Cost per interest/cost per lead ▪ Cost per mille	▪ Cost per order ▪ Ø contribution margin ▪ Return on advertising spendings (turnover or contribution margin to advertising costs)	▪ Costs of follow-up ▪ ROI over the campaign

◻ Fig. 3.22 Metrics for the evaluation of e-communication – II

In addition, the results achieved must be set in relation to the costs incurred in order to determine the **cost-effectiveness of the measures**. The KPIs to be used for this are summarised in ◻ Fig. 3.22 and have already been defined for other online instruments. Of particular importance is the **profitability calculation**, which compares the contribution margin or – even more meaningful – the profit of the orders generated with the advertising costs used. In the longer-term, **individual customer-oriented profitability calculation,** the costs incurred in the after-sales phase as well as other results achieved here must be taken into account in order to be able to determine the **customer value** (cf. Kreutzer 2021a, pp. 28-43).

3

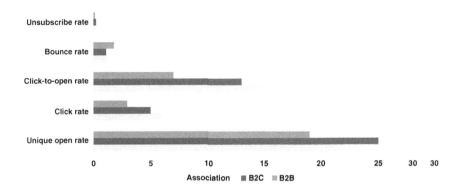

☐ Fig. 3.23   E-mail marketing performance metrics worldwide – in %

A study of **global e-mail marketing performance metrics** in the year 2020 analyzed e-mails sent out by different business types in ☐ Fig. 3.23. According to the findings of this study, B2C e-mails achieved slightly higher **unique open rates**, at 25% compared to 22% for B2B e-mails. Messages sent out by associations recorded a 19% unique open rate at that time. The **click rate** and the **click-to-open rate** are higher for B2B e-mails. The bounce rate is between 1% and 2%. The unsubscribe rate is between 0.1% and 0.2% (cf. Statista 2021e).

The values shown in ☐ Fig. 3.23 can be compared with the values achieved in your own company. In this way, impulses for further optimization can be gained.

3.6 Mobile Marketing

Learning Agenda
What is the importance of mobile marketing today and in the future? How has mobile usage behavior changed? Which possibilities for the use of mobile marketing are to be distinguished? What are the tasks associated with voice marketing? After reading …

- ▶ Section 3.6.1 you will master the basics of mobile marketing.
- ▶ Section 3.6.2 you can distinguish between the different fields of application of mobile marketing.
- ▶ Section 3.6.3 you know the fields of action of voice marketing.

3.6.1 Basics of Mobile Marketing

The increasing spread of mobile, Internet-capable devices is an important **driver of mobile marketing**. The development from mobile phones weighing several kilograms to smartphones has opened up **new fields of application and use for companies and customers**. Various **wearables** will reinforce this development. Fitness trackers, smart fashion and smart tattoos are just a few examples. Here, "smart" always signals access to the Internet.

The **intensity of mobile online access** and thus the **relevance of mobile marketing** will continue to increase for several reasons: First, **the number of mobile device users** continues to increase dramatically. As the number of mobile Internet users increases, so does **mobile access to online offerings**. On the other hand, the trend towards mobile Internet use is being further reinforced by the increasing **spread of powerful mobile end devices**. The **smartphone** is developing into a **smart service terminal** that is becoming the central, holistic and, above all, very personal **control and navigation tool** in the online and offline world. Car keys, credit cards, airline tickets, coupons, wallets and much more are managed via the smartphone. This leads to further changes in purchasing behavior, as information relevant to purchasing processes is becoming increasingly available on the go.

Easy online access to a lot of information comes from reading barcodes, using apps to recognize physical products, identifying music (through *Shazam*), and the varied use of QR codes. The move towards a cashless world is also already apparent. Smartphone usage will dramatically change the entire payment infrastructure over the next few years. With *Apple Pay, Facebook Pay, Google Pay*, *WeChat Pay, Alipay* & Co. corresponding payment concepts are already available. It turns out that many functions have now become apps for smartphones, tablets and other mobile devices. We are on the way to an **app economy**.

Notice!

That's why it's mobile first!

However, we should already be preparing for the next challenge: **voice first!** In the future, interactions will increasingly take place via voice control (► Sect. 3.6.2).

The **trend towards digitalization across the value chain** is becoming ever stronger. Not only **data** and processes are becoming increasingly digitalized and thus mobile. Previously predominantly **physical products** are also losing

3

their physicality. For example, flashlights, the compass or the dictaphone come to mind here. These are either replaced by apps or represent pre-installed functions of the smartphone. At the same time, this **overcomes physical boundaries** that were previously very important in our business models and often formed their basis. This development is promoted by the **increasing use of apps.** There are approximately five million different **apps** available for **download in** the *Google Play Store*, the *Apple App Store* and the *Amazon App Store* (cf. Statista 2020b, p. 27).

This development is referred to by the terms **dematerialization** and **zero-gravity thinking:** objects lose the physical limitations they had in the real world when they are digitized. The lasting effects of these developments on entire industries can be seen in the music and newspaper markets, but also in the retail and financial services sectors. Against this background, every company should address the question of how not only its own communication, but also the products and/or services it offers can be made available on the move.

The **digital transport to the buyer** in order to physically store content on an end device is also eliminated to the extent that content is stored in the cloud and only made available via streaming at the moment of use. **Decentralized data storage** per user is replaced by **centralized data storage** in the cloud. This trend towards relocation to the cloud is not limited to data, but encompasses further processes and entire business applications. Digitization thus encompasses entire business processes (cf. Kreutzer 2022b for further details).

Against the background of these developments, **mobile marketing** can be understood as a form of marketing that uses wireless devices with Internet access to achieve marketing goals. A special feature of mobile marketing is that many applications allow the user to be identified. This is usually based on corresponding permissions that the user often grants when downloading apps. For this purpose, the user is often asked the following questions to **achieve opt-ins by the companies**:

- Can the application send you push notifications?
- Is the application allowed to access your location?
- Is the application allowed to access your contacts?
- Is the application allowed to access your calendar?
- Is the application allowed to access your microphone?
- Is the application allowed to access your camera?
- Is the application allowed to access your photos?

Clicking on the corresponding confirmations leads to the granting of the respective permission. All these forms of permission granting show that **transparency and traceability** must be given to the user.

If the user answers the first two questions in the affirmative, for example, then the companies can not only localize the respective location, but also independently forward information. By aligning this information with the respective location, it can tend to achieve a higher relevance. This is referred to as **location-based services** (LBS) or **geo-sensitive applications.** In this way, a particularly high level of interactivity between the company and the user can be achieved in mobile marketing. The possibilities for action and reaction are influenced here by the mobile usage environment. Processes and content must therefore be aligned with the specific usage situation of the recipients. At the same time, the apps can query a variety of data that can lead not only to **personalization**, but also to **individualization** of the messages.

Basically, two different campaign types can be used in mobile marketing. In the so-called **push approach,** advertising companies use the permission received for the push notifications already mentioned. In addition, advertising messages are increasingly used in apps to draw users' attention to their own online offers. In contrast, with the **pull approach,** users actively request content from companies. In the course of content marketing, exciting content is offered via newsletters, apps, etc., which the user must actively request.

3.6.2 Fields of Application of Mobile Marketing

Mobile marketing offers companies the areas of application shown in ◘ Fig. 3.24.
 Mobile transmission of information by companies
  – The type of information made available on mobile devices initially includes **advertising** (also called **mobile display advertising**). This can be delivered on mobile – based on a wide variety of targeting concepts.

◘ **Fig. 3.24** Areas of application of mobile marketing

Due to the increasing spread of mobile applications, it is understandable why mobile online advertising is gaining dramatically in importance. By 2022, investments in mobile online advertising will grow worldwide from approximately US-$ 200 billion in 2020 to around US-$ 250 billion (see Statista 2021f, p. 5).

- Due to the relevance of apps for mobile Internet use, **in-app ads** – advertising that is integrated into the apps themselves – are increasingly being used. These forms of advertising tend to be more effective than classic mobile display advertising, as users are actively engaged with the app in question at the moment the ad is displayed. However, it must be examined which goal is to be achieved with the app: monetization via advertising or engagement with the content of the app provider itself.
- In addition to advertising, information as an expression of **location-based services** can refer to the location of the user if the user has given his permission. For example, coupons from customer loyalty programs can be targeted to the region in which the target person is located. At the same time, route planners make it easier to find the relevant providers. Other projects aim to deliver "matching" coupons directly at the POS if the user is in their vicinity. In addition, **location-independent information** can be accessed on the move, such as the free news from many newspaper publishers and TV and radio stations. Free information (e.g. from travel services) also belongs to this segment.

- **Mobile acquisition of information by companies**
  - Mobile contact with prospective customers and customers can also be used to gain further information. **Surveys** or **competitions** can be used for this purpose. In addition, the permission-based localization of users generates exciting data streams that can be analyzed in depth through the use and non-use of offers.
- **Mobile sales and mobile delivery of virtual products and services**
  - Virtually available products can not only be ordered mobile, but also delivered mobile. This applies to online games, music, videos, e-books, e-newspapers and e-magazines. Some of these contents are presented in special apps and allow the purchased contents to be listened to, watched, read or otherwise used immediately. Services can also be accessed on the move; for example, the free or paid services of streaming service providers such as *Amazon Prime, DAZN, Netflix* and *Spotify.*
  - The purchase of virtual products and services is accompanied by **payment transactions**. The payment of these transactions, which belong to

mobile commerce or **m-commerce,** can also be made via digital platforms (such as *PayPal*), via *Apple Pay, Facebook Pay, Google Pay, WeChat Pay* & Co. or classically via credit card as well as bank transfer or direct debit.

— **Mobile sales of real products and services**
- Ordering real products (e.g. clothing from *Zara* or *H&M)* can also be done on the move. The same applies to the booking of services that are used in the physical world (such as a flight, an overnight stay or the use of a rental car). This is also accompanied by **payment transactions.** While there is no connection to the user's location in the case of an order for clothing, there is in the case of a mobile purchase of a ticket for the parking machine or for the use of a subway. All of these purchase transactions that are triggered by mobile devices also count as **m-commerce.**

Many of the applications described here are based on apps, which continue to spread at an inflationary rate. This development is also fueled by the fact that most apps are offered free of charge. Paid apps have also only had an average price of around US-$ 2 worldwide since 2009 (cf. Statista 2020d).

In the case of apps, a distinction can be made between various **app business models**, some of which also occur in combinations:

— **Free apps for different services**
- These apps tend to have the largest user base and are funded by in-app advertising and/or the sale of data obtained in the course of use.

— **Freemium apps**
- In addition to a free basic version, there is a premium version for a fee, which has additional functionalities and is then also often free of advertising.

— **Subscription apps**
- Media companies often use such an app to offer their content behind a paywall. Often, a few online accesses to the content provided are initially offered free of charge. This is similar to the freemium strategy.

— **Paid apps**
- These apps can only be purchased from the app store for a fee.

— **Shopping apps**
- These apps support the sale of digital and/or non-digital products and services and are therefore usually offered free of charge, as they function primarily as a further advertising channel as well as a dialogue channel.

3

In part, due to the relevance of these programs there is talk of an **app economy**. However, it should be noted that downloading an app does not automatically equate to its intensive use. This is also understandable when one considers that over 50% of smartphone users have installed 13 or more apps (cf. Statista 2020b, p. 21). Since not every app can become an intensively used **Pareto app**, a high proportion of **sleeper apps** can be assumed. Everyone can determine for themselves how many sleeper apps exist on their own device based on the apps downloaded compared to the apps used. However, if the functionalities of the apps generate a high added value for the user, their use will also keep pace with the increasing distribution.

Consequently, when using apps, a **budget** should first be set aside for **development** and **ongoing program maintenance**. Development can focus on the leading operating systems (*Apple's iOS* and *Google's Android*). In addition, app providers should also budget for **app marketing**. This should not be limited to the launch date alone, but should accompany the entire duration of the app. This is because many apps are not self-perpetuating and must be continuously promoted if they do not achieve outstanding relevance for users.

App marketing also includes the use of important keywords in the **app stores** so that the app can be found in searches. Furthermore, in addition to a **convincing app presentation, good app reviews** by users must be worked towards. Since app store operators monitor not only the number of downloads, but also app usage in some cases, the relevance of the various apps can be determined in this way. This in turn has an impact on the **presentation of the different apps** in the app stores themselves. In order to promote their own apps, companies are called upon to integrate them into their online and offline communications as standard. Such promotion can also take place via search engine ads.

3.6.3 Challenges of Voice Marketing

In ◘ Fig. 3.25, all the tasks associated with voice marketing are shown. The individual tasks need to be combined because one module builds on the other. The first task is to define the **corporate language** or **brand language** when a brand communicates with users via voice. Next, **voice branding** is about how a company or brand should sound when using voice. In the case of **voice search,** voice engine optimization is addressed. If convincing work has been done here, the next step towards **voice commerce** can take place – a

◘ Fig. 3.25 Tasks of voice marketing

complete sales transaction via the voice interface. The top of the pyramid is **voice integration** – an integration of voice systems into products and services. As with every marketing concept, the success of voice marketing must be determined by **voice controlling.**

The basis of voice marketing is first of all the definition of the **corporate language** or the **brand language,** if not the company but a brand is the focus of voice marketing. Here it is defined in which language or tonality the company or the brand would like to communicate in the course of the customer dialogue. Is it rather a language that one also uses with one's best friend, or should a certain distance also be communicated linguistically?

In this process, the positioning of the company or brand is transformed into a linguistic positioning. This also includes defining the **keywords** that should be used as often as possible in communication and associated with the company or brand. In addition, dos and don'ts can be defined that need to be taken into account when using language, e.g. the question of **text comprehensibility for the recipient.** In this process, the positioning of the company or the brand is transferred into a **linguistic positioning.**

In this context, not every sender is necessarily served by always presenting information in a "snackable" and "shareable" manner, as the saying goes today. Sophisticated language, the understanding of which requires a certain intellectual potential, can be a deliberate part of the linguistic positioning (for example with providers such as *New York Times, Washington Post* or *The Times*). This linguistic positioning can be rounded off by a **claim** or a **slogan,** possibly combined with a special **jingle.** Here, for example, the jingle of *Deutsche Telekom* or *Audi* comes to mind, which builds the bridge to sound branding.

3

Sound branding defines how the company and/or a brand should sound in a very concrete and literal sense, e.g. whether a male or a female voice should be used. Various studies have shown that users tend to react more positively to female voices than to male voices. It is not for nothing that female voices are used in the digital assistants *Alexa, Cortana* and *Siri.*

Voice search in ◘ Fig. 3.25 is about finding content in search processes in order to inform the user and, if necessary, prepare upcoming purchases. A particularly important area of voice marketing here is **voice search engine optimization** (**Voice SEO**). For this, the information provided by your company about the offer, location, etc. must be prepared in such a way that the probability of being played out as voice search results increases. A second important component of voice marketing is **voice search engine advertising** (**voice SEA**). Through ads in the context of search engines, users should be made aware of voice offers.

Voice search engines in the form of digital assistants are not only aimed at communicating content (**voice communication**), but also directly at selling products and services (**voice commerce**). But distribution in the sense of "delivery" can also take place for digital products and services via digital assistants (**voice distribution**), as is already the case today with streaming content from *Amazon Music, Spotify* & Co.

The development towards **conversational commerce** is of particular importance for customer dialogue. At its core, conversational commerce (also known as *voice commerce* or *v-commerce*) is about shopping processes that take place via **system-based dialogue processes.** Already today, an increasing trend towards interaction between customers and companies through messaging and chat applications can be observed. Tools such as *Facebook Messenger, WhatsApp* and *WeChat* are used here. However, digital assistants will play a key role in this **trend towards voice-based purchasing.** In this case, purchases are no longer made solely **face-to-face** (in brick-and-mortar stores), **ear-to-ear** (in telephone sales) or **text-to-machine** (in classic e-commerce), but rather – without manual activities – simply **voice-to-machine.**

The top challenge in ◘ Fig. 3.25 is **voice integration.** This is the integration of voice into the products and services of a company itself. One example is the integration of *Alexa* into the vehicles of various automobile brands.

The results of voice marketing must also be continuously reviewed with regard to their contribution to achieving higher-level marketing and corporate goals. **Voice controlling** must be installed for this purpose (cf. ◘ Fig. 3.25; cf. in-depth Kilian and Kreutzer 2022).

3.7 Social Media Marketing

Learning Agenda

What opportunities and risks are associated with the use of social media? What exactly is understood by social media marketing? Which marketing goals can be achieved through social media? Which platforms should be used and how? After reading …

— ▶ Section 3.7.1 you can classify social media and social media marketing in terms of content.

— ▶ Section 3.7.2 you will master the various forms and objectives of social media marketing.

— ▶ Section 3.7.3 you will be able to select the relevant platforms for social media marketing.

— ▶ Section 3.7.4 you know the possibilities to monitor the use of social media marketing.

3.7.1 Social Media and Social Media Marketing

In the course of social media marketing, companies try to harness social media to achieve their own marketing goals.

■ **Notice!**

The term **social media** subsumes online media and technologies that enable online users to exchange information online in a way that goes far beyond classic e-mail communication. In addition to social networks and media sharing platforms, social media also include blogs, online forums and online communities.

The enormous **importance of social media** is shown in ◖ Fig. 3.26. This shows that, for the first time, all sections of the population and all stakeholders of a company have extremely powerful, high-profile instruments at their disposal for evaluating and making use of services as well as for making direct contact and thus for dialogue. It is therefore important to point out that social media can contain both **value-creating** and **value-destroying content** – and it is largely up to the company's own commitment which content dominates!

3

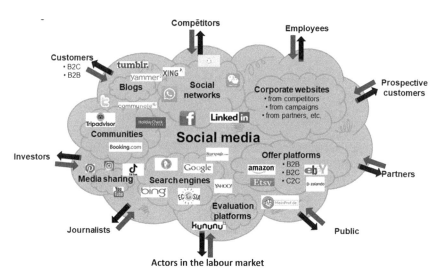

◻ Fig. 3.26 Increasingly uncontrollable and complex formation of stakeholder opinion through online media – networked through social media

Social media encourage **many-to-many exchanges,** where many users can communicate with many others. This exchange can be based on similar interests, a comparable professional environment, common projects, similar opinions or political attitudes. The exchange of information and the sharing of one's own achievements often primarily pursue **social goals.** It is about recognition, networking between the people involved and/or simply the exchange of a wide variety of content. **Commercial goals** usually take a back seat for private users of social networks. Companies and, in particular, purely promotional messages therefore do not initially play a dominant role in social media – from the user's point of view. Companies should therefore avoid turning social media into such a **spamming hotbed** if they want to build up and maintain the attention and trust of their target audience in the long term. Therefore, one thing must be emphasized already at this point:

❯ In a nutshell: **Social media** should not be misunderstood as another pure sales, advertising or PR channel. Rather, social media open up interesting new opportunities to enter into dialogue with stakeholders, to involve them in creative and evaluation processes, and to provide one-to-one services – and of course to generate enthusiasm for one's own offerings there. In addition to content, this can also be done through various advertising formats.

When creating content for social media, one should always keep in mind that it is primarily about the dialogue of brands and companies with their (prospective) customers and fans. In order to achieve **relevance of one's own messages,** the following aspects should be considered:

- **Content** should be **useful/educational/informative, exciting** and/or **entertaining/humorous** for readers to read and ideally like, share and/or comment on.
- At its core, it's about **conversations.** That's why the content should always be a bit more personal, authentic and appealing than classic advertising copy.
- **Dominantly sales-oriented content** should be **avoided,** except for direct promotional activities.
- A transparent **content calendar** must be defined that regulates which topics are to be covered by whom and when – and when content is to be deleted again because it is outdated (the latter is still too often neglected).
- Communication in social media should be based on clear – external and internal – **social media guidelines** (cf. in-depth Kreutzer 2021b, pp. 544-548).

But what motivates customers to engage with companies via social sites? In sum, the following **areas of a content strategy** for social media can be defined as relevant:

- **General and exclusive information** about products, services, the company and/or the industry (e.g. also through references to websites, blog entries or forums)
- **Information about new products/services** (e.g. in the run-up to or accompanying new product launches)
- **Information about offered customer services**
- **Texts, photos and videos on products/services** that encourage people to engage with them and/or buy them
- **Reference to (new) shopping sources** (e.g. through links to online shops or references to stationary shopping locations)
- The **granting of discounts** (including special price advantages, limited offers which may be aimed at different target groups)
- **Expressions of opinion on current products/services** (e.g. as a dialogue platform for exchange with other users)
- **Invitation to participate in events** (e.g. invitation to product or company presentations, like fashion shows)
- **Invitation to participate in a fan community**
- **Encouraging the development of ideas for new products/services** (e.g. idea competitions)
- **Motivation to submit ratings** on relevant rating platforms

3

At its core, social media is about **interaction between online users** – combined with the exchange of information and user-generated content. This can take place exclusively between private individuals or between private individuals and companies. On the one hand, **social relationships** are created between users who meet on the same hierarchical level. On the other hand, **opinion leader-follower relationships** can develop, which concretize themselves in the joint creation, further development and distribution of content, for example via blogs and communities (keyword "**influencer marketing**"). The low entry barriers to the use of social media – such as low costs, simple options for uploading content, ease of use (also known as usability) – promote their spread. The **key differences between "classic" and "social" media** are shown in ◘ Table 3.1. Classic media include TV, radio, newspapers and magazines.

◘ **Table 3.1**   Differences between "classic media" and "social media"

Classic media	Social media
Unidirectional alignment Traditional media communicate one-to-mass and one-to-many.	**Multi-directional alignment** In addition to one-to-mass and one-to-many communication, social media also enable one-to-one and many-to-many communication.
Linearity of the presentation Content is presented in a linear fashion. This content (also of an advertising nature) cannot be changed after publication or can only be changed at great expense (e.g. in the case of advertisements, posters, TV/radio spots).	**Non-linearity of the presentation** Communication in social media can take place in an intensive linkage with a high degree of parallelism and jumps back and forth. In addition, content can be changed here immediately – often without major effort.
Limited user engagement There is only a limited possibility of reacting to the content of the classic media (e.g. through letters to the editor and telephone calls) – or in the social media.	**User engagement as the DNA of social media** Social media thrives on user engagement – that's why it's called "social media". Reactions to online content can take place in real time. As soon as a tweet is sent or a post is placed, likes, shares and comments are received. Often, communication even jumps from social media to traditional media and back.
Restricted media combinations Classic media often still function stand-alone. Networking is only partially possible or given. For example, TV and radio spots are only very rarely linked with print measures.	**Social media live from networking** The core of social media is networking – with each other and with websites and online stores – and also with classic media.

□ Table 3.1   (continued)

Classic media	Social media
Time limit Activities in the classic media are usually limited in time – not least for cost reasons.	**Social media are "timeless" and borderless** Actions in social media can be extended indefinitely and revived again and again; also because the Internet forgets nothing. Thus, content – often even unwanted – remains findable online for years.
Rather planned action An engagement in the classic media often requires extensive planning – also due to lead times, the high costs and partly also due to limited media capacities.	**High agility in media use** Social media allow – preferably based on a strategic approach – a high degree of flexibility and spontaneity. This is part of the appeal of social media. Speed is the trump card – 24/7!
Stronger control of content Content in classic media usually goes through more comprehensive approval processes before publication. This often leads to a higher level of formalization – and quality.	**Lack of (any) control** Anyone can create content on social media – with all the opportunities and risks of this lack of control. Informal language often dominates.

While the use of **classic media** is reserved for **professional users**, engagement in **social media** is open to **every online user**. Another distinguishing feature between social and classic media is that social media often enable **real-time communication** – both in terms of providing and changing content. This enables a disproportionately higher speed in the exchange of information than is the case with most classic media due to the largely linear communication. This **linearity of communication** in classic media consists of a company placing an advertisement, for example. Ideally, this is read by many people after it appears. If the advertisement contains dialogue elements, the readers can now react individually. One step follows the other; a parallel communication between the recipients and the company will not occur.

In contrast, **social media** encourages **non-linear dialogue,** which can be characterized by the acronym **KIIS** as follows:
- **Collaborative**
  - Cooperation of users in favour of or against a company, a brand or an offer
- **Interactive**
  - Exchange between users and/or with the company

3

▬ **Iterative**
  – Repetitive, as e.g. complaints, suggestions, etc. are presented online until an appropriate reaction takes place from the user's point of view
▬ **Simultaneous**
  – Simultaneity of different communication strands and contents

People no longer use social media just to get information. Rather, they use them to communicate intensively, to give and receive ratings, and to present their own creations. The user is no longer a passive participant, but the already mentioned **prosumer**. He can basically search for information about companies, brands and offers at any time and from any place and create content of various kinds himself and present it online.

The most important **classes of use and examples of use of social media** can be found in ◘ Fig. 3.27. One group consists of offerings primarily aimed at **communication**, such as blogs, microblogs (e.g. *Twitter*), private and professional social networks (such as *Facebook, Pinterest* or *LinkedIn*), messenger services (such as *Facebook* Messenger, *Snapchat, WhatsApp*), social bookmarking platforms and forums and communities. Another group focuses on **cooperation between users.** Here wikis are set up jointly (such as *Wiktionary, Wikipedia, Wikiquote* or *Wikileaks*), existing services are assessed within the framework of rating and information platforms (such as ▶ *holidaycheck.com,* ▶ *tripadvisor.com,* ▶ *yelp.com*) or new services are cre-

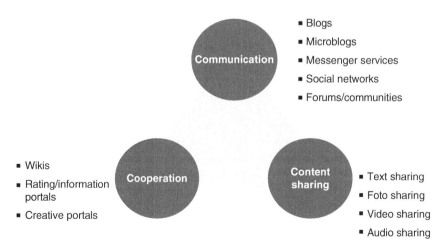

◘ **Fig. 3.27**   Use classes and application examples of social media

ated within the framework of creative and information portals. The third group is about **content sharing,** i.e. the sharing of content via specific media sharing platforms such as *Instagram, TikTok, Pinterest, Flickr, Vimeo* and *YouTube*. This content can be texts, videos, photos or audio files. However, such content sharing also takes place in the social networks, because here, too, a wide variety of content is shared with others.

At this point, it should be noted that the **transitions between the various social media** as well as the **classification of the various concepts,** e.g. to the social networks, to the media sharing platforms and to the messenger services, are becoming increasingly blurred. A contributing factor is that proven functionalities of a concept are adopted by other providers. *Facebook* is a social network, but it also offers a variety of media sharing options and has installed its own *Facebook Messenger* service. *Instagram* is a media sharing application, but it also has traits of a social network. *Pinterest* is more of a social network; but it too is about media sharing. *Snapchat* is a messenger service that focuses on sharing messages and pictures. The classification of the various concepts made in this work is based on the perceived focus of the providers.

Complex **social media applications** can be created by networking the concepts shown with each other and with the other media of online and offline marketing. The objective here is to address the target groups on the platforms where they are on the move in order to offer them relevant content there, which should also pay off here on the central corporate goal: the sale of own services!

But how important are the various **social media** on a **worldwide basis** today? The market leader is *Facebook*. This social network has around 2.8 billion monthly active users. *Facebook* also owns four of the biggest social media platforms, all with over one billion monthly active users each. These are – besides *Facebook* – *WhatsApp, Facebook Messenge,* and *Instagram*. In the first quarter of 2021, *Facebook* reported over 3.45 billion monthly users of their platforms. Chinese social networks *WeChat, QQ* or video sharing app *Douyin* have also garnered mainstream appeal in their respective regions due to local context and content. *Douyin's* popularity has led to the platform releasing an international version of its network: the name of this app is *TikTok*. The **leading social networks** are often available in several languages and enable users to connect with people across geographical, political, cultural or economic borders. In 2021, social networking sites reach close to 4 billion users. This number is expected to grow as mobile device usage and mobile social networks increasingly gain traction in previously underserved markets (cf. Statista 2021g) (◘ Fig. 3.28).

3

*Platforms have not published updated user figures in the past 12 months, figures may be out of date and less reliable

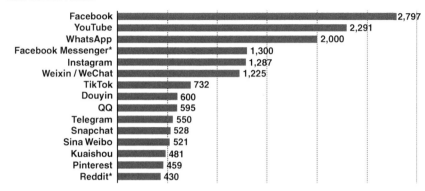

Facebook	2,797
YouTube	2,291
WhatsApp	2,000
Facebook Messenger*	1,300
Instagram	1,287
Weixin / WeChat	1,225
TikTok	732
Douyin	600
QQ	595
Telegram	550
Snapchat	528
Sina Weibo	521
Kuaishou	481
Pinterest	459
Reddit*	430

◘ **Fig. 3.28**   Most popular social networks worldwide ranked by number of active users – in millions

Social media plays a paramount role in the everyday life of more and more people. Therefore, these media are also another important channel to customers and they are of great importance.

> ┌─ Notice! ──────────────────────────────────
>
> An **engagement in the social media** is not a self-runner. It requires financial and human resources, a good strategy and staying power to succeed in social media! Those who cannot sustainably provide the necessary resources should rather do without such an engagement.

Therefore, many companies – especially smaller ones – do well to refrain from half-hearted activity in social media. As far as such an engagement is not demanded by the own target group, it often makes more sense to focus on the development of the own website (incl. search engine optimization) or on a consistent e-mail marketing.

> ┌─ Notice! ──────────────────────────────────
>
> **Social media marketing** is a procedural concept that makes use of social media to achieve marketing goals and involves users in various ways.

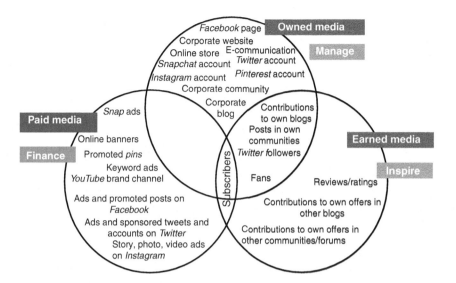

Fig. 3.29 Overview of different media classes

In social media marketing, a distinction must be made between different **media categories** (cf. Mayer-Uellner 2010, p. 16; Oetting 2010). The online activities for which the companies themselves are responsible are referred to as **owned media** (cf. Fig. 3.29). These include the corporate website, e-communications and the company's own online shop. Offers for communication with users via the company's own corporate blog and its own forums and communities are also part of this. The presences generated by companies on *Facebook, Google My Business, Instagram, Pinterest, Twitter* and *YouTube* platforms are often also counted as owned media, although the companies only have a right of use there and do not acquire ownership of the structures and data that develop. The owned media must be managed in order to achieve the defined goals (keyword **"manage"**).

These media are to be distinguished from **paid media**, which comprises the measures that companies buy from third-party partners. Examples of this are banners and keyword ads. This also includes the possibility on *Facebook* to pay not only for ads, but also for the delivery of posts (recognizable by the indication "sponsored"). *Twitter* offers analogous possibilities with *Twitter* ads and promoted tweets. *Instagram* offers story, photo, video and carousel ads, among others. Here we can speak of **social media stamps**,

3

with which companies must stamp their messages on social platforms so that they are delivered comprehensively. All other forms of advertising – be it on *Facebook, Instagram, LinkedIn, Pinterest, Snapchat, YouTube* & Co. – also fall into the paid media category. Access to these opportunities is simply a question of available finances (keyword "**finance**").

The third category of **earned media** in ❏ Fig. 3.29 refers to the platforms and, in particular, the content that companies have earned from online users through their activities – for better or for worse. This is user-generated content in various forms. This includes social bookmarks for the company's own websites as well as contributions to the company's own and external blogs, forums and communities. An important prerequisite for achieving a high (positive) share of earned media is gaining attention and engagement in the social networks. In addition to the necessary investment of time and money, this also requires the ability to tell good stories. The keyword here is therefore: "**inspire**".

Particularly interesting content lies in the **overlapping fields of the different media categories**. If, for example, users are invited to create their own content on platforms operated by companies, this part of the user-generated content belongs to the overlapping field between owned and earned media. *Starbucks Ideas* provides an example of this. Here, customers are invited to share their ideas with *Starbucks* (cf. Starbucks 2021). The same applies when a company invites users to dialogue on a corporate blog or in its own forums and communities, and users accept this invitation. Fans or followers gained on *Facebook, Instagram, Pinterest* or *Twitter are* also part of this. If users subscribe to a brand-specific *YouTube* channel, they belong as subscribers to the overlap area between paid and earned media.

Every company is well advised to strive for a **balanced mix between the different media categories**.

3.7.2 Forms and Goals of Social Media Marketing

Companies need to decide if and if so in what way they will participate within social media. Often, their prospects and customers are already there talking about the company, brands and/or specific offers – and no one is listening or caring about the people engaged there. Businesses have three social media marketing **courses of action** to choose from. These can be described by the terms **listening** and/or having a **say** (by **reacting** and **acting**):

- **Listening: social media monitoring**
  - The minimum level of social media engagement that all companies should implement with regard to social media is listening through effective **social media monitoring**. It is important to find out how people talk about your own services in social media. Because even without your own participation in social media, something is usually already being said, written or visually published there about the company and/ or its products and services. This monitoring should – at least for large companies – ideally take place 24/7. Because it applies:

Notice!

Social media never sleeps!

  - Therefore, the monitoring must not be based on traditional working hours (including a free weekend). Otherwise, companies run the risk that dramatic developments may begin on Friday evening and are literally "slept through" by the companies concerned. News could spread overnight or over the weekend without comment at viral speed and reach thousands, hundreds of thousands or even millions of people.
- **Reacting: integration**
  - Companies can step out of the passivity of social media monitoring and get involved in the communicative processes within social media. This may become necessary if discussions taking place there are not acceptable for a company. This may involve false accusations, one-sided portrayals or other disparagement against which a company wishes to defend itself.

Notice!

Social media not only amplifies the wisdom, but also the stupidity of the many!

- **Acting: creation**
  - The most comprehensive form of engagement involves setting up one's own platforms in social media. Here, for example, own forums or communities are developed in order to actively participate in the formation of opinion via these. This also includes the development of a corporate blog or the creation of an own video channel on *YouTube*.

3

When harnessing social media through social media marketing in the forms mentioned, one thing should be kept in mind:
The type, timing and frequency of access to social media are primarily determined by the users themselves.
In the case of classic media, the use or, more precisely, the possibilities of use are determined by the communicating companies, the media agencies, and the publishers or broadcasters. With regard to social media, it can happen that a company communicates a message on *Twitter* and online users respond to it in blogs or on *Facebook*. The principle here is that the company should follow the channel preferences of the users in order not to let the dialogue break off.

Which goals of a social media deployment can be aimed at – oriented to the described possibilities "listening, reacting and acting"? There is still a great deal of uncertainty here in many companies. First of all, it is generally true that the social media goals are to be derived consistently from the corporate goals and not to invent "completely new goals" just for the social media! The following **social media goals** are highly relevant for many companies:

▬ **Increasing the awareness of the offer/brand/company**
   – With the use of social media, many companies aim to increase the awareness of offers, brands and its own company in general. This goal is based on the realization that relationships with brands and companies today – in addition to advertising impulses, the experience at the online or offline POS, and through use itself – are increasingly shaped by the **experience in social media.**

▬ **Position yourself as an expert**
   – Companies additionally strive to position themselves as experts in social media. This goal is closely linked to the important topic of content marketing: **reputation building**. B2B companies in particular are very active in this area.

▬ **Demonstrate willingness to engage in dialogue**
   – One goal is also to expand relationships with customers through a willingness to engage in dialogue. Social media offer ideal conditions for promoting direct dialogue through **integration into corporate information flows** and the opportunities for a **direct exchange of information** between companies and users.

▬ **Attract applicants**
   – Meanwhile, more and more companies are also aiming to attract **new employees** through social media.

- **Customer acquisition**
  - Companies are also trying to gain new customers through their social media activities. Here, however, the realization is increasingly gaining ground that social media do not represent a classic sales channel. It has been learned that "social media" must not and cannot be redefined as **"commercial media"**. This is because using social media to sell directly will rarely meet with much approval from users. Social media is more likely to offer communication "through the grapevine", which of course is also intended to pay in sales – but often rather indirectly. This can be achieved well through the aforementioned goals of "positioning oneself as an expert" and "showing a willingness to engage in dialogue". However, more and more efforts are being made by companies today to integrate shop functionalities into social media.
- **Maintain contacts with journalists and other stakeholders**
  - Social media also offer the opportunity to build and maintain relationships with journalists and other stakeholders. What is important here is that it is no longer the **classic offline opinion leaders** (such as editors and journalists from the established media) alone who should be the focus of such activities. **Online opinion leaders,** who as bloggers, *Instagrammers, YouTubers* or *Twitterers* with a large reader and/or follower community can significantly influence opinion on the net, are becoming increasingly relevant.
- **Customer service**
  - Customer service can also be provided via social media. This is referred to as **social service.** *WhatsApp* plays an important role here.
- **Market research and market observation**
  - Opinions expressed in social media offer an unhindered and unadorned view of the evaluation of one's own performance in the eyes of stakeholders – often even in real time! Companies should definitely take advantage of this **opportunity to gather information** – knowing that only a (biased) sample of their own customers is ever engaged here!
- **Collaboration with customers to expand the product and service portfolio (crowdsourcing)**
  - Crowdsourcing is made up of the terms "crowd" (for mass) and "source" (for origin). Swarm intelligence can be used for **creative competitions.**

To ensure that an engagement in social media does not turn into a flash in the pan, every company has to develop **goals** and a **strategy for social media marketing** before getting started. This also includes providing the necessary

3

financial and human resources. Similar to customer loyalty systems, the various social media offerings will initially attract the fans or those individuals who have already established the greatest closeness to the company and its brands. If an engagement on *Facebook, Instagram, Pinterest, Twitter* or *YouTube is* discontinued after a short period of time or is only implemented uncharitably, the contacts to the company's most important partners may be cut off or at least damaged.

Therefore, an **exit strategy** should always be considered when entering social media. In concrete terms, this means that it should be made clear, for example, when engaging in *Facebook* or *Twitter* for the first time, that this is initially a "six-month test phase". If the corresponding activities are subsequently terminated – due to a lack of target achievement or resources – no one should be surprised. If, on the other hand, the activities are continued, there should be no protest. Therefore:

❯ In a nutshell, any business would be well advised to think ahead to a possible exit when getting into social media marketing.

The basic **procedure for opening up social media for a company** is shown by the **social media house** in ◻ Fig. 3.30. The prerequisite for any measures is first of all a comprehensive **analysis of the status quo of the use of social media** by the relevant target groups and the relevant competitors. Based on this, a **social media concept** can be developed. The crucial question is whether one's own company offers enough **substance** to provide attractive and thus

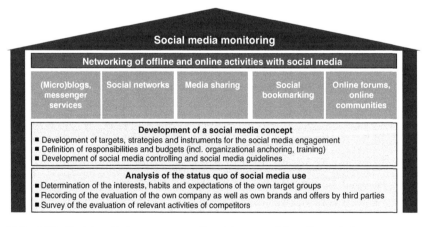

◻ **Fig. 3.30** Social media house – process for setting up social media marketing

relevant content for users. Without convincing substance, no social media engagement will succeed. Consequently, "content is king!" – and not just the reach achieved.

When developing and, in particular, implementing a social media concept (including the organizational anchoring and training of employees), care must be taken to ensure that the individual social media are not only networked in a target group-oriented manner, but also networked with the company's other communicative measures. Only in this way can a coherent overall presence of the company be achieved. The entire social media engagement must be integrated into a comprehensive **social media monitoring** in order to determine the – desired and undesired – results early and comprehensively. The basis for this monitoring is not only concrete usage data but also unstructured public data available in the form of text posts, photos and videos on the various social media platforms. This content must be evaluated with regard to its relevance for the company.

3.7.3 Platforms for the Use of Social Media Marketing

◘ Figure 3.31 shows which **social media platforms** dominate the use of companies. 5243 marketing managers worldwide were surveyed for this purpose. 94% of companies that use social media use *Facebook*. Compared to previous years, *Instagram* has gained in importance and is now used by 76% of companies. The business network *LinkedIn* follows at 59%. *Twitter* has become significantly less important, with only 53% of businesses now incorporating it

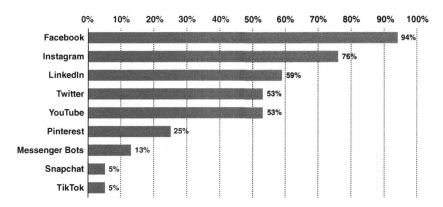

◘ **Fig. 3.31** Use of social media platforms by companies worldwide 2020 – in %

3

into their communications. Also 53% of the companies use the video platform *YouTube*. Other platforms such as *Pinterest* (25%), Messenger Bots (5%), *Snapchat* (5%) and *TikTok* (5%) are used significantly less (cf. Statista 2020h).

The own **corporate website** does not lose its relevance next to the various social media platforms. China is an exception here; there, a representation on *WeChat is* already more important than a website of one's own in many cases. In contrast, in the Western world, the website can be both the **starting point and the target of an engagement in social media,** in order to prepare or initiate the desired further steps towards conversion here. Here, the user can find out more about the company and in some cases also purchase its products or services, as well as receive information about stationary sources of supply.

A connection of the corporate website to social media is done by **adding links**: For each social media tool, there are corresponding buttons that can be integrated into the website. These are also called **social plug-ins.** In this way, users are directed to the various social media platforms on which the company is present at the click of a button. At the same time, links can lead from the social media presence to the company's own homepage, specific landing pages or the online shop, in order to direct prospective customers into corresponding information, consultation and/or purchasing processes. The type of design required depends on the respective business concept.

◻ Figure 3.32 helps to classify the **social media and their content orientation** by illustrating – ironically and exaggeratedly – the **basic tendencies**

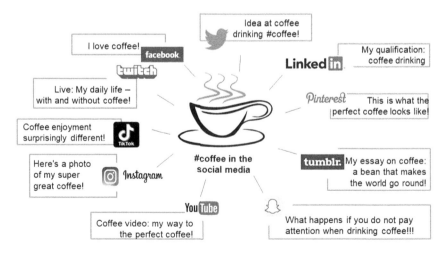

◻ **Fig. 3.32**   Basic trends in the content orientation of the most important social media

of the social platforms. *Twitter* and *Snapchat* are strongly fixated on the moment and can – in the case of *Snapchat* and also *TikTok* – also present a mishap once in a while. *Twitch* allows users to follow the daily lives of idols – with and without coffee – live. On *Facebook,* people make a commitment to a brand or company, get into a dialogue and report what's what. *Instagram* and *Pinterest* focus on pictorial staging, and on *YouTube,* video messages dominate. With *LinkedIn,* people switch to the business side. Here, professional exchange and the presentation of one's own qualifications and business interests predominate. With *Tumblr,* a blog platform has been created that allows in-depth discussion of all possible and impossible topics.

▪ Blogs

A blog is a website that can be run by individuals, groups or companies. On a blog, the owner and possibly also other invited or interested persons – the **bloggers** – can write about a wide variety of topics. At the same time, third parties can react to these entries with their own comments, steer discussions in other directions or link to their own blogs.

The main component of any blog is the **blogposts** or **posts** that are written by the blogger. Most blogs also provide for readers to write comments on the blog entries, which are displayed under the respective entries. This gives blogs their **interactive, conversational nature.** In addition to content, **permalinks** can be installed. These are fixed connections ("permanent links") to other blog entries. This makes it easier to search for certain categories in blogs. Through the use of **trackbacks,** visitors can also create a link to their own blog, which was written on similar issues.

Blogs play a major role in the acquisition of information. Increasingly, not only private individuals, but also company representatives or other special target groups inform themselves here. Therefore, it is indispensable for companies to gain an overview of the "mood" regarding their own company, their own brands or their own offers through **blog monitoring**.

▪ Microblogging

Microblogging is a form of blogging in which the length of posts is limited to a certain number of characters (on *Twitter* now 280). That is the reason why it is called **microblogging**. The world's best-known microblogging service is *Twitter*. To date, *Twitter* has not yet become a mass phenomenon. In the evaluation, a distinction must be made between the quantity of followers and their quality.

❯ In a nutshell: If important opinion leaders are reached via *Twitter*, they can have a far greater influence on the overall perception of the company than is reflected in the sheer number of followers. This is because the direct followers can in turn feed relevant messages into their networks and thus trigger viral effects.

3

In order to make tweets on certain terms and topics easier to find for a keyword search, they should be identified by a hashtag (#) (e.g. #socialmedia). *Followers* follow other users whose activities, opinions or information they are interested in and whose messages they want to receive regularly.

❯ In a nutshell: The decisive factor is that it is not the sender who determines who receives his messages, but the recipient.

▪ **Social Networks**

A social network is a **social media platform** that allows users to build new relationships with business partners and/or private individuals, find like-minded people, and get and stay in touch with them. In the Western world, the most important social network for private users is by far *Facebook*. In the professional sphere *LinkedIn* is very important.

The **basic structures of** social networks have the same characteristics:

- **Creating a profile** that tells who you are, what you do, what you are interested in, and how you can be contacted.
- **Enrichment of the profile with further elements** (including CV/resume, posts, photos, videos, links to own website, publications, etc.)
- **Identification of the connection to other persons** within the respective network
- **Communication between the users of the social network,** whereby a distinction is sometimes made between private messages (only visible to the individual) and public messages (visible to a larger circle of users, e.g. on a pinboard); in addition, communication via SMS, e-mail and chat functions is also supported in some cases.

From a company's point of view, there are several good reasons for engaging with social networks:

The demonstrated **intensity of access** to social networks shows where online users spend their time. In accordance with the motto **"fish were the fish are"**, companies are forced to engage in communication in these networks if their most important target groups spend a lot of time there. In ▶ Sect. 3.1, it was already worked out that **Internet use** in Germany today averages

133 minutes per day. For many target groups, this time is not only significantly higher, but is also concentrated to a large extent on social media. This must be taken into account in corporate communication.

Social networks offer the opportunity to **build a relationship with users** beyond traditional advertising communication. This can also take on dialogical forms and actively involve users in creative or selection processes. Involvement in social media is also relevant for companies because the content presented here and especially the ratings found there have an influence on the **positioning in** *Google's* **organic hit list** (keyword "social signals"; cf. ◗ Fig. 3.16).

Even though *Facebook* dominates social networks worldwide, every company should check whether *Facebook* is still relevant for its own target group. In the segment of users aged 14 to 39, daily usage time has fallen in Germany from 28 minutes in 2015 to just 13 minutes in the meantime. The intensity of use has also decreased slightly in the other age groups (cf. Statista 2020f). Many young people now regard *Facebook* as the network for the "older generations".

The start for a company or a brand on *Facebook* begins classically with the creation of a **fan page**. For this purpose, the company presents itself with photos and also defines who is behind the corresponding page. The check mark behind the company indicates that this page has been verified. This sender note is important because fans of companies and brands may also have built their own fan pages. Those responsible for the presence of companies and brands should know if there are such unofficial *Facebook sites*, which are often maintained by enthusiastic followers. It might be a worthwhile approach to contact the administrators of these unofficial sites. If it is possible to meet them in an appreciative manner and provide relevant material for them, positive communication for the company and/or the brand can be achieved – beyond one's own *Facebook presence*.

Calls-to-action are offered on a fan page, too. Since it is an important goal of a fan page to gain as many **"likes"** as possible, this call-to-action is often positioned prominently below the photo. Via the "Like" button, a fan can also say goodbye to the relationship ("Don't like you anymore"). Here you will also find the option to **subscribe to posts** as well as the option to **share the content** in your own chronicle. Clicking on "Buy now" can take you directly to an online store. In addition, there is often the option to send the company a message via *Facebook Messenger*. Visitors of the Facebook page are regularly invited to invite friends to become also fans of the company.

To support the fan advertising socially, the **fans of the brand or the company** are displayed at the same time **among the friends** with photo. In addition, a **rating of the page** is given. This rating is based on the number of people who recommend or do not recommend the page, as well as any existing ratings. Interesting information can be found in the **community box**. At this point, the visitor of the fan page is often requested to **suggest** the corresponding **fan page to their own friends**. Many additional information can be found on the **wall of the own fan page**. Various contents (information, photos, videos, articles, events) can be presented here in order to regularly provide new contents for the users.

With *Facebook,* however, it is not enough to just gain fans and hope for the highest possible ROI on the *Facebook* investment. Those who act in this way do not meet the requirements of a *Facebook* engagement. This is because a **fan page** on *Facebook* is – from the user's point of view – not the most important communication anchor, as can be the case with a corporate website. A fan page on *Facebook* does not represent a second corporate website, but rather a push channel through which – similar to a newsletter – interesting things can be announced. After the first visit to the fan page and "becoming a fan", many fans will no longer (regularly) visit this fan page, although they are interested in the offer and companies often present interesting content on their fan page and invite dialogue.

Becoming a fan represents only a **minimal commitment from users**, which is not very resilient. Those who solely trust that a large fan base will lead to a **high reach** and **increase ROI** will find themselves disappointed. The reason lies in the dynamics of social networks. In order to get communication going here and keep it going, interesting content is necessary. The fan page on *Facebook* is **not a pull medium**. The relationship building and thus the traffic between company and user are primarily achieved through **posts** and **advertising**. The following applies: **a lke is not enough!**

To achieve high engagement on *Facebook,* the steps shown in ◘ Fig. 3.33 are necessary. The goal of *Facebook* engagement does not end with collecting fans – quite the opposite. Those who have gained many *Facebook* fans are virtually obliged to offer them something as well. Because an engagement in the social media and on *Facebook* is like an invitation to a party. This must then also take place! In sum, a **fourfold leap plus 1** is required for success in social media (cf. ◘ Fig. 3.33). This fourfold leap begins with the **acquisition of fans** as the **first step**. The goal is to turn as many visitors to the fan page as possible into fans.

After the customer has entered into a certain relationship by becoming a fan, the **second step** is to cultivate this trust potential by sending relevant **posts** to the fans (cf. ◘ Fig. 3.33). Against this background, the permission to **send push messages** to one's own fans is of great importance. It becomes clear: The relationship between company and fan shifts from the fan page to the – hopefully exciting, interesting, new and thus relevant – **company mes-**

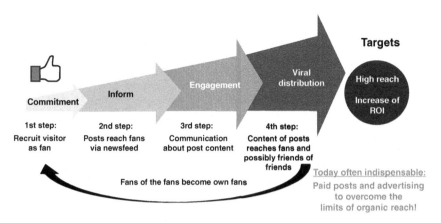

Fig. 3.33 Fourfold leap plus 1 to success in social media

sages that appear in the fans' news feeds. It must be taken into account that these posts are not delivered to 100% of the company's own fans – as is still often wrongly assumed. Organic reach today is much closer to 1% than 100% for large numbers of fans. **Organic reach** is the term used to describe the number of people on whose screens a company's unpaid posts are displayed. In contrast, **paid reach** refers to the number of people on whose screens a company's paid posts are displayed.

The relevance of the posted articles is also the prerequisite for the desired **engagement,** so that the own fans report on the communicated content in their respective network in the **third step** (cf. ☐ Fig. 3.33). Here, it can succeed in turning *Facebook* into a **social recommendation engine.**

> **Notice!**
>
> Recommendation is the new Search!

With the activities mentioned, the prerequisite for a **viral spread of the content** in the **fourth step** is already fulfilled (cf. ☐ Fig. 3.33). If the friends of the fans are enthusiastic and share the content in turn, **second-order virality** is achieved: the friends of the friends learn about the company's activities. Through this **viral reach,** these friends can also become fans. Engagement can also reinforce the initially acquired fans that they have engaged with the "right content" because it is also well received by their own friends. It is only through the intermediate steps shown that a **high reach** is made possible.

3

However, even this is no longer sufficient in many cases to achieve a **positive ROI of the measures**. Finally, as already mentioned, it must be noted that the **organic reach** on *Facebook* is continuously decreasing. The reason for this is easy to explain. As more and more companies and individuals are active on *Facebook*, the number of posts available to a single user is also constantly increasing. Estimates say that between 500 and 50,000 posts would be available per user per day. However, that would be too much even for an intensive *Facebook* user and would tend to scare them off. *Facebook* ultimately pursues the goal of keeping users on the platform as long and frequently as possible. Therefore, *Facebook* uses an algorithm that is not known in detail and also frequently changed to determine the **relevance of posts** for each individual user.

This ***Facebook* algorithm** initially takes into account **information about all content** that is available for display. This includes the posts of one's own friends and family members as well as other content that is shared outside of one's own network. In addition, a variety of **signals** are evaluated that can provide indicators of the relevance of a post. These include, for example, answers to the following questions: What topics does a user talk about with his friends? How much time did users spend looking at different posts? How many likes did the different posts get, how often were they shared and/or commented on? Based on such information, *Facebook* makes a **prediction** about how likely a user is to like a specific post. This prediction also uses an analysis of user history about the type of content that has been previously read, liked, shared and/or commented on. The totality of this information is incorporated into a **score**, based on which a post is delivered organically – or not.

> ❯ In a nutshell: *Facebook,* and not the user, decides which posts are visible in the newsfeed. *Facebook* therefore determines what is relevant for the individual user. This opens the door to manipulation of *Facebook users* (cf. in-depth Kreutzer 2020, pp. 67-94).

However, how the *Facebook* algorithm turns out in detail is not known and also not static (like the *Google* algorithm). Therefore, every company is called upon to intensively monitor the reactions of users to their own *Facebook* engagement and – in the event of changes to the *Facebook* algorithm – to adapt accordingly.

The key question of *Facebook* use, which every company should answer for itself, is: How can the company's own (prospective) customers be won over as fans and contribute to sustainable value creation for the company? The four relevant **fields of action** are shown in ◼ Fig. 3.34. First of all, con-

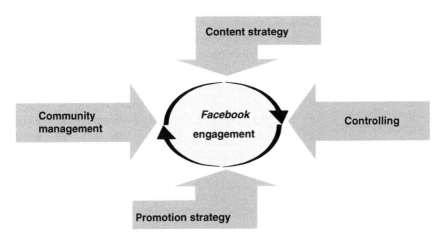

□ Fig. 3.34 Fields of action of a *Facebook* engagement

sistent **community management is** required. The first task is to define the goals for *Facebook* engagement. In addition, the interests and expectations of this core target group with regard to the content provided must be determined at the beginning and on an ongoing basis.

Based on the interests and expectations of the core target group, the **content strategy** for *Facebook* must be developed, which consistently revolves around the company, its brands and offers and ideally exciting stories about them (keyword "content marketing"). Here, a **consultative approach** is becoming increasingly important, because customers are often not looking for a very specific product (e.g. the *WELEDA Citrus Refreshing Bath*), but rather a problem solution (e.g. "refreshing bath additive") or even more general ("How can I relax healthily?"). Therefore, companies should define so-called **content claims** – based on their core competencies. This can be "health", "conscious nutrition" or "fashion advice for 50+ customers".

In line with the guiding principle **"content is king"** and **"relationship is queen",** a further field of action for *Facebook* engagement in the course of a **promotion strategy** is to activate users so that they actually make use of the offers (cf. **□** Fig. 3.34). In addition to *Facebook* posts, a wide variety of online instruments (such as banners, blog entries, notices in communities) and offline instruments (such as classic advertisements, posters or TV spots with corresponding notices) can be used for this purpose. In addition, *Facebook* offers – as already mentioned – various paid options to draw the attention of *Facebook* users to their own activities. These are becoming increasingly important due to the decreasing organic reach.

3

Finally, all measures taken must be reviewed with regard to their effectiveness by means of comprehensive **controlling** as a further field of action of *Facebook* engagement (cf. ◘ Fig. 3.34) in order to identify optimization opportunities as early and comprehensively as possible. But how can it ultimately be determined whether a *Facebook* engagement has been worthwhile? This requires a comparison between the *Facebook* goals, the investments in *Facebook* engagement, and the results achieved using **Facebook** **KPIs** that are also relevant for other social media.

■ **Media sharing platforms**

Media sharing platforms allow companies and private Internet users to upload content such as videos, photos, presentations and audio files on the Internet and thus make them accessible to other prospective customers. Two types can be distinguished:

▬ **Content created and published by the company itself**
  – Companies can provide interested users with information about the company, its brands and offers online on these platforms. These can serve to build up the image, create concrete offers, inform about correct product use or extend campaigns by uploading TV spots and/or their "making-of". In addition, training films can be presented.

▬ **Independently created and published content**
  – In positive cases, users who are independent of the company can post contributions that are conducive to the company and/or brand image and thus underline their enthusiasm for the offerings. In this way, Internet users can also be integrated into the company's creative processes. However, user contributions can also counteract the company's advertising statements and/or expose errors and omissions on the part of the. The critical public has a wide range of opportunities to make its voice heard via these platforms. This type of "material" constitutes **user-generated content**.
  – The media sharing platforms are also the big "stomping ground" for digital influencers. In addition to *YouTube, Instagram* and increasingly also *TikTok* are particularly popular platforms here.

■ **Instant messenger services**

Instant messaging is a kind of online chat which offers real-time text transmission via the Internet. The appearance of smartphone and the availability of mobile apps, low-cost or free chat and social messaging apps have proven themselves as a cheap alternative to operator-based text messaging via SMS. Many messenger apps support group chats, the exchange of graphics,

*Have not published updated users numbers in the past 12 months. All values are the last reported figures. Telegram figures from company blog.

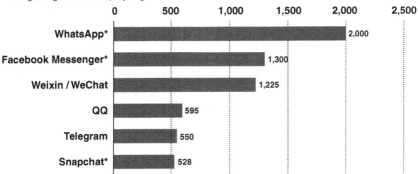

◻ **Fig. 3.35** Most popular global mobile messaging apps based on number of monthly active users – in millions

video and even audio messages as well as stickers or emoticons. ◻ Fig. 3.35 shows which messenger services may be relevant for corporate communications. Two billion users are accessing the *WhatsApp* messenger on a monthly basis. *WhatsApp* is one of the most popular mobile social apps worldwide. *WhatsApp is* followed – already at a considerable distance – by *Facebook Messenger*. On the next places we find the Chinese solutions *Weixin/WeChat* and *QQ*. Then follow – by a wide margin – *Telegram* and *Snapchat* (cf. Statista 2021h, p. 10).

One reason why messenger services are also gaining traction with companies is the high level of user engagement with the various messenger apps. This is often many times higher than with other apps. Additionally, the **"one-to-one" communication with users** that can be achieved here promises much greater immediacy and proximity to (prospective) customers through instant messaging. While the presented social networks and microblogging services primarily represent "one-to-many" communication, messenger services focus on direct communication, although many recipients can also be reached here through one message. At the same time, it is visible that the leading messaging apps are becoming increasingly commercialized.

The term **instant messaging** stands for the immediate online transmission of messages between two or more participants. Consequently, it is a **push transmission** in which the message reaches the recipient immediately and is seen there as long as the recipient is online. Otherwise, the message is delivered as soon as the person is online again. In addition to text-only messages,

3

many instant messenger services also support the sending of various files (e.g. photos, video and audio files, word documents). In addition, various service providers offer further functions such as voice and video chats, greeting cards, text messaging or online games.

WhatsApp offers different services to different user groups. The ***WhatsApp*** app itself is only intended for **private communication**. In the case of **solutions for companies,** a distinction is made between *WhatsApp for Business* and the *WhatsApp Business API.* ***WhatsApp for Business*** (also *WhatsApp* business app) is free, i.e., here you pay again with your data. The use is recommended only for smaller companies. *WhatsApp Business API* makes it easier to communicate with customers with features to automate, organize and quickly reply to messages. It works and feels similar to *WhatsApp* messenger.

- **Online forums and online communities**

Online forums are the oldest form of social media. An online forum is a virtual place for exchanging and often also archiving ideas, opinions and experiences. As a rule, communication does not take place in real time, but on a time-delayed basis. There are a large number of forums that address different subject areas and thus different target groups. After registering in a forum, one can ask questions within the forum that are answered by other members and/or deal with the questions and answers of the other participants. In addition, one's own topics can be introduced into the discussion. The questions and answers form the so-called **threads,** which have the character of conversations.

Online communities can be distinguished from online forums by a more intensive relationship between the members. Often their goals go beyond the mere exchange of information and include the joint processing of topics or the generation of new content through intensive collaboration (e.g. in the *Vodafone community*). However, this kind of distinction between forums and communities is not strictly taken into account by all authors.

3.7.4 Controlling of Social Media Marketing

Determining **ROMI** (return on marketing investment) is particularly difficult when evaluating social media engagement. Many aspects of these media, such as the value of an appreciative dialogue, are difficult to express quantitatively. What KPIs can be used to evaluate the successes achieved in social media? An overview is provided by ◻ Figs. 3.36 and 3.37. There, **social media KPIs** are defined that are to be integrated into a **social media dash-**

KPI	Metric	Formula	Data discovery
Reach	Social buzz	Number of mentions	Count
	Share of buzz	Number of "own" mentions compared to the total number/competition numbers	Determination via tags (according to categories)
	Development of social buzz/share of buzz	Number of mentions over time	Count
	Number of fans, follower, etc. (in the broadest sense)	Values from *Facebook, Instagram, Pinterest, Tumblr, Twitter, YouTube*	Count
	1st and 2nd degree reach	Number of people reached directly (1st degree) and indirectly (2nd degree)	Count
Sentiment	Number of positive, negative and neutral mentions (determination of sentiments)	Sentiment analysis (allocation of the contributions to rating classes)	Count
	Relative number of positive, negative and neutral mentions (determination of sentiments)	Number of posts per rating class in relation to the total number of mentions	Count
	Recommendation rate	Number of recommending mentions in relation to the total number of mentions	Determination via tags (according to categories)
Engagement	Number of posts (total) and comments/likes/shares (per post)	Values from *Facebook, Instagram, Pinterest, Tumblr, Twitter, YouTube*	Count
	Posts in communities and forums, incl. determination of sentiments	Values from communities and forums with sentiment analysis (allocation of posts to rating classes)	Count
	Participation in sweepstakes, rating contests, creative processes, etc.	Number of participants compared to total number of customers	Count

☐ **Fig. 3.36** Social media KPIs – I

KPI	Metric	Formula	Data discovery
Influence	Social buzz by channels/sites	Number of mentions by channels/sites	Count
	Social buzz by relevant authors (influencers)	Number of mentions by authors	Count by authors
	Cast of relevant topics	Most mentioned topics about the brand	Count via topic cloud
Conversions	Newsletter subscriptions	Number of new newsletter subscriptions	Count
	Downloads	Number of downloads made	Count
	Corporate website traffic	Website visits, session duration, bounce rate, pages views, downloads, requests, subscriptions, etc.	Count (e.g. via *Google Analytics*)
	Online store visits	Online store visits, session duration, bounce rate, page views, downloads, requests, subscriptions, purchases, etc.	Count via store software
	Offline store visits	Offline store visits (recorded via coupons, customer cards, etc.), test drives	Count

☐ **Fig. 3.37** Social media KPIs – II

board in order to have a continuous overview of the relevant developments. It is exciting to also have an overview of the results of the most important competitors.

The **reach of social media marketing** measured in ☐ Fig. 3.36 tells us something about how many people were reached by the distributed message.

3

The frequency with which the company is mentioned by users on other social media platforms, for example on blogs, on *Pinterest,* in online forums or in *Twitter* tweets, is also an indicator of reach. But again, the aforementioned applies: A social media mention can be beneficial or detrimental to businesses. Here, too, there is a need for supplementary evaluative information on the tonality of the messages, which in sum represent the **mood picture** to be surveyed.

On the topic of **engagement,** other terms need to be introduced. Regarding the likes/ratings of content, the term **content appreciation** is used. Regarding interaction, the term **conversational exchange** is also used. Sharing or distributing content is referred to as **content amplification.**

When measuring **influence,** it is important to consider that not only the buzz of (prospective) customers is to be measured, but also the buzz of (digital) opinion leaders. In addition, the extent to which it is possible to achieve agenda setting by defining the relevant topics must be recorded ◘ Fig. 3.37.

Social media KPIs, and thus social media dashboards, often still lack the capture of **conversions.** However, it is precisely these that are crucial in order to systematically record whether engagement in social media contributes beyond buzz and engagement to achieving sales and profit-oriented marketing goals. It is possible to measure how many users converted to prospective customers after watching a relevant company video on *YouTube,* for example, signing up to receive a newsletter or downloading an app. It is also possible to measure whether more information was requested and/or direct purchases were made after the launch of a campaign on *Twitter* – both online and offline.

These are different forms of conversion mentioned in ◘ Fig. 3.37. These criteria correspond to a great extent with the goals of the company, because they pay off on the development of non-knowers of the company into (prospective) customers.

3.8 Learning Control

🖥 Short and Sweet

The selection of the online marketing instruments to be used is based on the marketing objectives. A variety of instruments is available within the scope of online marketing. Before a company enters into the selection of individual instruments, precise goals for online marketing should be defined. Then it has to be decided which of the available instruments are best suited to achieve the online goals.

Often, the online presence starts with a convincing corporate website, which can be the central anchor point for many online and offline measures. If relevant information for the various target groups is available there, online and offline measures must be developed to generate traffic on one's own website. Here, too, it must be systematically determined which successes are achieved in each case.

In addition, it must be examined which online advertising and search engine optimization measures can be used to achieve a high frequency on the website. The fields of application of e-mail marketing, mobile marketing and social media marketing must also be evaluated with regard to the achievement of corporate goals.

❓ Let's Check

1. What is the importance of the corporate website in the context of a company's online and offline engagement?
2. Which target groups have to be considered when building the corporate website?
3. Through which **offline activities** can a high visitor frequency be built up for a corporate website?
4. Through which **online activities** can a high visitor frequency be built up for a corporate website?
5. What is targeting in online advertising?
6. What is the difference between search engine advertising (SEA) and search engine optimization (SEO)?
7. How can the basic concept of affiliate marketing be characterized?
8. What is keyword density?
9. What are the key guiding ideas in search engine optimization?
10. How can e-mail marketing be characterized?
11. What is the importance of e-newsletters and why?
12. What is A/B testing?
13. How can mobile marketing be characterized?
14. What are the key activities of voice marketing?
15. How can social media marketing be characterized?
16. What goals can be pursued through social media marketing?
17. What are the central fields of action of a *Facebook* engagement?
18. What is behind the term media sharing platform?
19. What are the most important KPIs to evaluate a social media engagement?

3

❓ Networking Tasks

Analyse the corporate website of *Zalando*. What content is presented here – presumably with what goal? Additionally, check on which social media platforms *Zalando* is present. Which platforms are chosen? What could be the reasons for this? In what way are users invited to present themselves on these platforms? What content are users presenting here? What are the motives of the online users? In which fields has the *Zalando* offering been supplemented in recent months?

ℹ️ Reading and Deepening

- Chaffrey, D./Ellis-Chadwick, F. (2019). *Digital marketing.* 7th Edition. New York.
- Chaffey, D./Smith, P. R. (2018). *Digital marketing excellence.* 5th Edition. London.
- Kingsnorth, S. (2019). *Digital marketing strategy: An integrated approach to online marketing.* 2nd Edition. London.
- Stokes, R. (2018). *eMarketing: The essential guide to marketing in a digital world.* 6th Edition. Red & Yellow.

e-Commerce

Contents

© Springer Fachmedien Wiesbaden GmbH, part of Springer Nature 2022
R. T. Kreutzer, *Online Marketing*, https://doi.org/10.1007/978-3-658-35369-8_4

Learning Agenda

Which phases are to be distinguished in e-commerce? Which requirements for goods, information and financial logistics have to be considered when setting up e-commerce? How can the online presence for retailers be designed in a target-oriented manner? How can a convincing offer positioning be done before the development of an online shop? After reading ...

4

- ► Section 4.1 you will understand the basics of e-commerce and be able to classify its forms.
- ► Section 4.2 you can design the omni-channel approach in a communicative and distributive way.

4.1   Basics and Forms of e-Commerce

The following applies to every **form of e-commerce**:

If the potential customer cannot find an offer, he cannot buy!

Because it is much more difficult to "stumble" across an offer online if you are not specifically looking for it. That is why all the explanations, especially those concerning the areas of corporate website, online advertising, search engine optimization, e-mail marketing and social media, are the basis for the successful design of e-commerce. At the same time, e-commerce poses a dramatic challenge for every stationary retail business. Because with the world's leading online shop *Amazon,* every household with an Internet connection has a showroom and a sales counter, both of which are open 24/7 and 365 days a year!

Online retail websites have made strong traffic gains due to the global coronavirus pandemic in 2020 as large parts of the population are staying at home and ordering items online which they usually would purchase in-store. ► *Amazon.com* had a monthly traffic average of almost 3.68 billion visitors in 2020, followed by ► *ebay.com* with 1.01 billion visits on average each month. ◘ Figure 4.1 shows the leading retail websites worldwide – based on the number of monthy visitors.

Companies can **enter e-commerce** in different ways and to different degrees (cf. ◘ Fig. 4.2; cf. also Merkle 2020; Heinemann 2020; Wirtz 2020; Kollmann 2019). These options are available to start-ups, stationary retailers and manufacturers alike. A **first stage of e-commerce** can be the engagement of a company on **sales platforms** or so-called **online marketplaces** (such as ►

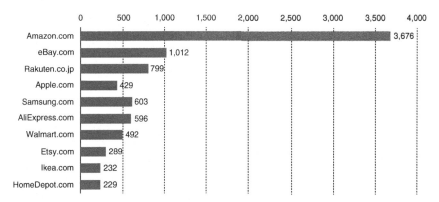

◘ Fig. 4.1 Leading retail websites worldwide by average monthly visitors – in millions

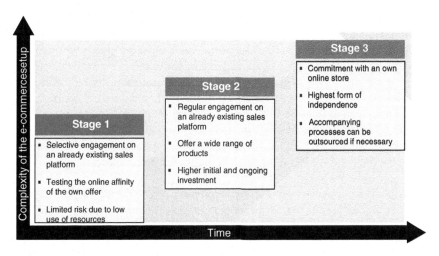

◘ Fig. 4.2 Process stages for setting up e-commerce

amazon. com, ► *ebay.com,* ► *rakuten.com,* ► *yatego.com*) that already exist on the Internet. For this purpose, the company does not have to establish its own online presence or the accompanying logistics processes described below entirely on its own. The articles to be sold are merely to be integrated into the already existing platforms. Communication and billing are often handled by the platform operators. Shipping is in the company's own hands, but can also be outsourced to the platform operators. This type of entry into e-commerce is thus a very quickly implementable and cost-effective variant. Such an approach can be chosen, for example, to determine the online affinity of one's own offering if this is not possible through an evaluation of already existing competitor activities.

A **second stage of e-commerce** is the continuous engagement on one or more of the platforms already mentioned, which is pursued with significantly higher resources. The various providers offer different ways to lead such a more comprehensive commitment to success in the long term. *Amazon* offers the program **Sell on** *Amazon*. *Ebay* supports here with a **premium shop**. A **professional package** is offered by ▶ *yatego.com*.

Finally, the **third stage of e-commerce** can be the **development of an online shop under one's own name** with the independent implementation of all or several of the necessary flanking systems (cf. ◘ Fig. 4.2). Solutions such as *Magento*, *Shopify*, *Shopware* or *WooCommerce* can be used for this purpose. Such a step represents a long-term investment in a new sales channel that can often only become profitable after a start-up phase of several years. No one planning such a move should be under any illusions about the large **time and budget requirements** *involved*. Without a **viable business plan** – with realistic assumptions! – such a project should not be tackled.

The figures shown in ◘ Fig. 4.1 therefore do not mean that all stationary retailers must necessarily open an online shop. If that were the case, many companies would only be in the red. **Entering the field of e-commerce** (also called "**digital shelf extension**") must be well considered. Often, several years of investment with simultaneous losses have to be managed before an online shop becomes profitable. And there is no guarantee of success!

> ❯ In a nutshell: An **entry into e-commerce** should only be tackled by those who have an exciting business idea and/or the sufficient resources (personnel and capital) to survive even a long lean period without endangering the core business!

The reason why correspondingly high investments for an online shop are to be expected is answered by ◘ Fig. 4.3. with a focus on Germany (cf. Statista 2020c, p. 13). The **drivers for online shopping from the customer's point of view** are shown there. For this purpose, 1550 people aged 18 and over were surveyed in Germany. **Free returns** and free **delivery are** named in the first places. In addition, **modern payment procedures** are expected. Customers also expect **detailed product descriptions, tools for price comparisons, transparent cost structures, flexible ordering processes** and **fast delivery** (cf. the

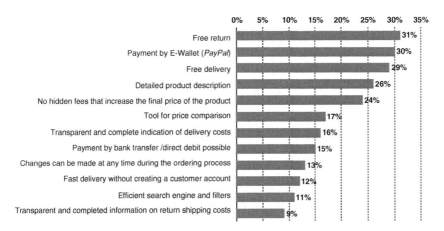

❑ **Fig. 4.3** Drivers for online shopping from the customer's perspective in Germany

customer expectations in ► Fig. 1.12). Customers can afford to ignore the associated costs on the part of the shop operator. The shop operator, however, may not do so.

The different **stages for setting up e-commerce** are relevant because establishing an online shop is not exhausted by having one's own web presence or purchasing shop software, as can be observed time and again. The biggest problems that many e-commerce newcomers fail with are the **procedural requirements of e-commerce**. These task areas can be described by the following terms:

- Information logistics
- Merchandise logistics
- Financial logistics

Of course, the **online offer** must first be convincing in order to demonstrate relevance for potential users. Pure me-too providers offering interchangeable products and services are quickly reduced to price on the Internet. Those who cannot offer attractive prices will not succeed in a transparent market environment. In contrast, niche providers who offer a specialized product range and thus address a precisely describable target group have a good opportunity to find customers and grow online. An indispensable prerequisite for all providers is that they have mastered the **logistics processes** outlined below and that this is ideally also reflected in positive customer reviews.

4.2 Information Logistics

The most important question of information logistics when setting up an online shop is: Should all or parts of the shop processes be outsourced or is programming and/or implementation in-house or under one's own responsibility planned? Companies have a variety of options at their disposal here. For example, a **rental shop can** be used, which is remunerated on a monthly and/or commission basis. This solution is based on the previous experience of third parties, so that teething troubles with the shop software itself are generally limited. Many corresponding offers can be found online.

4

Alternatively, **open source solutions** can be used for the development of your own shop software. Open source means, that the source code of the software used is publicly accessible. Various solutions available online can be accessed. Finally, a **shop software license** can also be purchased if the range of functionalities and/or the support intensity of the aforementioned solutions are not sufficient and the company is planning a strategic commitment with the online shop.

The transitions between the individual offerings are sometimes fluid because software developers also offer rental shops and many simultaneously offer other services. Software offers can also be hosted in the company's own data center (also called "on premise"), by the software provider itself or by an IT service provider. Such services are offered as **ASP solutions** (application service providing) or **SaaS solutions** (software as a service). In most cases, an outsourcing solution is initially recommended for start-ups because they often lack the necessary IT infrastructure of their own and their attention is primarily focused on their own offerings, the company presentation and the acquisition and support of customers.

Information logistics in the context of e-commerce also includes the **merging of supply and demand.** This is one of the core functions of search engines when providers have not yet achieved the importance that their domain address (such as with ▶ *amazon.com* or ▶ *ebay.com*) is entered directly or is recorded as a bookmark by the user. In order to support the online findability of one's own offers, the **shop software** used should be **optimised for search engines**. Only then can the content offered there also be indexed by the robots of the search engines. In addition, the shop should be entered in the relevant **online shop directories.**

In addition, **price comparison or rating platforms** can be used as an orientation for prospective customers to lead to one's own offer. Therefore, every online shop operator should monitor the opinions expressed there (keyword "**web monitoring**" or "**social media monitoring**"). The importance of these price search engines has led to the establishment of a new field of activity entitled **price search engine marketing** (PSM; cf. Kamps and Schetter 2018, pp. 247–250).

Another important task of e-commerce operators is to present their offers in an attractive way. For this purpose, not only **zoom functions** can be offered to display the products, but also **total, detail, side, back and/or 3-D views**. In addition, the possibility can be created to compile and view specific clothing collections online. A further development is the integration of a **product configurator** in order to implement individual preferences in product design. The Internet is the ideal platform for such **mass customization**.

In addition, a powerful information cycle in the course of **customer relationship management** serves to make the initiation and execution of business as professional as possible (cf. Kreutzer 2021a). This includes that all **purchase-relevant information** can be accessed online. This includes, among other things, the **availability of goods** and information on the planned **time of delivery**. It can be purposeful to provide alternative offers directly if products are not available. If the desired jacket in the colour red is not available, a comparable model in this colour can be offered as an alternative. If necessary, it can also be interesting to suggest complementary products (such as shoes to go with the dress or a book to go with the yoga set) to increase sales per transaction. Flanking the flow of goods with appropriate communication with **shipment tracking/delivery status** (i.e. "order has been received", "order has been processed", "shipment has been carried out") can not only avoid cost-intensive queries from the buyer, but also influence the customer's expectations in the desired direction.

In parallel, **help functions** can be offered to answer further questions. This primarily includes **FAQs** (frequently asked questions), where users search for solutions on their own and do not require company resources. In addition, appropriate **forums** and **opportunities for personal contact** can be offered. In addition to e-mail communication, telephone contact can also be offered, e.g. by means of a **call-back button**. Alternatively, a **call button** can be integrated into the website so that the user can establish direct telephone contact with the company. After entering one's own telephone number and the request "call now", the telephone contact is established within a few seconds. This immediate contact makes the filling out of an extensive contact form unnecessary. By means of a link between the respective website and the telephone system, the customer service center is immediately connected to the incoming telephone number. This minimizes waiting times when answering inquiries.

Another valuable support is **co-browsing** or **co-surfing**. This is the joint browsing on two or more computers with the help of a synchronization of the browsers. In this way, the online user can be guided through the company's own online shop with the help of a company representative in order to successfully complete a purchase process. Some companies now also integrate **chat offers via chatbots** or *WhatsApp* communication into their website.

Amazon shows a successful form of **customer-oriented communication.** After the order, the customer receives information from *Amazon* that helps to answer all possible questions of the buyer. Through this flanking information, the buyer is comprehensively informed about the status of the delivery, as all relevant areas are covered:

- **Confirmation of receipt of the order,** including information about the possibility to change the order
- **Confirmation that the ordered items have been shipped,** including the following options or information
  - Viewing of the customer account with the possibility to view and, if necessary, modify the order
  - Showing of the ordered products, incl. naming of the order time
  - Indication of the expected date of delivery
  - Information about the receiving address and the integrated logistics service provider
  - Reference to the possibility of parcel tracking by means of a designated parcel tracking number
  - If applicable, indication that part of the delivery will be sent separately
  - Reference to possible price fluctuations when paying with foreign currencies
  - Reference to the buyer's right of withdrawal (including offline and online address – in the case of the latter, in the form of a link to an online contact form)
  - Reference to the consequences of revocation
  - Information about the return guarantee and the return options (incl. link to further information)
  - Link to the general terms and conditions

What is achieved by such comprehensive, **transaction-accompanying information of the customer**? On the one hand, the customer feels well informed and thus valued. On the other hand – and this is at least as important for companies with a high customer frequency – the number of **customer-**

initiated contacts is significantly reduced by (more cost-effective) **company-initiated contacts** due to a timely provision of important information. Here, many questions are answered before the customer could even ask them! In this way, the important KPI **ConPO (Contacts per Order),** which is often decisive for commercial success, can be kept low. Every customer query reduces the profitability of a sales process due to the resulting communication costs, unless profitable follow-up orders are generated in the course of such customer queries.

For this reason, companies also anticipate the **FAQs** that may arise during a sales process from the customer's point of view and answer them in a proactive (i.e. anticipatory) communication. Explanatory videos are often used for this purpose. These measures keep a **company's support costs** down because appropriate "self-answering" reduces the need for written or telephone contact. An evaluation of the questions that occur at various customer touchpoints (such as in the customer service center or in sales) is very helpful in determining FAQs. The benchmark for the FAQs can be the already mentioned user defined as **DAU** ("dumbest assumable user") in order to cover the range of questions as comprehensively as possible. Another possibility to create a self-service for the users is the integration of a **buyer-help-buyer platform** in the own shop appearance.

4.3 Merchandise Logistics

Merchandise logistics encompasses all activities from **purchasing** to **warehousing, packaging** for shipping and the **shipping** itself to the return of goods. **Returns management** in particular, i.e. the acceptance of returned and possibly damaged goods as well as their re-packaging and re-feeding into the shipping chain, represents a major challenge for many companies. After all, many returns by customers contain damaged goods, which leads to a loss of sales due to low-quality returns. Often, such merchandise can only be sold at deep discounts – if at all. A problem can arise simply because the products arrive with damaged or without original packaging.

The logistics of goods is often outsourced by larger online shops to specialized external service providers. In addition to *Amazon, DHL* also offers corresponding services. It is important that the merchandise management system is linked to the online presence and the CRM system in order to provide real-time availability information. Such information should also be integrated into the e-communication with customers.

4.4 Financial Logistics

In the course of **financial logistics,** it is a matter of mapping secure payment flows. From the company's point of view, it is particularly important to **check the creditworthiness of potential buyers** (before delivery). Financial logistics must also include the further process stages up to collection and any necessary judicial **recovery of receivables.** From the customer's point of view, it is a question of whether **payment transactions** are reliable and whether bank or credit card data can therefore be transmitted securely.

Payments on the Internet can be made via advance payment, invoice, direct transfer, cash on delivery, direct debit and credit card or via specific online payment systems (such as ► *paypal.com*). Which payment method is offered to a customer may depend on the result of a credit check that takes place in the course of the online payment process. If a credit check is not carried out, a company may insist on advance payment, cash on delivery, credit card payment or settlement via an online payment system, especially for new customers.

4.5 Design of the Communicative and Distributive Multi- or Omni-Channel Approach

◻ Table 4.1 shows which forms of **e-commerce engagement** are possible. Various combinations of **communicative or distributive multi-/omni-channel concepts** can be seen here. Many stationary retailers have recognized that an online engagement is indispensable for the communication of stationary stores. The situation is different when it comes to setting up their own online shop. Such a step requires – as already mentioned – the necessary financial resources and the willingness to invest, if necessary over several years, before the online shop pays off. Many brand manufacturers not only serve wholesalers and retailers, but also enter into direct competition with their traditional sales partners with their own online shops. In addition, stationary service providers have developed the Internet as a supplementary sales channel for themselves. Other companies started out on the Internet and have supplemented their online involvement with catalogue-based sales or the (trial) establishment of stationary sales outlets. In addition, there are still pure Internet providers (Internet or digital pure players) such as ► *asos.com,* which – at present – rely solely on the online sales channel.

◘ Table 4.1 Forms of distributive multi-/omni-channel engagement

Forms of distributive multi-/omni-channel engagement	Example
Traditional retailers build online presence (no online shop)	*Many local retailers*
Traditional retailers build online shops	*H&M, Zara*
Traditional mail order companies build up online shops	*Bonprix, Conrad Electronic, Otto*
Traditional retailers and mail order companies are setting up online shops	*Tchibo, Manufactum*
Brand manufacturers build up online shops	*Adidas, BOSS, Esprit, Lacoste, Levi's, Nike, Nivea*
Traditional service providers build online shops	*ADAC, ATU*
Online shop operators build up a catalogue-supported distribution system	*Ebrosia, Zalando*
Online shop operators build up offline presence	*Amazon, ebay, MyMuesli, Zalando*

When **classic retailers** establish an **online presence without an online shop**, however, it is not possible to speak of omni-channel sales, even if the activities are comprehensively coordinated. It is rather a purely **communicative omni-channel approach**. In this case, it is important, to draw the attention of the online searcher to one's own offer. In order to prepare a visit to the brick-and-mortar store, the relevant information must be presented online in a way that is easy to find and highly topical.

For this purpose, it is necessary to present the **current brochures** or a more or less interactively designed **flip catalogue** (without ordering option) online. Parallel to this, **online platforms** can be used that additionally contribute to the **dissemination of information and offers from stationary providers**. These include ► *groupon.com*. In any case, it is crucial for the user to think about the **short- and long-term expected costs and returns** in the run-up to a corresponding booking. The ► *coupon-calculator.com* offers valuable support for this. It queries the relevant criteria and shows, for example, that a corresponding promotion can be profitable for the platform provider, but not for the offering company itself. Therefore, the calculation of a corresponding promotion is indispensable. This **coupon calculator** can also be used if the company – independent of the platforms mentioned – wants to use coupons.

A **local listing** is also important for stationary retailers. In order to offer many potential customers points of contact, they should be present with their locations on the relevant online platforms. In addition to social networks, these include map services, yellow pages, rating platforms and, increasingly, navigation systems. **Local listing services** can ensure that you are represented there with an entry. For this purpose, corresponding profiles can be set up, which, in addition to the important contact data, also include pictures, videos etc.

The old principle still applies here – especially for stationary shops:

4

> ┌─ **Notice!** ──────────────────────────────────────
> Only what is available online can be found online!

Stationary retailers see that due to the increasing importance of the information source "online", a web shop is becoming more and more significant to **secure the store business.** Potential customers often use the online shop to get a first overview and to check whether the range of services fits their own requirements. The online shop has an **information and orientation function** (quasi to support decision-making) and should, in the best case, arouse curiosity about the stationary store. However, an opposite effect can also be observed, which is called **showrooming.** In the case of showrooming, people interested in buying visit traditional shops in order to obtain information there – as in a showroom – and possibly also to try out or try on certain products. Afterwards, the "matching" products are ordered online. This is to be expected above all in the case of large (expected) price differences and high price transparency of standardised products. This procedure constitutes **theft of advice** because it deprives stationary retailers of their business basis. After all, retailers have to provide cost-intensive consulting services without being rewarded for it by the beneficiaries – through purchases.

An online shop can additionally contribute to the **expansion of the relevant catchment area** because regional borders lose their significance. At the same time, it has been shown in many cases that **omni-channel customers** who shop online and offline with the same provider often achieve a significantly higher **customer value.**

When **brick-and-mortar retailers** set **up an online store,** the following questions need to be answered:

- **Should the online and offline presence be under the same company retail brand?**
  - If this is the case, it is important to ensure **consistency** between offers and price levels in the online shop and in the stationary shop. If neces-

sary, existing price differences can be explained by different service levels. Through an online presence, customers who buy from the same retailer offline and online may become addressable for the first time for the stationary retailer, if the address acquisition in the stationary retailer has not already taken place via a customer card or similar. In this case, people can be addressed directly by the retailer and advertising material (e.g. catalogues, flyers) can be sent by post. If an e-mail permission is presented, **additional contacts** can be created regularly at low cost (e.g. with price advantages, coupons), further purchases can be triggered and, ideally, the customer can be retained in the long term.

– Through different **incentive programs,** purchasing behavior can be promoted either more online or more offline. Furthermore, an online shop offers additional possibilities for **staging the range of goods,** for example by presenting 3-D images, offering a product configurator and/or calling up videos of products and services.

▬ **Should the online and offline presence be under different retail brands of the company?**

– A separate brand presence in the online and offline areas is expedient if **different target groups** are to be addressed, possibly also with divergent offers and pricing. If significantly lower prices are demanded in the online shop in order to survive in online competition, a **two-brand strategy** avoids **cannibalization effects** between the channels.

– However, **cross-promotions** (online for offline and offline for online) cannot take place. This would therefore not be an omni-channel concept, but rather a multi-channel concept, because different channels are used in parallel.

However, the biggest **challenges for the stationary retail trade** result from the online shops that are being set up by **new providers** (such as *Amazon, ebay, Zalando) as* well as by classic mail order companies (e.g. *Otto mailorder house).* In addition, more and more manufacturers are distinguishing themselves by setting up their own online shops. Via discount campaigns that **manufacturers** initiate in their online shops – without consulting their retail partners – for identical products in order to stimulate their own sales, significant price pressure is exerted on established retailers.

Retailers are therefore well advised to critically analyse whether long-term profitable survival in this **sandwich position** can be ensured by a convincing online presence for brick-and-mortar retail and/or a stand-alone online shop. When setting up an **online shop,** every provider must strive for a convincing **positioning in the market** – just as with the stationary retail store.

An important contribution to this can be made by **carrying out a SWOT analysis**, which in particular includes identifying and analysing the relevant competitors and the expected market environment (cf. in-depth Kreutzer 2019, pp. 99–114). The **key questions** that every company must answer before setting up an online shop are:

- Why should a prospective customer choose my offer?
- How can my offer stand out from the competition?

4

Possible answers to these **questions about one's own positioning** can be provided by the following content:

- **Wide range of products** in order to be interesting for many target groups (e.g. full-range retailers such as ► *amazon.com*, ► *ebay.com* and *otto.de*)
- **High assortment depth,** in order to submit a large offer for completely special desires (e.g. dance shoes, clothing for large sizes)
- **High quality competence** through the offer of high-quality products (such as ► *ralphlauren.com*)
- **High brand competence** by offering all relevant brands in its own assortment
- **Price leadership** in order to achieve price advantages over the competition, achieved, among other things, by specializing in a few products or a certain segment of the product range (such as ► *primark.com*).
- **A wide range of services** (e.g. advice, customisation of products, 24-hour or same-day delivery, extended take-back arrangements, spare parts service, long-term guarantee – possibly for an appropriate surcharge)
- **Individualization of offers** through mass customization (e.g. for muesli at ► *mymuesli.com*).
- **Ecological orientation of the product range** (e.g. ► *hessnatur.com*)
- **Provision of interesting background information** about the own offer
- **Intensive prospect and customer support,** through which added value is created (e.g. individual advice for follow-up purchases)

The basic **questions about positioning** must be answered convincingly before designing an online shop in order to avoid a false start. A shop concept must be created, tested and implemented based on the defined customer expectations. Since the time schedule for the launch of a shop is often not adhered to, many online shop operators make a central mistake: they launch their online shop even though it is still in the shell stage and the "workmen" are coming and going. Interestingly, one would never do this with a classic retail store. And if they did, they would create an event out of it! In the online sector, you (unfortunately) often venture out of cover too early – and scare away the prospective customers who come to you first and perhaps have the highest affinity to your own offer. Those prospective customers who are driven away at the beginning due to an unconvincing performance of the online shop may never be won back. Because the competition never sleeps.

The following **options for action of a distributive omni-channel retailer** are to be examined for their relevance for the respective target group:

- Online research before visiting the store (**"webrooming"**)
- Buy in a store and have it delivered to your home (**"ship from store"**)
- Reserve/order online and then have it picked up in the store (**"click and reserve"** or **"click and collect"**)
- Retrieve further information online from the same provider via mobile device in the retail store (**"in-store research"**)
- Buy additional items online from the same supplier in the store using a mobile device (**"in-store ordering"**) – keyword "virtual product range expansion".
- Buy online and return in the store (**"return to store"**)

With this in mind, the following **guidelines for a successful online store** should be considered:

- **Provision of central information on the company** (incl. a – confidence-building – correspondence address in the target market).
- **Product presentations** that answer all relevant questions about the offer (incl. photos or videos of the services offered, in the case of clothing also information about possible combinations, if applicable).
- **Simple search option** for specific products or services or for corresponding groups. An error-tolerant search function ensures that even if product names are misspelled or incompletely known, a suitable hit is achieved. If necessary, a requirements query (e.g. colour, cut and size for clothing) can be made first in order to present the appropriate offer.
- **Smart purchase process** that has no distractions and answers all relevant questions early and transparently (e.g. on availability, delivery times, payment terms, payment methods, delivery costs, warranty services). This also means that only a few clicks lead to the desired purchase.
- **Simplified purchase process for existing customers** who log in with name and password. Delivery and payment preferences can be stored in a buyer profile here.
- **Personalized approach to (prospective) customers.**
- **Memory function for (prospective) customers,** so that they can access already made selections at a next visit in the online shop (e.g. in the form of notepads, wish lists).

- **Relevant payment methods** from which the customer can choose according to his own preferences.
- **Fast delivery** (customers often expect delivery within 2 days or sooner).
- **Presentation of trust-building elements** ("trust anchors"), e.g. quality seals (such as *Trusted Shops* or *TÜV* seal of approval), *ePrivacy* seal to document tested data protection (cf. ePrivacy 2021), easy-to-understand general terms and conditions, simple return options and/or, if applicable, references from customers; naming the number of customers served to date also represents a trust anchor.
- **Provision of transaction information** (e.g. about the delivery status, the planned receipt by the customer).
- **Offer meaningful FAQs** that cover the relevant questions of (prospective) customers, increase search success, and at the same time conserve the company's own consulting resources.
- **Dialogue and support services** to be easily accessible in the event of complaints and claims and to answer the questions of (prospective) customers relevant to a successful purchase (e.g. via call-back and e-mail functionalities, an online chat or co-browsing or co-surfing, *Facebook Messenger* or *WhatsApp*).
- **Cross-device functionality** so that the online shop can also be used via mobile devices such as smartphones and tablet PCs.
- **Linking to social media** to support an exchange of (prospective) customers with like-minded people and thus potential customers (e.g. through social bookmarks, "Like" or "Pin It" button, etc.).
- For omni-channel providers: **Reservation, pick-up and return option of the goods ordered online in the stationary store** (this additional procurement channel creates further sales opportunities for suppliers and customers).
- **Provide the budgets as well as the human resources** to meet the expectations of the (prospective) customers in terms of service delivery.

One way to present oneself to potential customers as a trustworthy online shop operator is to acquire the ***Trusted Shops*** seal of approval. Online shops that display this seal want to differentiate themselves from other providers by committing to buyer protection and customer service. Prerequisite for the award of this seal is a **certification of the online shop**, which includes the areas of creditworthiness, security technology, price transparency, information obligations, customer service and data protection. In Europe, more than 30,000 online retailers have already been certified; 20 million online shoppers use this service. Customers can contact the *Trusted Shops Service Centre* online, by e-mail or by telephone if they have problems with these retailers and thus have an additional contact person in case of emergency (cf. Trustedshops 2021).

As already mentioned, **retailer ratings** are also taken into account when awarding seals of approval. Independently of this, they also represent an important orientation factor, especially for new customers, because they promote the establishment of trust in a previously unknown retailer. That is why it is important for every online shop operator to look after its customers in an appreciative manner. While a disappointed customer in stationary trade often only ventilates himself in the private (offline) environment, online customers can make their displeasure known on rating portals for all Internet users to see.

The **quality of service** is therefore of particular importance when running an online shop. Since human-to-human communication is generally omitted here, the perceived service quality dominates as an influencing factor on customer satisfaction and customer loyalty in addition to the quality of the product range. Consequently, binding **service standards** must be defined for all service partners involved (internal and external), which are to be regularly checked for their achievement and the associated costs. These standards should also be incorporated into the remuneration systems in the form of the **service level agreements** (SLA) in order to make their relevance clear to all parties involved.

4.6 Form e-Commerce to m-Commerce and s-Commerce

The mobile Internet is leading to a smooth transition from e-commerce to m-commerce (mobile commerce), because online offers are also purchased via mobile devices. **M-commerce** can be characterized as business transactions of various types in which at least one of the transaction partners uses a mobile device in the course of initiating and/or carrying out the business process.

S-commerce (social commerce) is based on a connection between social media on the one hand and e- or m-commerce on the other. We speak of **social commerce platforms** when they enable people with the same interests to meet, exchange information and opinions and simultaneously access various online shops integrated there.

At its core, social commerce is therefore about selling services and products via social media platforms such as *Facebook* and *Instagram*. For this purpose, online shops link their presence in social media and the customer reviews and recommendations they receive with a direct option to purchase. In this way, it becomes possible for prospective customers to complete their orders directly where they come across an interesting product. An emotional (positive) appearance – created by the company itself and/or its customers – should be the **trigger for a purchase** here.

In this way, the customer journey should come to a conclusion (through purchase) as quickly as possible. Finally, the alternative is to search for an advertised product in the online shop, add it to the shopping cart and finally enter all payment-relevant data. Each of these steps represents a filter in which people willing to buy can get stuck – and not buy after all. How much more elegant is a click on the product and the immediate initiation of the payment process. This should turn a purchase into a real shopping experience.

In addition, these platforms often provide the opportunity to communicate directly with the corresponding brand and/or the company behind it. This is achieved through the classic **product review**. Companies should react promptly to both positive and negative statements. In addition, users can be invited to participate in **creative processes** related to the offer – be it fashion and decoration tips or cooking recipes. User-generated content also includes collages developed by users. These are posted online and include links to online shops where the products used can be purchased. The **possibility of such collaboration** offers identification potential for (potential) customers. According to the motto "Rattling is part of the trade", **advertising via and through social media** is also part of **social commerce**. Very well rated offers from one's own shop can be presented prominently or particularly exciting reviews can be presented – in this way, an emotional experience is reinforced. Finally, a professional use of **influencer marketing** can complement the activities.

The advantage of s-commerce for the providers is that the product or offer-related **exchange between like-minded people** and the **active integration of sales** via references to the relevant online shops go hand in hand. In the case of s-commerce, therefore, the sales-oriented intention does not have to be hidden, since references to purchasing possibilities are part of the rounding off of the offer of such platforms. Especially with fashion applications, a high conversion rate from viewing to buying can be assumed. Against this background, it is advisable to check the **integration into social commerce platforms** for your own company with a target group-affine offer.

4.7 Learning Control

🗨 Short and Sweet

E-commerce – a must for many companies! Retail is in a state of comprehensive upheaval these days. On the one hand, more and more retailers that started online are building stationary retail spaces. On the other hand, more and more stationary retailers see the need to not only be present with a convincing online storefront, but to build up an online shop themselves. However, the complexity and costs associated with such a development step must not be overlooked. Every decision to be made here must be strategically prepared and comprehensively reviewed.

❓ Let's Check

1. In which process stages can the development of e-commerce take place? Give concrete examples in each case and search for others on the Internet.
2. What are the possibilities of an online presence for a retailer?

❓ Networking Tasks

Analyse the goals with which *Amazon* opened its first brick-and-mortar bookstore in Seattle in 2016. What does *Amazon* hope to accomplish with it? Why did *Amazon* acquire the *Whole Food* retail chain in 2017? What are *Amazon's* goals with *Amazon Go* and *Amazon Fresh*? Analyse the targets of the offers of *Amazon's* basics and *Amazon's* essential products.

ℹ Reading and Deepening

- Chaffrey, D./Ellis-Chadwick, F. (2019). *Digital marketing.* 7th Edition. New York.
- Chaffey, D./Smith, P. R. (2018). *Digital marketing excellence.* 5th Edition. London.
- Kingsnorth, S. (2019). *Digital marketing strategy: An integrated approach to online marketing.* 2nd Edition. London.
- Stokes, R. (2018). *eMarketing: The essential guide to marketing in a digital world.* 6th Edition. Red & Yellow.

Supplementary Information

© Springer Fachmedien Wiesbaden GmbH, part of Springer Nature 2022
R. T. Kreutzer, *Online Marketing*, https://doi.org/10.1007/978-3-658-35369-8

Glossary

A/B test or A/B testing (also split run test) - An A/B test or A/B testing is a specific test method in which two design variants, e.g. when using a specific means of communication (such as an e-mail), are used in a real environment with regard to their effects in two structurally identical test groups (group A and B). In such a test, only one design variant may be different in the two alternatives so that the effect of this individual variant on the overall result can be determined.

Account - In online marketing, account refers to a user profile (also user or user account) in social media.

Acquisition - Acquisition is the totality of a company's activities aimed at approaching people and/or companies in order to persuade them to make a purchase. Customer acquisition measures attempt to gain new customers for a company. Acquisition activities can also motivate existing customers to make further purchases.

Act of purchase - The act of purchase is the completed purchase.

Ad - Ad is the short form of "advertisement", or for individual advertising media, such as a banner.

Ad click - A click on a linked advertising medium is referred to as an ad click. This records how many users were motivated by a communicative online impulse to click on a linked content of a website (e.g. an online advertising medium).

Ad impressions (also ad views) - The ad impressions metric is intended to indicate whether a user has made visual contact with the respective advertising medium. De facto, however, it is not a matter of recording the actual visual contact. Depending on the method, either the request for the advertising material is already counted, regardless of whether the user is still on the site at the time of delivery or not. Or the completed delivery of the advertising medium is recorded, where the user at least had the chance to actually see it. However, only if he had not already scrolled on or left the website.

Ad server - Ad servers refer to the technical infrastructure for the delivery of online advertising. Such systems can be used by website operators, marketers, agencies and advertisers themselves. The ad server delivers – based on different targeting variants – the selected advertising media when a website is called up. For this purpose, placeholders for the advertising are integrated on the website in the form of ad tags as a link.

Ad tag - An ad tag is a marker in the form of a program code on a website that addresses an ad server and retrieves an online advertisement there. This tag also gives the impulse to the browser to open a window in order to display the advertising banner that the ad server provides.

Address or address data - The address or address data is the central basis for many forms of dialogue communication (e.g. advertising letters, e-mails). The address usually consists of first and last name, title (for decision-makers also function and company) and postal address. E-mail addresses and telecommunications data (telephone and fax numbers) are also part of the address data.

Advertiser - cf. affiliate marketing

Advertising - Advertising is a communication instrument by means of which information, influence and control objectives with regard to the company's core performance are to be achieved among prospective customers, target and actual customers by means of specific advertising media.

Advertising banner - cf. banner

Advertising material - The advertising medium is the designed form of an advertising message, e.g. a TV/radio spot, an advertisement, an insert, an e-mail, a mailing or an advertising banner.

Advertising medium - An advertising medium is the medium that transmits various advertising materials to the target audience. Advertising mediums or advertising media include TV, radio, newspapers, magazines, Internet or cinema.

Advertising message - The advertising message is the core of an advertising statement that an advertiser wants to convey to the target group. It can be, for example, the formulation of the customer benefit or the problem-solving properties of a product or service.

Affiliate - cf. affiliate marketing

Affiliate marketing - Affiliate marketing (derived from "to affiliate" in the sense of "connected, associated") is generally an Internet-based sales cooperation. Here, a provider (the "advertiser" or "merchant") provides advertising material to another company so that this partner (the "affiliate" or "publisher") integrates it on its websites to promote the merchant's offer. This is an attempt to direct further advertising visitors to the merchant's website.

After-sales services - After-sales services are various services offered by a company to its customers after the purchase in the use phase. These include paid or free service hotlines, training, maintenance contracts and the like. After-sales services are intended to strengthen customer loyalty, generate additional sales and profits and, ideally, prepare and promote further purchases (more-sell, cross-sell, up-sell).

Algorithm - An algorithm is a unique set of instructions for solving a task. It consists of well-defined individual steps to solve a problem in a limited time.

App - App is a shortened form of the word application and mostly refers to application programs for mobile devices (such as smartphones or tablet PCs).

Backlink - Backlinks are links from websites of other companies or from blogs to one's own online offer, i.e., one's own corporate website.

Banner (also advertising banner) - Banners are a variety of different forms of online advertising, which are integrated into websites in a variety of ways. This integration can take place by embedding the banner in the layout or by (temporarily) overlaying the site with a banner. This refers to the advertising company as a hyperlink and is activated by clicking on it.

Behavioural targeting - Behavioral targeting is a targeting method based on analyses of the surfing and search behavior of online users in the past. Behavioral targeting distinguishes target groups, for example, according to the content environments (e.g. photo portals, hotel sites) in which a person is "on the move" online, in order to then provide them with content (e.g. advertising links, banners) that corresponds to the content preferred in the past.

Benefit - Benefit is the value of a product or service that a customer receives through the purchase or use of a product or use of a service.

Billboard ad - The billboard ad is an advertising banner with a size of 800 x 250 pixels and offers a large advertising opportunity within the website content below the navigation. The banner extends across the entire width of the website content and is therefore particularly attention-grabbing.

Blog (also weblog) - The term weblog, or blog for short, is an artificial word made up of web and log (book). Weblog describes an Internet notebook or diary on which private individuals or companies report on a wide variety of issues (from fashion to cars to cat care). Blogs are based on easy-to-use software that allows even unskilled users to publish their own posts online quickly and without cost. The content, known as blogposts or posts, is created and managed by the so-called bloggers.

Brand - A brand is the sum of all the ideas that a brand name or a trademark evokes in people (brand image) or should evoke (brand identity). The aim of a brand is to distinguish the products and services of a company from those of other companies through this brand.

Bounce - Bounces (from "to bounce" or "to bounce somebody" in the sense of "to throw somebody out") describe the undeliverability of e-mails which are sent to the dispatch address by the creation of messages of the corresponding mail server and thus become visible to the sender (bounce message or non-delivery notification, NDN). Since undeliverability can have various causes, a distinction is made between hard and soft bounces. Hard bounces are caused by permanent errors, for example, because the recipient's e-mail address no longer exists. Soft bounces occur when the undeliverability is due to temporary reasons, e.g. the mailbox is overfilled or there is a vacation notification.

Bounce management - Bounce management involves dealing with different types of bounces with the goal of reducing the number of bounces detected in order to maximize advertising impact.

Bounce rate - In relation to websites, the bounce rate quantifies the percentage of visitors who leave a website after a short period of time (e.g. 1–2 seconds) without having taken any action on the website.

In e-mail communication, the bounce rate refers to the proportion of unde-liverable e-mails in relation to the total quantity sent. A distinction is made here between hard and soft bounces (cf. bounce).

Brand ambassador - A brand ambassador is an often passionate advocate of a brand who positively highlights it in their personal and/or business envi-ronment. Brand ambassadors can be one's own employees, customers and/or other people (e.g. bloggers). If well-known personalities are paid to com-ment positively on one's own offers, they are usually referred to as testimo-nials or influencers. Such brand ambassadors are particularly important if they also assume an opinion leader function and have a large reach, i.e. exert a great influence on the purchasing decisions of others.

Brand building (also branding) - Brand building refers to the process of creat-ing a brand, in the course of which, among other things, the brand is identi-fied (e.g. by means of brand or word marks) and its content is defined. The aim of branding is to achieve distinctiveness and thus to differentiate one's own offering in the competitive environment. The development of a brand first requires the definition of the desired brand identity, e.g. by answering the question of what a brand stands for. In the further course of brand build-ing, brand building blocks such as logo, slogan, colors and tonality are to be developed. Through the integrated totality of the individual brand building blocks, a convincing brand identity is to be created, which is transported inter-nally and externally through the use of communication measures. Customers should perceive the brand as an important purchase decision criterion.

Break even point - At the break-even point, the sales and total cost curves of a product or other service offer cross. At this point, neither a profit nor a loss is generated. From the quantity marked by the break-even point, the revenue generated exceeds the costs, so that the company makes a profit.

Briefing - The briefing is the written or verbal description by a client of the objective as well as the framework conditions relevant to achieving the objec-tive. A briefing can refer to the development of a communication campaign, the establishment of a foreign branch or the development of a new product or service. Briefings can also be used by board members or managing direc-tors as well as by other executives as a target in the sense of an assignment to their employees. A briefing usually contains condensed information about the desired target state, available resources (time, budget, employees) as well as other relevant information (e.g. regarding competitor activities). "Brief" has the meaning of "short" – and the objectives addressed here should also be short and concise.

Browser (also web browser) - The term browser can be translated as "search program" and is derived from the verb "to browse". Web browsers are programs that allow you to call up and display Internet websites and other applications on the Web. Therefore, browsers are the basis for the use of the Internet.

Business model - The business model describes how a company operates and, in particular, the specific way in which it aims to generate profits or achieve a very specific business objective.

Business-to-business (B-to-B, also B2B) - Business-to-business is the term used to describe a market where the demand of businesses meets the supply of other businesses.

Business-to-consumer (B-to-C, also B2C) - Business-to-consumer is the term used to describe a market where consumer demand meets business supply.

Button - A button is a visual (button-like) representation on a website that triggers a defined function with a click.

Call-to-action - The request to users to perform certain actions is called call-to-action, especially in the online context. This call-to-action should be formulated as precisely as possible in order to give the user a concrete orientation aid, such as "order here" or "redeem coupon here".

Campaign (advertising) - A campaign is the totality of all designed advertising media and their use in selected media in a specific advertising period to achieve specific goals.

Campaign, multi-stage - The multi-stage campaign is an acquisition measure in which an attempt is first made to win over prospective customers for a specific offer. Only in the second or third stage is an attempt made to conclude a sale.

Campaign, single stage (also one shot) - The single-stage campaign is an acquisition measure that attempts to motivate the target person to make an immediate purchase. The objective here – in contrast to the multi-stage campaign – is not the generation of prospective customers or leads, but directly of customers. This approach is also called "one shot"; after all, "one shot" should be enough to achieve a purchase.

Channel - In marketing terminology, channels are on the one hand the communication or distribution channels.

On the other hand, accounts or user accounts (e.g. on *YouTube*) are also referred to in this way. Here, a distinction is made between user channels as the simplest form of brand channels and custom brand channels as more exclusive forms of brand presence.

In online advertising, delivery can be booked in channels. These channels denote specific genre-, offer- and/or target group-oriented summaries of websites.

Click rate - In online marketing, the click rate indicates how many users have clicked on a presented link. Such links can, for example, be part of the e-mail communication or part of advertising banners.

Click-through rate (CTR) - In online communication, click-through rate (CTR) refers to the percentage of users who clicked on a link – in relation to the total number of those who saw it.

Click-to-open rate - The click-to-open rate is an indicator of e-mail communication that determines the percentage of people who have opened an e-mail who have also clicked on a link.

Cloaking - With cloaking, the crawler of the search engine is presented with a different site or content under the same URL than the "normal" visitor. This second site is optimized solely for the requirements of the crawler (e.g. with an extremely high keyword density). This method contradicts the specifications of the search engine operators and should therefore be avoided.

Community - cf. online community

Competition - Competition describes the rivalry relationships between participants in economic processes in the achievement of a company's own goals. These goals can be pursued, for example, on sales and procurement markets, but also in the general public.

Confirmed opt-in - The confirmed opt-in is a concept for obtaining permissions (i.e. permission to contact by e-mail, telephone or fax) on the Internet. In this case, the interested party receives a confirmation that the permission has been received after expressing interest. This form of opt-in generation is not sufficient for evidentiary purposes.

Contacts per order (ConPO) - This success metric determines how many contacts were needed between a target person and a company to develop them into a customer.

Content marketing - The term content marketing refers to an orientation of marketing – and here in particular of communication – in which relevant and thus valuable content is created, provided and/or distributed for specific target groups. These activities are initiated with the aim of attracting or retaining certain target groups or motivating them to engage in a certain way in order to achieve overriding marketing objectives in this way.

Contribution margin - The contribution margin is the portion of sales that remains after deducting the costs directly attributable to the respective reference object (e.g. assortment, product, region, customer, sales channel) to cover all other costs and to generate profit.

Controlling - In the corporate environment, controlling is understood as a comprehensive control and coordination concept that supports the management or the heads of individual divisions and departments in their work by providing information, instruments, processes and systems.

Conversion - Conversion is a collective term that expresses that a person has reached another stage in the relationship with a company by taking certain actions. It therefore represents the transition from one stage to another, and this can come about through very different transactions or actions. For example, a transition from an anonymous website visitor to a prospective customer occurs when the visitor has left his e-mail address. Another conversion occurs when a prospect makes a purchase.

Conversion rate - The conversion rate expresses what percentage of visitors to a website have taken a desired action.

Cookies - Cookies are small files that are stored by the web server on the computer's local hard drive to identify the computer. In the further usage process on other websites or in subsequent visits at a later time, these files can be queried and the computer can thus be clearly identified. However, this cannot lead to personalisation if such information was not collected during the dialogue. Strictly speaking, a provider therefore only communicates with a specific computer, which may even be accessed by different users.

Corporate website - The corporate website of a company is the official online presence of a company. The homepage (start page) of the online presence represents the virtual entrance door to a company and thus becomes the main pillar of online marketing. The corporate website comprises the entire content of a company presented under one URL. The focus of a corporate website can be the company itself, its products, its services and the respective brands. In addition, links to the company's activities in social media, such as *Facebook, Pinterest, Twitter*, but also blogs, social bookmarks and online communities can be communicated here.

Cost per acquisition (CPA, also cost per conversion) - With this billing model, the advertiser must pay a defined price to the advertising partner if a person is acquired as a customer and thus acquired.

Cost per action (CPA) - With this billing model, the advertiser must pay a defined price to the advertising partner if the target person has shown a certain behaviour. Cost per action (CPA) is thus an overarching, rather imprecise term, which defines different actions of the user as a prerequisite for payment.

Cost per click (CPC)/pay per click (PPC) - In this pricing model, the advertiser must pay the advertising partner a certain amount per click (corresponding to the page view) of a user on an online advertising medium.

Cost per click out - With this billing model, a commission is only due for the advertising partner when the user clicks on an advertising medium embedded on the provider's site – often from a third-party provider. The hurdle for remuneration is significantly higher here, because the click on an advertising medium on the website of the advertising partner is not yet sufficient to trigger the payment of a commission.

Cost per coupon (CPCoup) - With the help of the key figure cost per coupon, the costs per distributed coupon can be shown. For this purpose, the total costs of a couponing campaign are divided by the number of coupons issued.

Cost per install - With this billing model, a commission is only due for the advertising partner when the user installs software on his computer for the first time. This can be, for example, demo versions of advertised offers.

Cost per interest (CPI)/cost per lead (CPL) - With this billing model, the advertiser must pay a certain price if a prospect is acquired by generating the corresponding address (contact address). The corresponding costs are invoiced by the online advertising partner.

The cost per interest (CPI) or cost per lead (CPL) key figure also makes the total costs of interest acquisition of a company transparent in order to compare these for different acquisition measures. To determine this, the total costs of interest acquisition – i.e. also the costs for the creation of advertising materials and the provision of incentives, etc. – are divided by the total number of prospective customers acquired.

Cost per mille (CPM)/thousand-contact-price (TCP) - The cost per mille value defines the amount an advertiser must pay to achieve 1000 ad impressions for an online ad.

Cost per order (CPO) - With this billing model, the advertiser must pay a certain price when a purchase is made. The corresponding amount is to be paid to the online advertising partner per order.

The key figure cost per order (CPO) can also be used to make the total costs of order acquisition of a company transparent in order to compare different order acquisition measures with each other. To determine these figures, the total costs of order acquisition – i.e. also the costs for the creation of advertising materials and the provision of incentives, etc. – are divided by the total number of orders won.

Cost per print out - With the cost-per-print-out billing model, the advertising partner is paid when the user initiates the output of advertising information via a print interface. This can take place, for example, at a self-service terminal in a bank branch or a department store, where the user – prompted by an advertising impulse – prints out information.

Cost per redemption (CPR) - Cost per redemption indicates the cost per coupon redeemed and thus per purchase act made. The value is determined by dividing the total costs of a couponing campaign by the number of coupons redeemed.

Cost per sale - cf. cost per order

Cost per sign-up - In some cases, it is not possible to make a direct purchase online (e.g. for larger purchases), because sales processes run through several stages or the customer is not willing to buy at the first contact. Here, cost per sign-up represents a meaningful remuneration criterion. A remuneration is paid to the advertising partner if the Internet user leaves his data by filling out contact forms. This can be done, for example, by subscribing to an e-newsletter or in the course of downloading information. Since in this case only one interested party is acquired, it can also be referred to as cost per lead.

Cost per view (CPV) - This cost parameter is used for video ads. This size corresponds with the CPC concept. However, the basis here is not a click, but the viewing of a video. Cost per view refers to the costs that are incurred per video when it is viewed.

Coupon - A coupon is a reaction medium in the form of an entitlement card with which the holder can obtain certain benefits. These can be, for example, price advantages or certain services.

Coupon display - In a coupon ad, a coupon is incorporated into a print ad as a response instrument. This is to be triggered from the ad and used as a response medium. By using a coupon, further desired information can be requested in a particularly elegant way (in addition to the postal or e-mail address, for example, also the telephone number or age).

Coupon booklet - In a coupon booklet, several offers from different companies are brought together in one booklet or catalogue.

Couponing - Couponing is a measure in which an issuer provides a selected group of people with a credential (a coupon), the use of which during a defined period promises a specific benefit if the target group engages in a certain behavior.

Crawler (also robot or bot) - Crawlers are the reading robots of the search engines. These robots are computer programs that search websites (worldwide), index them for search engine databases and thus make them findable. In addition to target persons (e.g. prospective customers, customers, suppliers, applicants, investors, etc.), they are therefore the second important target group that must be taken into account when creating online content.

Cross-media - Cross-media is a special form of using different communication channels within a campaign. Here, different media forms and genres are used in combined and/or staggered form and consequently interlocked with each other.

Cross-sell - Cross-sell aims to motivate a customer who has already been acquired to purchase other products or services from the same company. For example, a new car buyer should also take advantage of financial services from the same provider (e.g. financing).

Cross-validation - The term cross-validation describes the verification of the quality of the results of an (analytical) instrument, a model or practical experience. The results can be validated by repeating or comparing the results of other instruments, models or experiences of the same object of investigation, or they can be evaluated as invalid. If, on the other hand, different sources provide the same results, the reliability of these data tends to increase and with it their validity in the sense of their validity.

Crowdsourcing - The term crowdsourcing is composed of the words "crowd" and "sourcing" and includes the process of cooperation (e.g. with customers) to develop new service ideas or new products or services.

Customer card - A customer card is an identification card in the form of a plastic card that is used for customer loyalty purposes. This is a standardised card, usually the size of a credit card, which has various storage media (barcode, magnetic strip, chip). This makes it possible to identify the customer individually when using the card.

Customer cards, virtual - With virtual customer cards, no plastic card is issued, but a virtual customer account (e.g. via an app) is offered. Here, for example, loyalty points and the like can also be recorded.

Customer development management - cf. customer loyalty management

Customer experience management - Through customer experience management, companies strive to make the "customer experience" positive and at the same time create value for both sides. This "experience" includes all experiences that customers have throughout their relationship with a company. The customer experience therefore includes all experiences within the customer journey – across all customer touchpoints.

Customer journey - A customer journey is the "customer's trip to the company". This "journey" includes various phases that a customer goes through before deciding – starting from an initial contact – to buy a product or purchase a service.

Customer lifetime value (CLV) - The customer lifetime value represents the sum of the value contributions of a customer determined according to various criteria aggregated over the possible or desired duration of the relationship with a company. Often, it is only on the basis of such a CLV that a decision can be made as to which investments can be made in the long-term loyalty of a customer. The CLV can be determined for consumers and companies alike.

Customer loyalty - Customer loyalty is described as the goal of maintaining (valuable) customer relationships for as long as possible.

Customer loyalty management - Customer loyalty management is the systematic analysis, planning, implementation and control of all corporate activities aimed at the long-term preservation of (valuable) customer relationships.

Customer magazine - The classic customer magazine is traditionally produced as a glossy magazine or in newspaper format. Today, many customer magazines have an extension to the Internet. Despite its name, the customer magazine is also sent to non-customers as part of the prospecting process.

Customer management, value-oriented - Value-based customer management is essentially about developing concepts for selecting and processing profitable customer relationships. The measures of customer management are oriented to the respective customer values. The tasks of value-oriented customer management are the selection, development, design, maintenance and termination of business relationships with individual customers or customer groups – based on the value contributions generated in each case.

Customer relationship lifecycle - The customer relationship lifecycle divides a customer's relationship with a company into the three phases of prospect management, customer loyalty/customer development management and win-back management. The company's communication should be oriented towards the different needs of the respective persons associated with these phases.

Customer relationship management (CRM) - Customer relationship management is a conceptual approach to marketing that aims to provide holistic, individual customer-oriented support for target persons within the framework of the customer relationship lifecycle by means of integrated marketing measures. In essence, it is about the goal-oriented, mutually value-creating structuring of relationships with customers, based on the terms "customer", "relationship" and "management". The basis for this is a database that provides the information required to create added value in the relationship between the company and its customers. If the relevance of advertising messages for the recipient is increased by establishing a temporal, spatial and content-related proximity of the advertising influence, this is referred to as three-dimensional CRM.

Customer service center (also customer care center or more narrowly defined call center) - A customer service center is an organizational unit that handles a wide variety of incoming and outgoing communication channels from (prospective) customers. In addition to the telephone, this also includes communication via letters, e-mail and fax as well as the exchange via blogs, communities and social media.

Customer touchpoints (CTP) - Customer touchpoints are all points of contact between (prospective) customers on the one hand and the company on the other. Such touchpoints can be directly controlled by the company (company sphere), or they are beyond direct influence (non-company sphere). Touchpoints have a lasting influence on the image that a prospect or customer builds up of a brand, an offer and/or a company.

Customer value - Customer value serves as a benchmark for assessing the value of a customer relationship from the company's perspective. Monetary and non-monetary criteria can be used to determine customer value.

Dashboard - Dashboard is a control cockpit for management and/or marketing that provides detailed information about customer groups or individual customers. On the basis of such information, individualized customer approaches and support can be carried out.

Deep link - Deep links represent a category of hyperlinks that refer to sub-pages of a website – as opposed to surface links, which direct a user to the entry page of a website.

Delivery rate - The delivery rate shows how large the proportion of valid e-mail addresses or postal addresses is. It is determined by dividing the number of undeliverable addresses by the mailing quantity and multiplying by 100.

Demand - Demand refers to the purchasing power-based pursuit of the acquisition of certain economic goods; this means that a person who demands a product or service also has the necessary purchasing power to acquire it.

Dematerialization - Dematerialisation describes the process of converting analogue information and physical products into digital formats, which can be observed in many industries. As a result, these objects lose the limitations caused by their physicality (e.g. the need for physical transport in the case of money, images, texts and sounds). This overcomes physical boundaries that were previously of great importance in many business models and often formed their basis.

Desired customer - cf. segmentation, acquisition-oriented

Destination - Goals represent a concretization of desired states in the future. They thus provide the central points of orientation for human action.

Device - The term device usually refers to end devices such as stationary PCs, laptops, smartphones or tablet PCs, but also smart watches and other wearables (i.e. portable computer systems).

Dialogue marketing (also direct marketing) - Dialogue marketing is based on the guiding principle of market-oriented corporate management and provides a variety of instruments to support the implementation of marketing strategies. The dialogue marketing instruments aim at opening a direct relationship and thus a dialogue with the addressed target persons. Since "direct" reactions of the addressed persons are usually aimed at, the term direct marketing and dialogue marketing are often used synonymously.

Dialogue program - A dialogue programme is an on- and/or offline-supported retention concept that focuses on the communicative involvement of prospective and/or desired and actual customers in order to familiarise them with the company's own range of products and/or services through regular communication impulses and to motivate them to make use of it. The programs can be used for the support and retention of prospective customers as well as for the retention and further development of existing customers. Online and offline measures can be used for this purpose.

Dialogue/direct advertising - Dialogue or direct advertising is when communication instruments aimed at an immediate reaction or dialogue are used to achieve advertising objectives.

Digital pure player (also pure player) - Digital pure players are companies that are pure online providers. These are companies that only and originally operate online shops and are therefore not represented in the stationary trade.

Digitization - Digitization describes the entire process of converting analog information into a digital, electronically processable format. Not only data (e.g. customer information) and processes (e.g. consulting, sales, payment processes) are increasingly digitized and thus made available on a mobile basis, but also products that were previously provided primarily physically (e.g. CDs, books, videos).

Direct mail - cf. mailing

Direct response (DR) - The term direct response (in the sense of a "direct answer") expresses the fact that the viewer, listener or reader is to be directly stimulated to react by a communication medium. A corresponding call-to-action can be found in many online and offline communication media. Posters, flyers, TV and radio spots, advertisements, many online advertising media as well as the products themselves can call for an immediate response. Various response channels are offered for this purpose. In addition to the website, these include an e-mail or postal address as well as telephone or fax numbers, but also coupons and QR codes.

Direct response spot - A direct response spot is a spot on television, in the cinema or on the radio that is intended to motivate the listener or viewer to respond immediately (direct response). For this purpose, a telephone or fax number, a QR code, an e-mail or postal address or an Internet address is given, which the recipient should contact immediately. This call-to-action turns a TV spot into a DR TV spot and a radio spot into a DR radio spot. In cinemas, such spots often call for the purchase of ice cream and the like.

Display ad (also display advertising) - Display advertising (the term "display" means "monitor") uses the advertising space on non-own websites, i.e. mostly outside the own corporate website, to advertise own offers there. The most diverse forms of banner advertising are used for this purpose. However, depending on the business model, the company's own website can also be the delivery location for display advertising.

Domain (also domain name or domain address) - A domain is the name of an Internet presence or an Internet server that is assigned only once worldwide and under which it can be reached. It thus corresponds to the postal address of a company in order to address this company on the Internet.

Doorway pages (also bridge page) - Doorway pages are Internet pages that are optimised for the search engines with regard to a few search terms and registered there, which function as intermediate pages and usually automatically link from these to the respective web presence. This method contradicts the specifications of the search engine operators and should therefore be avoided.

Double opt-in - In the case of double opt-in – the most demanding type of permission – the interested party must click on a confirmation link after registering (e.g. for a newsletter) in order to communicate their expressed interest to the offering company a second time. This is why we speak of a "double" opt-in. Only then is an e-mail or fax message sent or a telephone contact established. This type of permission solicitation is the only one that is associated with sufficient legal certainty when obtaining a permission in many countries.

Download - When downloading, the data is tranfered to the user's digital device (laptop, computer, etc.) and can then be accessed even without Internet access.

Dwell time - cf. site stickiness

E- - The prefix "e-" expresses that something takes place electronically or specifically on the Internet or something is supported by electronic networks, media and technologies. Consequently, a distinction must be made here between communication and e-communication, mail and e-mail, coupon and e-coupon, commerce and e-commerce.

Earned media - Earned media refers to the content that companies have earned from online users through their activities – for better or worse. This is user-generated content in a wide variety of forms. Earned media includes posts in non-company and company blogs, forums and communities. Earned media also includes fan pages that users have developed and maintain on their own. To earn earned media, the call-to-action is to "inspire!"

E-commerce - E-commerce (short for "electronic commerce") is understood as the electronic initiation and handling of purchasing processes. These can include physical goods (e.g. flowers, clothing), non-physical products (e.g. e-books, music or software downloads) and services (e.g. hotel or flight bookings as well as music and video streaming).

Effectiveness - Effectiveness is about the question, "Are we doing the right things?" Effectiveness therefore examines whether a measure or an intermediate goal contributes positively to a higher-level goal. Thus, it is about the "degree of effectiveness" with regard to the achievement of the objective.

Efficiency - Efficiency is about the question: "Are we doing the things right?" Consequently, the input-output ratio is considered here – regardless of whether the result of this process contributes to the achievement of entrepreneurial goals. This addresses the "degree of economic efficiency".

E-mail marketing (also e-communication) - E-mail marketing comprises the systematic transmission of marketing-related information by e-mail to achieve marketing goals. One focus of e-mail marketing is often the goal of triggering a direct impulse to act or directing the recipient to the company's own online presence in order to carry out certain activities there. To this end, e-mails contain links which, when clicked on, establish a direct connection to other offers of the company available online.

E-newsletter - The e-newsletter is a variant of e-mail marketing that provides (prospective) customers and other stakeholders with information on a regular basis in order to achieve the highest possible level of loyalty to the company.

Engagement rate - Engagement rate is an e-mail marketing metric used to track all recipients who have taken action across all stages. Such activities can also be expressed separately in terms of revisit rates, repurchase rates and referral rates.

The engagement rate is a social media marketing metric that shows how many of the targeted people engaged with the presented content on social media. The forms of engagement include likes, shares and comments.

E-recruiting - E-recruiting means that the processes of personnel recruitment are supported by electronic networks, media and technologies.

Expectation management - In the course of expectation management, a consistent attempt is made to steer the expectations of the performance partners into a range that the company can also meet. Those who deliver more than promised will trigger enthusiasm. Those who deliver less than promised will disappoint customers. The guiding principle here is: Under promise and over deliver!

Eye-tracking - cf. gaze registration

Fan page - A fan page is a website or page in a social network (cf. account) that focuses on a topic, a person, a brand or a company in order to directly provide existing fans with information or to integrate them, on the one hand, and to attract new fans, e.g. prospective customers, on the other hand. Official fan pages only exist if the company, the brand or the person itself has created this page, manages it and thus presents itself.

Feed - cf. newsfeed

First screen - Increasingly, different communication channels, such as stationary computer, tablet PC, smartphone, laptop and/or TV are used in parallel. In this context, the communication channel – i.e. the "screen" – that receives the most attention is referred to as the first screen. If two communication channels are used simultaneously, the other device is referred to as the second screen. If three channels are used in parallel, the device with the second highest attention of the user is the second screen and the channel that receives the least attention is the third screen.

Followers - Followers are users registered on various social media who "follow" another user (person or company). Following refers to receiving future messages from the user.

Forwarding rate - The forwarding rate is a measure of the success of communication measures. It describes the number of forwards in relation to all recipients of an e-mail, tweet, post, etc.

Frequency capping - Frequency capping limits the frequency with which a person or, more precisely, an IP address is repeatedly shown the same or similar advertising, for example on a website or in advertising networks. This method is used for re-targeting. The number of advertisements can be limited for a visitor, for example, to four times within 24 hours.

Frequently asked questions (FAQs) - Frequently asked questions are questions anticipated by a company and published on the company website, for example, which may arise during a sales process from the customer's point of view.

Friendship advertising (also tip-a-friend) - Friendship advertising is a form of customer acquisition in which a customer – but increasingly also non-customers – wins a non-customer as a buyer. The referrer usually receives an incentive.

FTP - FTP stands for file transfer protocol and describes a protocol for transferring files over IP networks.

Gaze registration (also eye tracking) - Eye-tracking is a marketing research method that captures eye movements when viewing a template (e.g., an e-mail, mailing, ad, or website) to capture the information intake process for optimizing information delivery.

Geo fencing - The artificial word geo fencing is composed of the terms "geographic" and "fence". This is a (digital) fence that can be erected around a specific object. As soon as a person crosses this fence, certain dialogue processes can be triggered (permission-based).

Geo-targeting (also IP-targeting) - With geo-targeting, the spatial location of an online user is determined by identifying the dial-up node on the Internet. This makes it possible to offer location-based services that are geared to the respective location of the user.

Hardbounce - cf. bounce

Hashtag - In order to make posts on certain terms and topics easier to find for keyword searches (e.g. on *Instagram*), they are to be marked with a hashtag (#).

Hidden content - Hidden content is the term used to describe e.g. text with a font size of "0" or white text on a white background on websites. This method contradicts the specifications of search engine operators and should therefore be avoided.

Hit list, organic - In the context of search engine optimization, one speaks of organic hits or an organic hit list. This refers to the results determined by a search engine algorithm in the course of a search process initiated by an online user. The ranking on the organic hit lists results from a match – determined by the search engine operator – between the search terms used by a user and the content available online from various providers.

Hosting - Hosting or – more specifically – web hosting describes the provision of storage space for a website.

Household advertising - Household advertising (sometimes too narrowly labelled as brochure distribution) is understood to mean the delivery of flyers, brochures, catalogues and product samples, especially to private households. The delivery can – in rather rare cases – take place nationwide. Much more frequent is selective use. This concentrates on certain regions and in these on regional target areas which are selected, for example, on the basis of socio-demographic or micro-geographic characteristics with regard to an affinity for the offer.

HTML (also hypertext) - HTML stands for hypertext markup language and characterizes a text-based markup language for structuring content (such as text, images and hyperlinks) in documents. The individual pieces of information are linked by hyperlinks between the knowledge units known as nodes.

http - The abbreviation http stands for hypertext transfer protocol and represents a protocol for transferring data over a network. This protocol is mainly used for loading websites via a web browser.

Hyperlink (in short also link in the sense of connection, relationship) - Hyperlink means an electronic reference or cross-reference to another resource available online.

Image - The image (in the sense of a picture) is the sum of all ideas, knowledge, experiences of a person or a group of persons, which they have towards an object (company, service, product, brand) or towards a person or group of persons (actor, band, orchestra). The image has a high degree of action control.

Indexing - Indexing is understood as the inclusion in an index in the sense of a directory, which is created by a search engine, for example. These directories function like catalogues in which the information found can be quickly retrieved and evaluated.

Individualization - A provider achieves individualization when offers are geared to the specific needs of the user. The individualization can refer to the communicative approach (e.g. individual purchase recommendations at *Amazon*), but also to the offers themselves (e.g. an individually created muesli or perfume).

Influencer - Influencers are individuals who influence the purchasing decisions of others through recommendations and/or through the use of products and the use of services.

Info box - In the info box (also called direct answer box or featured snippet), *Google* summarizes the information obtained from various sources to present the searcher with a compact result. This is displayed above or next to the classic search results – in position zero.

Internet - The Internet is a globally distributed network. It is the basis for the use of Internet services that enable the international transfer of data in a wide variety of forms. Data is transferred via standardized Internet protocols. The terms "Internet" and "www" are often used synonymously for "World Wide Web" because the www is the most widely used Internet service.

Internet community - cf. online community

Interstitial - An interstitial is a form of online advertising that is displayed as an interrupt ad before accessing the homepage or between two pages when visiting a website. They often occupy the entire browser window and disappear after a few seconds to allow access to the intended page.

IP - IP is the abbreviation for Internet protocol. It divides the data to be sent into small packets and writes the unique address of the recipient in their head. This is called an IP address, which is uniquely assigned to the individual devices that are on a network.

IP targeting - cf. geo-targeting

Key performance indicator (KPI) - Key performance indicators (KPIs) are particularly important key figures that are used to measure the success of, for example, individual communication instruments or to evaluate the company's overall performance.

Keyword - Keywords are the terms that a user enters into the search engine's search mask. These keywords are important for website optimization as well as for the display of advertisements in search engines.

Keyword ad (also sponsored links and text ads) - Keyword ads are developed in the course of search engine advertising and placed on search engine results pages. These are purchased placements on these results pages, usually awarded via bidding procedures.

Keyword Advertising - cf. search engine advertising

Keyword stuffing - With keyword stuffing, the texts of the website as well as their tags and meta tags are "stuffed" with the relevant keywords in order to achieve a good ranking in the organic hit list of the search engine. This method contradicts the specifications of the search engine operators and should therefore be refrained from.

Keyword targeting - Keyword targeting refers to the specific delivery of advertising by search engine providers depending on the search terms entered by the user.

KISS ("Keep it short and simple") - KISS is the central guiding principle for the simple design of advertising communication, for example, in order to achieve a high level of understanding of the content by the recipients and at the same time to make it as easy as possible for the recipients to react.

Landing page - The landing page is the page on which one "lands" by clicking on an advertisement or hyperlink in the course of marketing campaigns. Landing pages are often specifically promoted as part of a campaign, ideally to facilitate the user's entry into a website. The landing page should ideally contain all the information needed to successfully complete the customer journey.

Link - cf. hyperlink

Location-based services (LBS) - The term location-based services is used to describe all communicative measures and services that a company tailors to the spatial location of the target person and plays out via (mobile) devices. This is intended to achieve greater relevance.

Log-in - Log-in is the registration of a user with a special service or a special provider. For this purpose, a combination of customer number, user name and/or e-mail address must usually be entered in conjunction with a password. Through a log-in, a personalization or individualization of the website content can be achieved.

Mail order - Mail order is a form of retailing in which goods are bought and sold "at a distance".

Mailing (also direct mail, advertising letter, white mail) - A mailing is classically a paper-based advertising approach to target persons by post. A mailing can be sent addressed and unaddressed.

Marketing - Marketing characterizes the concept of market-oriented corporate management and comprises the planning, organization, implementation and control of all market-oriented activities. Marketing can be understood both as a guiding principle of management as a whole. Marketing can also be understood "only" as a corporate function that is located in the company alongside procurement, production, human resources and others.

Marketing controlling - Marketing controlling is an integral part of marketing management and is intended to ensure the effectiveness and efficiency of market-oriented corporate management. It comprises the development and design of the organizational basis for marketing planning and controlling, the provision of decision-oriented planning and controlling instruments, the informational support of the planning and controlling processes as well as their coordination.

Marketing goal - A marketing goal is a desired state of a company, which is to be achieved through the use of marketing strategies, the design of the marketing diamond, the marketing execution with appropriate use of marketing controlling and the marketing organization.

Mass customization - Mass customization describes the mass provision of individual offers, which, in addition to the advantages of mass production for the company, also tries to take into account the customer's wishes for individualization – and this at an acceptable cost.

M-commerce (also mobile commerce) - M-commerce can be characterized as business transactions of various types in which at least one of the transaction partners uses a mobile device in the course of initiating and/or carrying out the business process.

Media planning - Media planning comprises the temporal and instrumental allocation of the communication budget to the available advertising media and means of advertising. The objective is an optimal distribution of the communication budget with regard to the communication goals.

Media sharing platform - Media sharing platforms allow to "share" media (such as videos, presentations, pieces of music, photos, texts, etc.) with others. Examples of media sharing platforms are *SlideShare*, *YouTube* or *Instagram*.

Merchant - cf. affiliate marketing

Meta - "Meta" means "standing on a higher level" or "superior". Thus, the term meta-data means that "data about data" is provided. Meta-data can be used, for example, to describe telephoning behaviour or the intensity of online use, without analysing the content of the telephone calls or the websites visited.

The meta-level itself describes the superordinate area of observation for the topic in focus. For example, the meta-level can be used to talk about how people interact with each other and what improvements might be necessary – again, independent of the content being discussed.

Mircoblogging - Microblogging is a form of blogging in which posts are limited to a certain number of characters (on *Twitter*, for example, to 280 characters).

Microsite - The microsite is thematically and formally an independent small online presence, which usually has only a few subpages and only a low navigation depth within a larger online presence. Microsites are somewhat independent of the parent website and are often used for temporary promotions for a product or service.

Mobile marketing - Mobile marketing includes all communicative measures that a company initiates using telephone contact via mobile devices in order to influence customer behavior. If the information or services are tailored to the exact location of the target person, this is also referred to as location-based services.

Monitoring - Monitoring stands for the direct and systematic observation, recording and supervision of ongoing processes and developments. The objective of monitoring is to intervene in the ongoing process on the basis of the knowledge gained. In monitoring, answers are sought to the following question: What is currently happening?

More-sell - More-sell aims to motivate an already acquired customer to repeatedly purchase the same products or services from the same company.

Multi-channel - Multi-channel refers to the parallel, often independent use of several channels (in the sense of communication or distribution channels).

Narrative marketing - cf. storytelling

Net range - cf. range

New customer acquisition - New customer acquisition refers to all measures that a company uses to motivate people or companies to enter into a buying relationship with its own company for the first time.

Newsfeed (also feed) - Via newsfeeds, companies provide users online with continuous information about news of all kinds. Interested users can subscribe to such feeds in order to be informed about the latest developments without having to visit the relevant pages themselves.

Noline - The term "noline" refers to the approach that all online and offline activities are developed in an integrated procedure, thereby overcoming the distinction between "online" and "offline". In this way, the often prevailing customer expectations are to be better taken into account.

Off-site optimization (also off-site search engine optimization) - Off-site optimization is one of two basic measures of search engine optimization. Off-site optimization includes all measures to improve the ranking in search results that are carried out on third-party websites.

One shot - cf. campaign, single-stage

One-to-many - One-to-many is a mode of market communication in which a communicator (e.g. a company) sends out a message differentiated by market segment. The persons belonging to a segment are therefore addressed in the same way. However, there are differences between the addresses of different segments.

One-to-mass - One-to-mass is a mode of market communication in which a communicator (e.g. a company) sends an undifferentiated message to the general public (the "masses").

One-to-one - One-to-one is a mode of market communication in which a communicator (e.g. a company) directs a message in a highly personalised and, if necessary, individualised manner precisely at a target person.

Online advertising - The term online advertising covers all advertising measures that are carried out via the Internet.

Online community - An online community is an online platform that allows interaction between users and also provides the possibility for users to contribute to the design of the community by posting their own texts, images and/or videos. In addition, contributions by other members of the community can usually also be used, commented on and/or modified.

Online communication - Online communication describes the communication policy activities of a company, which are supported by online media.

Online marketing (also Internet or web marketing) - Online marketing comprises the planning, organisation, implementation and control of all market-oriented activities with the help of the Internet.

On-site optimization (also on-site search engine optimization) - On-site optimization is one of two basic measures of search engine optimization. On-site optimization includes all measures that are taken on the website itself, whose position in the organic hit list of the search engine is to be optimized. This includes, among other things, a – from the crawlers' point of view – reader-friendly design and structuring of relevant and thus up-to-date content.

Opening rate - In order to determine the opening rate (e.g. for e-mails), the total number of openings in relation to the delivery quantity must be determined as a percentage. If an e-mail is opened 600 times for every 1000 e-mails delivered, this results in an opening rate of 60%.

Open source - Open Source means "open" in the sense that the source code of the software used is publicly accessible and nothing has to be paid for its use.

Opt-in - Opt-in is a process whereby the user must explicitly allow promotional contact (by e-mail, fax and telephone) and/or access to contacts, camera, photos, calendar, location, etc. by companies in advance.

Order rate - The order rate is a specific characteristic of the conversion rate and describes the percentage of orders, e.g. in response to an e-mail or a mailing, in relation to the quantity sent.

Owned media - Communication channels that are used directly and exclusively by the company are referred to as owned media. These include, for example, the corporate website, a corporate blog or a social media presence. The responsibility for the design of these channels lies with the companies themselves.

Package inserts - Package inserts are, for example, letters, catalogues, product samples, vouchers or special offers that are sent as inserts in mailings from other companies to prospective customers and/or customers.

Paid media - Paid media refers to media services that companies purchase from third-party partners in order to advertise their offers. This includes, for example, advertising banners, keyword ads and paid posts.

Pareto principle/Pareto effect (also 80:20 rule) - This rule is based on the realization that there are concentration effects in all areas of life that need to be recognized. For example, 80% of a company's turnover is often generated with only 20% of its customers. Or 20% of all products or services of a company achieve 80% of the turnover or 80% of the profit. The decisive factor is not whether the ratio "20:80" is achieved in each case, but rather that it becomes clear overall that in most cases there is no equal distribution.

Pay per action - cf. cost per action

Pay per click - cf. cost per click

Pay per click-out - cf. cost per click-out

Pay per install - cf. cost per install

Pay per lead - cf. cost per lead

Pay per print - cf. cost per print-out

Pay per sale (PPS) - cf. cost per sale

Pay per sign-up - cf. cost per sign-up

Paywall - A paywall is a mechanism by which specific content presented online is only released by the content provider after a fee has been paid or a subscription has been taken out. Various newspapers and magazines have now installed such a paywall for their content.

Permission (also opt-in) - A permission is a specific permission given by a prospect or customer to a company regarding the "permitted" way of contacting and/or accessing certain data. These permissions can be revoked at any time by the prospect or customer. Companies are generally legally obligated to strictly observe these permissions to contact.

Personalization - Personalisation is the personal, i.e. named, address of the user by an advertising company.

Podcast - Podcast is a made-up word made up of the most popular MP3 player, *Apple's* iPod (where pod stands for "play on demand") and the term broadcast. Podcasts are audio and video contributions that are distributed online and can be subscribed to. Podcasting refers to the production and offering of media files via the Internet.

Point of sale (POS)/point of purchase (POP) - Point of sale refers to the place where the purchase or sale takes place. These activities can take place online or offline.

Position zero - The position zero is the search result that is displayed above the organic hit list. The goal of voice search engine optimization is to reach this position.

Positioning - Positioning describes the desired and planned "position" of a product, a service, a brand and/or a company with regard to the dimensions relevant to the target persons in comparison to relevant competitors. The positioning is to be designed in such a way that the own product, the own service, the own brand and/or the company differentiates itself from the other offers available on the market.

Post - On the Internet, term "post" is used for contributions in communities, blogs, social networks, etc.

Predictive behavioral targeting - Predictive behavioral targeting is a specific form of addressing target groups in online marketing. Here, the provision of online advertising is aligned with the expected behavior of the online user. For this purpose, information on online usage behaviour is linked with further data from other online users in order to "extrapolate" to the expected behaviour or expected areas of interest.

Pretest - A pretest is a marketing research tool that is used to determine the effects of planned marketing measures – before they are fully implemented – in a test environment.

Profile data - For consumers, profile data provides information about demographics (such as age, gender), psychographics (such as lifestyle orientation) and the social life of a consumer (such as family situation, social media engagement). In the case of a company, profile data provides information about the size of the company and the respective industry; it can also include psychographic data such as expectations and wishes of the company's internal decision-makers.

Prospect management - The aim of prospect management is to acquire prospective customers, to develop a purchase intention in them and ultimately to persuade them to make a purchase.

Publisher - cf. affiliate marketing

Pull approach - With the pull approach, the customer is wooed to become active himself and thus explicitly request something (e.g. by downloading studies, white papers as part of content marketing). With pull messages, the initiative to transmit content comes from the customer.

Purchasing power - Purchasing power is the amount of money consumers have available for consumption purposes.

Push approach - With the push approach, the customer is provided with advertising messages without being asked. For example, advertising companies use rented address lists to send advertising messages to target groups. In their apps, companies also frequently request permission to send users so-called push messages. With push messages, the initiative to transmit content comes from the company.

QR code - QR stands for quick response. The QR code consists of a square matrix and contains data that can be read by mobile phones and other readers using software. Through a QR code, information available online can be accessed very quickly and easily.

Reach - Reach is a contact measure used to assess the broad impact of media. It indicates the proportion of people who come into contact with one or more advertising media or advertising materials. The quantitative reach indicates how many people come into contact with the advertising medium in a unit of time, regardless of whether they belong to the respective target group. Qualitative reach indicates the extent to which an advertising medium reaches the exact group of people it is trying to attract. Net reach refers to how many people have seen the advertisement at least once; multiple contacts are therefore not counted in net reach.

Reach, organic - Organic reach describes the number or percentage of posts (on *Facebook*, for example) that a company can play out to its own fans or followers without paying the platform operator.

Reach, paid - Paid reach describes the number or percentage of posts (on *Facebook*, for example) that a company can play out by paying the platform operator.

Reactance - Reactance occurs when an individual feels exposed to an unwanted influence and withdraws from the expected behavior through a defiant reaction. Reactance is the opposite of acceptance.

Reaction - cf. response

Reaction amplifier - cf. response amplifier

Receiver orientation - In corporate communication, one speaks of recipient orientation when messages are directed at the target persons. In this case, content is designed in such a way that, for example, the focus is on the benefits of the advertised object from the customer's point of view. Through a consistent recipient orientation, a higher relevance of the messages can be achieved – in the eyes of the recipients.

Recommendation engine - A recommendation engine is an algorithm. It derives personal recommendations for individual persons or groups of persons from the previous purchasing behavior of all customers. Classic shopping cart analyses can be used for this purpose. Today, artificial intelligence algorithms are increasingly used in this area. Since these recommendations are automatically determined by a system, the term "recommendation engine" is used.

Recommendation rate - The recommendation rate indicates how many of the users or non-users of an offer have recommended it to others.

Rectangle - Rectangles are online advertising banners that are placed directly in the editorial environment of websites and are surrounded by several pages of editorial content. This is intended to increase their credibility.

Redemption rate - The redemption rate shows the number of people in percent who redeemed a coupon out of the total number of people addressed (e.g. in a coupon distribution).

Referrer - Referrers (from "to refer") are the URLs of the pages from which a user clicked on the website to be analyzed. These can be, for example, the hit lists of search engines, keyword ads or advertising banners.

Relaunch - A relaunch (in the sense of a "new start") is a strategy for extending the product lifecycle – mainly initiated at the end of the saturation phase. In the sense of this relaunch, the product design as well as other elements of the marketing diamond are often adapted to specific target groups. A relaunch can also be carried out analogously for services.

Reminder - A reminder is a hint to a target person (e.g. after receiving a catalogue or an e-mail) to make a purchase or fill out a form. A reminder therefore refers to a previous advertising activity of a company.

Reporting - Reporting is about the preparation of central company data through reports. For example, it is necessary to document which customers have ordered or cancelled a particularly large number of orders and which have been newly acquired. Reporting is essentially about the question: What happened?

Repurchase rate - The repurchase rate indicates the percentage of buyers of a product or service who make another purchase within a certain period of time.

Request rate - The request rate is a specific characteristic of the conversion rate and describes the percentage of, for example, information requests in response to an e-mail in relation to the quantity sent.

Response (also reaction) - Response is the reaction of a target person. The response can be a query, a request for information, a recommendation or an order.

Response amplifier - A response amplifier is a benefit designed to motivate the recipient of an advertising message to respond. Consequently, a response amplifier is intended to increase response. A response amplifier can be a time-limited discount or a gift that is promised to the responder. If the response is to be as fast as possible, the speed of the recipient's response is rewarded. Then, for example, the first 100 senders receive a special reward. In this case, one also speaks of a speed premium or an early bird incentive.

Response element - A response element offers the recipient of a message the opportunity to react. A response element can, for example, be designed as a coupon, reply card or order form.

Response management - Response management includes all the measures that are used to record and process the response from marketing activities. Response management concludes with a response analysis.

Response media, classic - The classic response media include above all TV, radio, newspapers and magazines. Spots and advertisements placed there become dialogue measures if they are aimed at an immediate response. This can be done by providing a telephone number, a QR code, an e-mail or Internet address or a postal address. In this way, spots become DR spots and ads become DR ads, where DR stands for direct response. Through these measures, the classic media become response media.

Response rate - The response rate indicates how many recipients responded directly to an e-mail, mailing or other type of direct response advertising medium. To determine this, the number of responses is reported as a percentage of the mailing volume. Responses can be orders, arrangements of visit or test drive appointments, retrieval of information as well as referrals.

Response rate (also reaction rate) - The response rate is a central key figure in marketing. It shows in percentages how many responses were recorded in relation to the advertising media used, for example.

Responsive (Web) design - The goal of responsive (Web) design is an "optimal" view of the website ("viewing experience") regardless of which device is used. For this purpose, the content of a website, but also of an e-newsletter, for example, automatically adapts to the size of the end device used. This makes it easier to read and navigate a website or an e-newsletter.

Retail media - Retail media refers to the possibility of placing ads within online shops and on marketplaces (such as *Amazon, ebay, Otto Group Media* and *Zalando*).

Re-targeting - Re-targeting is the name given to a tracking process in which an online visitor to a website is marked to be retargeted with targeted advertising on the same or other websites in order to increase the conversion rate. The core target group of re-targeting consists of visitors to a website who have taken certain actions there without completing the company's preferred transaction. Users are (usually) marked by cookies when they visit certain websites and are later identified by them on other websites. There they are then shown again the corresponding products or services of the visited website as part of an advertising network. This is an attempt to motivate users to make further conversions that did not occur during the first visit.

Return - A return is a letter or merchandise item that was undeliverable for some reason.

Return on investment (ROI) - Return on investment is a key indicator for determining the profitability of an investment. For this purpose, the profit achieved is set in relation to the investment amount. The key figure return on investment is expressed as a percentage.

Retweet - Retweets are the tweets forwarded to one's followers by other users on the microblogging service *Twitter*.

Revenue per visit (RPV)/revenue per visitor (RPV) - The key figure vevenue per visit shows how much revenue was generated per website visitor or per website visit.

Rich media - Rich media refers to Internet content that is visually or acoustically enhanced by the integration of video, audio and/or other animation elements. This is intended to increase engagement with the content and thus the viewing time.

Robots - cf. crawler

Roseshower - A roseshower is the counterpart of the shitstorm. In a roseshower, a large number of positive messages about a product, a service, a brand or a company are spread virally.

RSS feed - RSS stands for really simple syndication. So-called RSS feeds offer users the possibility of being regularly informed about new information on a website. For this purpose, the contents prepared in a standardized, machine-readable form can be subscribed to.

Sales letter - cf. mailing

Scalability - We speak of good scalability when, for example, software can also be used for other tasks or for a larger amount of data without incurring disproportionately high additional costs. In the context of advertising, scalability refers, for example, to the phenomenon that multiplying online advertisements does not itself cause (large) expenses. Additional costs are only incurred due to the additional click costs, which, however, also go hand in hand with a desired advertising effect.

Scattering loss - Scatter losses are non-targeted contacts in advertising measures. These occur when people or companies are confronted with an advertising medium (a TV spot, an ad, an advertising banner or a mailing) although they do not belong to the target group. This is a case of misdirection, which should be reduced as far as possible by optimization measures.

Search engine advertising (SEA) (also keyword advertising, sponsored links) - With search engine advertising, companies place advertising banners to appear on the search engine's result pages for matching search queries.

Search engine optimization (SEO) - Through search engine optimization, companies try to achieve good rankings in the organic hit lists of search engine providers due to a specific design of their online presence as well as through measures on third-party websites.

Second screen - cf. first Screen

Segmentation, acquisition-oriented - In the course of an acquisition-oriented segmentation, the company defines which persons or companies or groups the own company would like to win as customers ("definition of the prey scheme"). This definition of the acquisition focus is not only important for the design of the marketing concept, but also for the definition of the relevant information needs and for the selection of the marketing instruments to be used for the acquisition.

Segmentation, microgeographic - In microgeographic segmentation, a large amount of information is brought together at the smallest geographic level in order to either evaluate one's own customer base or to enter into the acquisition of new customers in a targeted manner. This segmentation is based on area-wide databases that compile as much information as possible about consumers on a small-scale structure (on a cell basis) that is relevant to purchasing behavior. The households grouped together in a cell are regarded as homogeneous and are given a "stamp" in the sense of being assigned to a certain pattern of characteristics and behaviour. The reason why different households in a small cell are considered homogeneous is the so-called neighbourhood hypothesis. This hypothesis assumes that people live in areas where "like-minded" people have already settled (motto: "birds of a feather flock together").

Segmentation, transaction-oriented - A transaction-oriented segmentation can be carried out for the already acquired leads and customers of a company. This segmentation is based on information already gained in the course of transactions between leads and customers on the one hand and the company on the other. Transaction-oriented segmentation allows a much greater depth and sharpness in the segment description and processing than acquisition-oriented segmentation.

Sentiment - "Sentiment" means "mood" and describes the positive, neutral or negative statements regarding a person, a company, a product, a service or a brand in social media. By means of corresponding sentiment analyses, the posts in the social media can be evaluated on the basis of their tonality.

SERPs (search engine result pages) - The term search engine result pages (SERPs) is used to describe the results achieved by a search engine, which include the organic hit lists as well as the keyword ads, the info box and, if applicable, shopping results.

Service - Services are non-tangible goods, such as the advice of a company or the services of a hairdresser.

Shipping quantity - The total number of units sent, e.g. mailings, e-mails, newsletters or coupons, is referred to as the dispatch quantity.

Shitstorm - A shitstorm is a phenomenon of social media and refers to the mass emergence ("storm") of critical statements ("shit") against companies, certain offers and/or persons.

Showrooming - In the case of showrooming, prospective buyers visit traditional offline stores to obtain information – as in a showroom – and possibly also to try out or try on certain products. The purchase is then completed via the Internet. Showrooming therefore goes hand in hand with theft of advice.

Sign-up - When signing up, the user actively communicates his data to the company. This often takes the form of an entry in a mailing list for regular receipt of a newsletter, for receipt of a customer card, when downloading an app or when making a purchase in an online shop.

Silo - In management, a silo in connection with information and processes is understood to mean thinking in closed units (such as departments or specialist areas). One speaks of a silo mentality, for example, when people do not want to share the information they hold with other people or areas.

Single opt-in - The single opt-in is a concept for obtaining permission to be contacted by e-mail, fax or telephone. In this case, a prospective customer informs us that he is interested in receiving an e-mail newsletter, for example. With single opt-in, this order/registration does not have to be confirmed again as with double opt-in. However, this procedure is not legally secure and is not sufficient in the event of legal disputes regarding the legality of an advertising approach. A double opt-in is required here.

Single view of customer (also single point of information or single point of truth) - The single view of customer is about creating a uniform view of leads and customers in terms of systems and data technology – regardless of which channel was used to obtain which information. In essence, it is about creating a customer database in which this different information is consolidated and recorded in a way that can be evaluated.

Site stickiness - cf. stickiness

Sitemap (also page overview) - A sitemap is a clear and complete presentation of the individual documents or websites of an online presence. In addition to the overall structure, the hierarchical links between the individual pages of the website are often shown. Sitemaps are intended to make it easier for users and search engines to find content. They are an example of meta data.

Skyscraper - Skyscrapers are banners that resemble skyscrapers because of their shape (high and narrow) and are usually seen on the right edge of the website.

Sleeper rate - The sleeper rate is the percentage of issued customer cards that are not used or not used with the desired frequency. The sleeper rate is also used for apps when referring to the percentage of those who have downloaded an app but do not use it.

Social bookmarking - Social bookmarking refers to the possibility of marking interesting websites and informing other users about one's own website preferences.

Social commerce/s-commerce) (also referral commerce or social shopping) - Social commerce is a specific form of e-commerce that contains a "social component" through the active involvement of other users in the purchasing process. Central elements of s-commerce are customer participation in the design or sales via recommendations from other customers.

Social log-in - Social log-ins are used to facilitate the registration process for users and at the same time to gain access to further user data. With social log-ins, the user's existing log-in information (e.g. from social networks, *Microsoft* or *Google*) is used to log in to third-party websites. This means that the user does not have to create a new account for each new platform protected by a log-in.

Social media (also social sites) - The term social media covers online media and technologies that enable users to exchange information online, which goes far beyond classic e-mail communication and has a high degree of interaction. In addition to social networks and media sharing platforms, examples of social media include blogs, online forums and online communities.

Social media marketing - Social media marketing encompasses the planning, organization, implementation and control of measures in which a company uses social media to achieve marketing goals.

Social media targeting - Social media targeting refers to the narrowing down and reaching of target groups in social media. The provision of online advertising is based on the information published about and by the user in the social networks.

Social networks - Social networks represent a form of social media, which is characterized by the networking of registered users. The presentation through created user profiles and the sending of messages to specific persons are particularly characteristic.

Social plugin - Social plugins are functions of social media platforms that can be integrated on your own websites. Probably the most important social plugin is the "Like" button from *Facebook*. It allows visitors to interact with the network via the simple click of such a button. They also serve as tools to offer users personalized user experiences on one's own website, as these are also shared outside of social networks through interaction with social plugins.

Social signals - Social signals are expressions and activities that users show on social media. The central social signals are likes, shares and comments.

Social sites - cf. social media

Softbounce - cf. bounce

Spam - Unsolicited e-mails are referred to as spam. The term is derived from spiced ham, sometimes also spiced pork and meat, because the unwanted e-mails – just like the canned meat mentioned – are pushed into the mailbox. The mass sending of unsolicited advertising e-mails that often underlies this is referred to as spamming or spamming.

Spider - cf. crawler

Split run test - cf. A/B test

Sponsor link - cf. keyword advertising

Sponsored link - cf. keyword advertising

Stakeholder - The term "stakeholder" is derived from "to have a stake in something". The stakeholders of a company include the employees, the customers, the cooperation partners, the shareholders, but also society as a whole.

Stickiness - The term stickiness is derived from the verb "to stick". Site stickiness is often used to measure the success of online presences and refers to the average time spent on a website. This is also referred to as "time on site".

Storytelling - In storytelling, values and information are conveyed through a narrative story in order to reach customers emotionally with the advertising message. The prescriptive function sets standards and thereby defines what the relevant values of the company and brand are. The descriptive function additionally provides an idea of the form in which values can be lived out in concrete terms.

Strategy - Strategies are characterized as the fundamental, long-term behavior and orientation of the company and relevant sub-areas towards their environment in order to achieve the long-term goals of the company. Here, the entire company, complete strategic business fields (SBFs) or strategic business Units (SBUs) are often the focus of strategy development. Strategies involve the development of concepts for the long-term creation, safeguarding and exploitation of success potentials. These set the framework for operational planning. Strategic tasks also include the design of systems that underlie entrepreneurial activities. This includes, for example, a re-organization, i.e. the revision of the organizational structure, which is reflected in the company's organizational chart. But it also includes the further development of the process organization, as it underlies planning, implementation and controlling.

Streaming - Streaming refers to a data transmission in which audio or video content is received from a computer network and played back at the same moment.

SWYN - SWYN stands for "share with your network" and describes the sharing of content via *Facebook* or *Twitter*, for example. This is also referred to as social sharing.

Tag - A tag is a label or marking of a dataset with additional information. In the process of tagging, databases are provided with suitable keywords or categories. As a rule, this is intended to ensure easier retrieval. Hashtags (#) are often used for tagging.

Target customer - cf. segmentation, acquisition-oriented

Target definition - For a precise definition of a goal, the goal content (What is to be achieved?), goal extent (How much is to be achieved?), time horizon (By when is it to be achieved?) and scope of a goal (Where is it to be achieved?) must be fixed.

Target group - The target group represents a defined group of people and/or companies who are to be addressed, for example, with an advertising campaign.

Target group selection - In the course of a target group selection, it is determined which prospect and/or customer groups are to be processed by instruments of the marketing diamond. The selection of the target groups is based – like the design of the instruments – on the company and marketing objectives.

Targeting - The exact addressing of target groups is referred to as targeting. The most important prerequisite for this is the determination of the target group in advance of any advertising campaign.

Telephone marketing - Telephone marketing describes the totality of marketing activities that are carried out and supported by the use of the telephone.

A distinction is made between active (outbound) and passive (inbound) telephone marketing.

Template - A template is a frame for the design of the communication. This template determines, for example, where the logo, photos, body text, etc. are to be positioned and which font type and font size are to be used. Templates can be developed for e-mails, e-newsletters, flyers, mailings, advertisements, etc. to ensure a recognizable handwriting in the communication.

Text ad - cf. text link

Text link - A text link is a text ad that is directly linked to the advertiser's website. Such a text link can either be integrated in the editorial content of a website or in the navigation bar. It is distinguished from the actual content of the website by the addition "advertisement". With this form of online advertising, there is a risk that the boundaries between editorial and advertising content become blurred.

Third screen - cf. first screen

Thousand-contact-price (TCP) - cf. cost per mille

Tonality - Tonality is the basic tone of address of advertising messages, for example. The brand tonality is part of the brand identity and should take into account not only the personality traits of a brand but also its experiences and relationship characteristics.

We also speak of tonality in the posts of users on social networks in order to evaluate the different moods or sentiments of the expressions of opinion.

Twitter - *Twitter* is an information service on the Internet. Registered users can enter their own text messages (maximum 280 characters) and forward them to others. This communication process is called twittering (equivalent to "tweeting"). The posts are called tweets (equivalent to "beeping"), are displayed as a chronological list and can be subscribed to and forwarded (retweeted) by interested persons (followers).

Unsubscribe rate - The unsubscribe rate is a metric for measuring the success of e-mail campaigns. It describes the ratio of the number of unsubscribes in relation to all recipients of an e-mail. It is calculated by multiplying the number of unsubscribes of the last e-mail newsletter by 100 and dividing it by the number of all recipients (i.e. the mailing quantity, reduced by the number of bounces) of this newsletter.

Up-sell - Up-sell aims to motivate an already acquired customer to purchase higher value products or services from the same company.

URL - URL is the abbreviation for uniform resource locator. URL is colloquially translated as web or Internet address (e.g. ▶ *audi.com*). A URL can identify and locate a resource/website via the access method to be used, such as the network protocol used (http or FTP).

Usability - Usability means "user-friendliness" or "ease of use" and refers, for example, to a corporate website. A high usability is advantageous from the customer's point of view and should therefore be strived for. Among other things, it consists of the process of navigation, clarity and the relevance and timeliness of the content.

User-generated content - Internet content that is generated by "normal" users of a site is referred to as user-generated content. This includes, for example, texts, photos, audio files and videos from customers, but also social signals in the form of comments and ratings.

Visit - Visits are used to indicate the number of visits to a website. As long as a visitor makes several page impressions within the same website, this is shown as only one "visit". The allocation of several page impressions to one user can be done, for example, via the IP address or cookies. Visits are to be distinguished from unique visits.

Voice marketing - Voice marketing describes the planning, implementation and control of all company activities aimed at current and potential markets that use spoken language and/or voice engines as a communication, sales and distribution channel in order to establish, maintain and further develop profitable customer relationships in the long term.

Wallpaper - The wallpaper is composed of a super banner (a large-format banner) and a skyscraper. It frames the editorial content at the top and on the right edge.

Web - The term web is the abbreviation for World Wide Web (www).

Web 2.0 - Web 2.0 describes an evolutionary stage with regard to the offer and use of the Internet. Instead of the pure dissemination of information, the participation of the user comes to the fore. The consumer thus takes on an active role and consequently becomes a prosumer – a mixture of producer and consumer. This is why the term "participatory web" is used instead of Web 2.0.

Web browser - cf. browser

Web monitoring - Web monitoring involves a systematic evaluation of the contributions made by online users in Web 2.0. Through this, a company can receive feedback regarding its own performance or even impulses for innovation management. A simple way of web monitoring is the installation of *Google Alert*.

Weblog - cf. blog

Website - In the Internet, website refers to the location of an Internet presence, which usually consists of a large number of pages.

Wiki - Wikis (like *Wikipedia*) are pages published on the Internet that allow easy editing of content by users due to a simplified syntax.

Win-back management - Win-back management is about renewing an endangered or declining relationship between a customer and a company in order to retain (valuable) customers. Various measures can be used for this purpose, e.g. so-called win-back calls.

World Wide Web (www) - cf. Internet

Zero click search - Zero click search involves search queries that do not trigger any further clicks after a glance at the info box (for example, on *Google*), because all the desired information can already be found in this info box and no further research is necessary. Consequently, none of the other hit results are clicked on anymore.

Literature

Auto1. (2021). *Über uns.* https://www.auto1.com/de/company. Accessed 23 Feb 2021.

Becker, J. (2018). *Marketing-Konzeption, Grundlagen des zielstrategischen und operativen marketing-managements* (11. Aufl.). Vahlen.

Beilharz, F. (2020). *Page experience: Googles neuer Focus auf Nutzererfahrung.* https://plus. marketing-boerse.de/fachartikel/details/2023-Page-Experience-Googles-neuer-Focus-auf-Nutzererfahrung/168123. Accessed 8 Feb 2021.

Blind, J., & Stumpfrock, R. (2021). Rechtliche rahmenbedingungen des online-marketings. In R. T. Kreutzer, *Praxisorientiertes online-marketing* (4. Aufl., S. 607–633). Springer Gabler.

Böckenholt, I., Mehn, A., & Westermann, A. (2018). (Hrsg.). *Konzepte und Strategien für Omnichannel-Exzellenz, Innovatives Retail-Marketing mit mehrdimensionalen Vertriebs- und Kommunikationskanälen.* Springer Gabler.

Dean, B. (2019). *We analyzed 5 million Google search results Here's what we learned about organic click through rate.* https://backlinko.com/google-ctr-stats. Accessed 12 Feb 2021.

DGUV. (2010). Manchmal neben der Spur! Was geschieht beim multi-tasking? *IAG, 4*(3037). Berlin.

ePrivacy. (2021). *ePrivacyseal.* https://www.eprivacy.eu/guetesiegel/eprivacyseal/. Accessed 25 Feb 2021.

Esch, F.-R., Langner, T., & Remperl, E. (2005). Ansätze zur Erfassung und Entwicklung der Markenidentität. In F.-R. Esch (Hrsg.), *Moderne Markenführung. Grundlagen – Innovative Ansätze – Praktische Umsetzungen* (4. Aufl., S. 103–129). Springer Gabler.

Google. (2021). *Attribution.* https://support.google.com/analytics/answer/9397590?hl=de. Accessed 24 Feb 2021.

Heinemann, G. (2020). *Der neue Online-Handel* (11. Aufl.). Springer Gabler.

Hundertmark, S. (2021). *Digitale Freunde. Wie Unternehmen Chatbots erfolgreich einsetzen können.* Wiley.

Innomega. (2021). *Qualität – Dialog – Antwortzeit – Kundenanfragen in Zeiten von Social Media.* https://www.innomega.se/de/hilfe-center/thema-social-media-soziale-netzwerke-nutzen/qualitaet-dialog-antwortzeit-kundenanfragen-in-zeiten-von-social-media/. Accessed 5 Aug 2020.

Kamps, I., & Schetter, D. (2018). Performance marketing. In *Der Wegweiser zu einem mess- und steuerbaren Marketing – Einführung in Instrumente, Methoden und Technik.* Springer Gabler.

Kilian, K. (2020). Influencer-marketing – mehr Reichweite und Resonanz mit medialen Multiplikatoren. In M. Stumpf (Hrsg.), *Die 10 wichtigsten Zukunftstrends im Marketing* (2. Aufl., S. 71–105). Haufe.

Kilian, K., & Kreutzer, R. T. (2022). *Digitale Markenführung.* Springer Gabler. (im Druck).

Kollmann, T. (2019). *E-Business, Grundlagen elektronischer Geschäftsprozesse in der Digitalen Wirtschaft* (7. Aufl.). Springer Gabler.

Kost, J. F., & Seeger, C. (2020). *Influencer marketing. grundlagen, strategie und management* (2. Aufl.). UTB.

Kreutzer, R. T. (2019). *Toolbox for marketing and management. Creative concepts, forecasting methods, and analytical instruments.* Springer.

Kreutzer, R. T. (2020). *Die digitale Verführung. Selbstbestimmt leben trotz Smartphone, Social Media & Co.* Springer Gabler.

Kreutzer, R. T. (2021a). *Kundendialog online und offline. Das große 1x1 der Kundenakquisition, Kundenbindung und Kundenrückgewinnung.* Springer Gabler.

Kreutzer, R. T. (2021b). *Praxisorientiertes online-marketing. Konzepte – Instrumente – Checklisten* (4. Aufl.). Springer Gabler.

Kreutzer, R. T. (2022a). *Praxisorientiertes Marketing. Konzepte – Instrumente – Fallbeispiele* (6. Aufl.). Springer Gabler.

Kreutzer, R. T. (2022b). *Toolbox digital business.* Springer.

Kreutzer, R. T., & Sirrenberg, M. (2020). *Understanding artificial intelligence. Fundamentals, use cases and methods for a corporate AI journey.* Springer.

Kreutzer, R. T., & Vousoghi, D. (2020). *Voice-Marketing. Der Siegeszug der digitalen Assistenten.* Springer Gabler.

Kreutzer, R. T., Rumler, A., & Wille-Baumkauff, B. (2020). *B2B-online-marketing und social media* (2. Aufl.). Springer Gabler.

Lammenett, E. (2019). *Praxiswissen online-marketing* (7. Aufl.). Springer Gabler.

Mayer-Uellner, R. (2010). Der Weg ins soziale Netz. *Markenartikel, 7,* 16–18.

Merkle, W. (2020). *Erfolgreich im stationären Einzelhandel, Wege zur konsequenten Profilierung im digitalen Zeitalter.* Springer Gabler.

Nielsen Global Trust in Advertising Survey. (2015). *Global trust in advertising.* https://www. nielsen.com. Accessed 10.3.2021.

Oetting, M. (2010). *Ein Überblick: Paid, curated, owned and earned media.* https://www. connectedmarketing.de/cm/2010/02/ein-ueberblick-paid-curated-owned-and-earned-media.html. Accessed 25 Feb 2021.

Peppers, D., & Rogers, M. (2017). *Managing customer relationships. A strategic framework* (3. Aufl.). Wiley.

Pilot. (2021). *Addressable TV.* https://www.pilot.de/leistungen/addressable-tv/. Accessed 23. Feb. 2021.

Ranganath, A. (2020). *Understanding and using Core Web Vitals.* https://akshayranganath. github.io/Understanding-And-Using-Core-Web-Vitals/. Accessed 12. Feb. 2021.

Rusnjak, A., & Schallmo, D. (Eds.). (2017). *Customer Experience im Zeitalter des Kunden. Best Practices, Lessons Learned und Forschungsergebnisse.* Springer Gabler.

Sherman, L. E., Payton, A. A., Hernandez, L. M., Greenfield, P. M., & Dapretto, M. (2016). *The power of the like in adolescence, effects of peer influence on neural and behavioral responses to social media, psychological science.* http://journals.sagepub.com/doi/pdf/1 0.1177/0956797616645673. Accessed 22. Feb. 2021.

Smart Insights. (2020). *Average display advertising clickthrough rates (CTRs) – 2020 compilation.* https://www.smartinsights.com/Internet-advertising/Internet-advertising-analytics/ display-advertising-clickthrough-rates/. Accessed 24. Feb. 2021.

Solis, B. (2012). *Your brand is more important than you think: BrandSTOKE's 9 criteria for brand essence.* briansolis.com. Accessed 22 Feb 2021.

Starbucks. (2021). *What's your Starbucks idea?.* https://ideas.starbucks.com/. Accessed 25 Feb 2021.

Statista. (2020a). *E-Mail-Nutzung.* https://de-statista-com.ezproxy.hwr-berlin.de/statistik/ studie/id/24350/dokument/e-mail-nutzung-statista-dossier/ . Accessed 24 Feb 2021.

Statista. (2020b). *Mobile apps.* https://de-statista-com.ezproxy.hwr-berlin.de/statistik/studie/ id/11697/dokument/mobile-apps-statista-dossier/. Accessed 24 Feb 2021.

Statista. (2020c). *E-Commerce in Deutschland.* https://de-statista-com.ezproxy.hwr-berlin.de/ statistik/studie/id/6387/dokument/e-commerce-statista-dossier/. Accessed 25 Feb 2021.

Statista. (2020d). *Schätzung des durchschnittlichen Preises kostenpflichtiger Apps für das iPhone und iPad weltweit in den Jahren 2009 bis 2023 (in US-Dollar).* https://de-statista-com.ezproxy.hwr-berlin.de/statistik/daten/studie/170003/umfrage/preisentwicklung-von-apps-in-den-fuehrenden-app-stores-weltweit/. Accessed 18 Feb 2021.

Statista. (2020e). *Social-Media-Werbung.* https://de-statista-com.ezproxy.hwr-berlin.de/statistik/studie/id/60506/dokument/social-media-werbung/. Accessed 25 Feb 2021.

Statista. (2020f). *Durchschnittliche tägliche Nutzungsdauer von Facebook nach Altersgruppen in Deutschland in den Jahren 2015 bis 2019.* https://de-statista-com.ezproxy.hwr-berlin.de/statistik/daten/studie/601946/umfrage/taegliche-nutzungsdauer-von-facebook-in-deutschland/. Accessed 25 Feb 2021.

Statista. (2020h). *Anteil der Unternehmen, die folgende Social-Media-Plattformen nutzen weltweit im Januar 2020.* https://de-statista-com.ezproxy.hwr-berlin.de/statistik/daten/studie/71251/umfrage/einsatz-von-social-media-durch-unternehmen/. Accessed 25 Feb 2021.

Statista. (2021a). *Tägliche Nutzungsdauer ausgewählter Medien in Deutschland 2020.* https://de-statista-com.ezproxy.hwr-berlin.de/statistik/daten/studie/165834/umfrage/taegliche-nutzungsdauer-von-medien-in-deutschland/. Accessed 23 Feb 2021.

Statista. (2021b). *Ausgabenanteil von Programmatic Advertising im Markt für digitale Werbung in Deutschland in den Jahren 2017 bis 2019 sowie eine Prognose bis 2025.* https://de-statista-com.ezproxy.hwr-berlin.de/prognosen/831081/umsatzanteil-von-programmatic-advertising-im-markt-fuer-digitale-werbung-in-deutschland. Accessed 24 Feb 2021.

Statista. (2021e). *E-mail marketing performance metrics worldwide in 1st half 2020, by sender type.* https://www-statista-com.ezproxy.hwr-berlin.de/statistics/961418/e-mail-marketing-performance-metrics-worldwide-sender-type/. Accessed 14 July 2021.

Statista. (2021f). *Mobile marketing and advertising worldwide.* https://www-statista-com.ezproxy.hwr-berlin.de/study/66883/mobile-marketing-and-advertising-worldwide/. Accessed 14 July 2021.

Statista. (2021g). *Most popular social networks worldwide.* https://www-statista-com.ezproxy.hwr-berlin.de/statistics/272014/global-social-networks-ranked-by-number-of-users/. Accessed 14 July 2021.

Statista. (2021h). *Most popular global mobile messaging apps 2021.* https://www-statista-com.ezproxy.hwr-berlin.de/study/15257/mobile-messenger-apps-statista-dossier/. Accessed 14 July 2021.

Stauss, B. (2000). Perspektivenwandel: Vom Produkt-Lebenszyklus zum Kundenbeziehungs-Lebenszyklus. *Thexis, 17*(2), 15–18.

Trustedshops. (2021). *Our business solutions.* https://www.trustedshops.com/solutions/business/. Accessed 15 July 2021.

Vögele, S. (2005). *Dialogmethode: das Verkaufsgespräch per Brief und Antwortkarte.* Redline Wirtschaft.

Wirtz, B. W. (2020). *Electronic business* (7. Aufl.). Springer Gabler.

Printed by Printforce, the Netherlands